Energy Efficiency
and Conservation in Mexico

About the Book and Authors

In comparing the degree of efficiency in energy production and the uses to which energy resources are allocated
in Mexico with those in other countries, this book addresses
three basic questions: What are the major reasons for differences in energy efficiency between industrial economies
and a newly industrializing country like Mexico? To what extent is energy conservation possible in the Mexican economy?
And what are the social and economic benefits of more efficient use and conservation of energy in comparison with
their costs? Using the history and operations of two state-
owned energy agencies, PEMEX and the Federal Electricity
Commission, as case studies, the authors explore the patterns of energy use in all major sectors of the economy and
discuss the prospects for energy-saving policies between
the mid-1980s and the end of the century.

Oscar Guzmán is a researcher at the Energy Research
Program at El Colegio de México. He is coauthor of Perspectivas energéticas y crecimiento económico en Argentina.
Antonio Yúnez-Naude is a professor of economics at the Center of Economic Studies, El Colegio de México. Miguel S.
Wionczek is a senior fellow and the head of the long-term
Energy Research Program at El Colegio de México. He is co-
editor of Mexico's Energy Resources (Westview) and editor
of Politics and Economics of External Debt Crisis (Westview).

Published in cooperation
with El Colegio de México

Energy Efficiency and Conservation in Mexico

Oscar Guzmán, Antonio Yúnez-Naude, and Miguel S. Wionczek

translated by Glenn Gardner
and Rodney Williamson

Routledge
Taylor & Francis Group

LONDON AND NEW YORK

First published 1987 by Westview Press

Published 2018 by Routledge
52 Vanderbilt Avenue, New York, NY 10017
2 Park Square, Milton Park, Abingdon, Oxon OX14 4RN

Routledge is an imprint of the Taylor & Francis Group, an informa business

Library of Congress Cataloging-in-Publication Data
Main entry under title:
Energy efficiency and conservation in Mexico.
   (Westview special studies on Latin America and the
Caribbean)
   Bibliography: p.
   Includes index.
   1. Energy consumption--Mexico. 2. Energy
conservation--Mexico. 3. Petróleos Mexicanos.
4. Petroleum industry and trade--Mexico--Energy
consumption. 5. Mexico. Comisión Federal de
Electricidad. 6. Electric utilities--Mexico--Energy
consumption. I. Guzmán, Oscar. II. Yúnez-Naude,
Antonio. III. Wionczek, Miguel S. IV. Series.
HD9502.M62E54 1987   333.79'16'0972   85-22636

ISBN 13: 978-0-367-00623-5 (hbk)
ISBN 13: 978-0-367-15610-7 (pbk)

Contents

Tables and Figures

FIGURES

Preface

This book presents the results of a study entitled "Conservation and Efficient Use of Energy in Mexico," conceived and designed with cooperation of the Energy Directorate of the Commission of the European Communities in Brussels in the fall of 1983. According to the initial agreement between El Colegio de México's Energy Research Program and the Commission's Energy Directorate, the study was to undertake the first phase of an analysis of the efficient use of energy and the obstacles and possibilities for more efficient energy use in Mexico. This first phase was to include the design of a methodology for the study, the collection and strengthening of the national data base, and the preliminary and tentative analysis of the data collected for the purpose of increasing the efficiency of energy uses in the country.

In accordance with the project plan, four particular questions, among others, were to be addressed in the study:

1. What are the basic reasons for differences in energy efficiency among industrial and developing countries, given the basic assumption that energy conservation should not be viewed simply in terms of thermal efficiency and even less in terms of oil use?
2. To what extent is energy conservation possible?
3. What are the social and economic costs of energy conservation at the macro and micro levels compared to its benefits?
4. Are analytical methods used in the industrial countries transferable to less developed economies, and to what extent are such transfers of methodologies valid in view of the structural, institutional, and social differences between these two types of societies? For the sake of brevity, the two societies might be described as postindustrial and preindustrial countries; some countries, such as Mexico, would represent borderline cases.

As this book demonstrates, the study's terms of reference, set by mutual agreement and in the project outline, were largely exceeded. The book does not intend to report only on the first phase of an analysis of the degree of efficiency in the use of energy and the obstacles and possibilities in that field in Mexico; instead, it covers these subjects fully and in great detail, with due emphasis on the possibilities for improving energy use and performance at both the macro and micro levels.

Analysis offered by the study was made possible by mobilizing a considerable group of Mexican experts, from both the academic and public sectors, who worked to collect and organize data, which were often extremely scarce, incomplete, and contradictory, on energy uses in the 1970s and the early 1980s in all sectors of the Mexican economy. This coordinated exercise was integrated within the Energy Research Program of El Colegio de México.

This was the first research project of its kind conducted in Mexico and perhaps one of the first undertaken in any developing country. It is hoped that the study will be of considerable use to the country's energy policymakers in the public sector, who, as of late and particularly since the appearance of the official Programa Nacional de Energéticos 1984-1988 in August 1984, have given the highest priority to measures aimed at increasing conservation and the rational use of energy in an economy presently going through serious development difficulties.

The views presented in this book should be considered those of a group of independent researchers associated directly or indirectly with El Colegio de México. Although some participants in the project occupy official positions, both the opinions and the policy-oriented proposals contained in the study should in no way be taken as reflecting the official viewpoints of the publicly owned entities that form the energy sector in Mexico.

The study of energy uses in Mexico required a wide range of technical contributions that would not have been possible without the collaboration of a large group of experts on energy issues from both the public and academic sectors. We would like to thank Jaime Mario Willars and Antonio Souza for their help in analyzing the energy and industrial sectors as well as for their participation in the study of several other branches. Thanks are also due to Fernando Schutz, whose knowledge provided the basis for the quantitative analysis of the electric power, industrial, housing, commercial, and public sectors and who provided overall assistance in organizing the study.

The authors of the final version of the study would also like to thank Juan Francisco Bueno for his opinions regarding the energy sector as a whole; Gerardo Bazán for his participation in the study of the transportation sector; Manuel Betancourt, for his aid in the study of the indus-

trial sector; Jesús Cervantes for his participation in the
study of the rural sector; Miguel Angel Cóseres for his research on the sugar industry; Eliut González for his collaboration in the work on the transportation sector; Omar Ma-
cera and Marco Martínez Negrete for their contributions to
the study of the rural sector; Roberto Mendoza for his efforts in obtaining the information used in the analysis of
the housing, commercial, and public sectors; Dolores Nieto
for her help in gathering information analyzed in the macroeconomic study; Alma Parrilla for her participation in the
study of the iron and steel industry; and Gustavo Pastrana
for his collaboration in the research on transportation. We
would like to thank our two translators, Glenn Gardner and
Rodney Williamson, for their care in translating the original Spanish-language manuscript. Last, thanks should be
given to the secretarial personnel--Leticia Cabrera, Juana
Socorro Cervantes, Elizabeth Caso, and Rosa María Valenzue-
la--and to the staff of the program's Documentation Center,
particularly Blanca Laura Aguirre and Pilar Torres.

The completion of the study and the publication of its
results were made possible by the institutional support of
El Colegio de México and by the generous financial assistance of the European Communities Commission.

Miguel S. Wionczek
Director, Energy Research Program
El Colegio de México

1

Introduction

Initial studies on the question of energy conservation and savings in developing countries, including Mexico, strongly suggest that the issue is not exclusively economic or technological, as is argued by many studies undertaken in advanced industrial countries and suggested by the declining energy demand per unit of production in the latter countries since 1973 and especially after 1979. In the less-developed countries (LDCs) on the whole, the relatively inefficient use of energy, both in the monetarized and the nonmonetarized (subsistence agriculture and marginated urban) sectors, also has institutional and social aspects that have hardly been studied. Large differences in the absolute levels of energy used by the major economic sectors and income groups of a developing country, whether per unit of gross domestic product (GDP) or per capita, and in how efficiently it is used, as well as the different ways of wasting energy, whether primary or end-use, indicate that a great deal of research needs to be conducted on the issue of conservation and savings before a consistent conservation policy can be worked out and implemented.

Research in Mexico, as in all developing countries, is hampered by an extremely limited and weak data base. This is particularly true in countries richly endowed with energy resources, where the unlimited supply of primary energy is often taken for granted and where, moreover, energy resources are often considered a "public good."

Recent experiences in the industrial countries and in some of the developing countries show the impact of their efforts to use energy more rationally. Their experiences raise a number of questions that are particularly important for developing countries such as Mexico, torn between the general, implicit goals of energy conservation for the bene-

fit of future generations and the current practice of
wasting energy.

The main rationale behind El Colegio de México's research program, which falls within the scope of its activities in the field of energy research, is that under the
persistent and increasingly unstable conditions of world
energy markets and acute domestic constraints, it is of the
utmost importance to Mexico to decelerate its inordinate
growth in domestic energy demand. Otherwise, the Mexican energy sector will need considerable new investments, particularly in the oil sector, investments that do not seem fi-
nancially feasible at the present time or in the near
future.

Because concern with energy conservation and savings
is relatively new to Mexico, the quantitative information
base from both the major energy-producing enterprises and
the energy-consuming sectors is weak and incomplete. Also
incomplete are data about the degree of interfuel substitution and the nature of technological change in the field
of conservation, both of which are of great importance to
the study of energy use and conservation in Mexico. These
problems are magnified by methodological uncertainties. It
is not always valid to transfer methods of analysis designed for studying the industrial world to less-developed
countries such as Mexico.

This book, therefore, is the result of an intense effort to tackle these questions, so as to better understand
the problems of energy use and waste in developing countries. General aspects of energy consumption trends in
Mexico as well as sectoral problema are analyzed. The study
begins by demonstrating that Mexico has been wasting considerable amounts of energy at all levels, particularly
since the beginning of the 1970s (Chapter 1). These findings
are supported by sectoral and micro analyses that identify
the major energy-wasting sectors and activities (Chapter 2).

The sectoral discussion contains a quantitative diagnosis of energy consumption and waste, a projection of the
trends observed, and proposals for a more rational use of energy that would modify those tendencies and result in large
financial and resource savings and in the increased efficiency of the economy as a whole. The discussion takes up,
first, the performance of the two key energy-producing,
state-owned enterprises, which are, at the same time, the
major net energy consumers in Mexico: Petróleos Mexicanos
(Chapter 3) and the Comisión Federal de Electricidad (Chapter 4). This is followed by the analysis of one of the consuming sectors that wastes a large amount of energy: trans-

portation (Chapter 5). Energy behavior in the manufacturing industry, including a detailed analysis of three of the major energy-intensive industries--iron and steel, cement, and sugar--is then discussed (Chapter 6), followed by an analysis of energy consumption and waste in the housing, commercial, and public sectors (Chapter 7). The sectoral discussion ends with an analysis of the rural sector, singled out because of its special characteristics in LDCs such as Mexico (Chapter 8).

The final part of the study includes rough estimates of the possible levels of energy savings in the years to come, savings that could be obtained after an integrated, longer term program for rational energy use is implemented in Mexico (Chapter 9).

2

Energy Production and Consumption: Historical Patterns and Current Situation

The object of this chapter is to explain why Mexico has experienced a considerable increase in energy consumption since the beginning of the 1970s and has developed its extreme dependence on hydrocarbons. In the first section, the dynamics of energy production and consumption from the 1960s to the present are analyzed according to energy sources and sectors. A series of explanations are presented, which together could elucidate Mexico's trend toward increasing energy consumption and the national economy's growing dependency on hydrocarbons. The explanations are of a technical, economic, and political nature.

One explanation appears to be the speed with which the country grew and industrialized during the oil boom of 1976-1981. During the oil-boom years, there was massive extraction of oil, and internal prices for energy were kept low. However, it is clear that even though these pricing policies coincided with the view that the country was extremely rich in hydrocarbons, these policies nonetheless led to the wasting of hydrocarbons.

In the second section of the chapter the validity of this hypothesis is confirmed by a comparative study that attempts to answer two questions: Has the rate of increase in Mexico's energy consumption been greater than that of countries with a similar degree of development? Does this rate correspond to a more or a less pronounced process of industrialization?

A comparison is made between the experience in economic growth and energy consumption of a group of underdeveloped countries in southeast Asia and Latin America, including Mexico, and that of capitalist industrial countries. The conclusion is that due to the marked differences between these two distinct groups of countries, a detailed comparison between Mexico's energy patterns and trends and those of other underdeveloped countries undergoing rapid growth is more relevant than comparisons between Mexico's experiences and those of industrialized nations. Results of this comparative study show that Mexico, as well as the other energy-exporting countries with dynamic economies, experienced a considerable increase in its energy consumption when compared to both the rest of the industrializing nations and the industrialized nations. Using this comparative analysis as a foundation, one can define more precise guidelines for studies leading to detailed comparisons of growth patterns, industrialization, and the evolution of transportation and energy consumption in Mexico, on the one hand, and in particular countries in southeast Asia and Latin America, on the other.

In the last section of this chapter, the domestic energy prices of these countries, and their evolution, are considered. We examine whether sharp rises in price may correspond to less marked trends in consumption. We also examine whether the notable energy price increases in some countries are part of a broader policy toward energy conservation and efficient energy use.

It is worth pointing out that this analysis emphasizes mostly those aspects of energy related to end use. It has been impossible, so far, to cover in detail all aspects related to energy production. This is, therefore, a limitation of the study. As is well known, the energy sector is a strong consumer of its own product. It has enormous potential for conservation and efficient use of nonrenewable energy resources. This limitation is dealt with in the first section of this chapter and, in more detail, in two of the sectoral studies in this book (see Chapters 4 and 5): one on the electric power industry (CFE) and the other on the oil industry (PEMEX).

MEXICO

Notwithstanding the acute structural and financial imbalance in Mexico from the mid-1960s to mid-1980s, Mexico registered an accelerated process of growth and industrialization. The average annual growth rate (AAGR) for its GDP was 7% in the 1960s and almost 5% in the 1970s. In per capita terms, it was 3.5% and 2.2%, respectively.1/

An analysis of Mexican energy consumption from 1960 on

shows a clear tendency toward a rapid expansion of Mexico's
energy demands.2/ Oil and electrical end use grew at a
5.1% annual rate in the 1960s and at 8.6% in the following
decade. According to energy sector information, the AAGR
for end use energy rose from 7.9% in 1970-1975 to 8.8% in
1975-1980 (see Table 2.1).3/

The evolution of per capita energy consumption shows
similar tendencies: The AAGR of per capita consumption of
oil and electricity, which was on the order of 1.7% in the
1960s, rose to 5.2% in the following decade, and the AAGR
of total per capita energy consumption increased from 3.7%
in the first half of the 1970s to 6.5% during the second
half of the decade.4/

These tendencies were not accompanied by corresponding
increases in the national product. The product elasticity
of energy consumption, fluctuating around 1.0 in the 1960s,
increased to 1.3 and 1.7 in the following two five-year
periods.

The AAGR for energy consumption per unit of GDP was
0.69% for the first half of the 1970s and 3.3% for the second half of the 1970s.5/ It is therefore evident that Mexico's energy consumption increased more rapidly than the
growth of its product. This trend grew stronger with time.

During the second half of the 1970s, the industrialization process was characterized by, among other things, a notable increase in energy production, in particular, of hydrocarbons. Domestic production of oil, gas, and energy as
a whole grew at a very rapid pace during this time, as compared to the first half of the decade: The AAGR for energy
production increased from 7.4% to 17.9%; for oil, from 10.8%
to 22%; and for gas, from 3.4% to 10.5% (see Table 2.1).

Notwithstanding the fact that a growing percentage of
domestic hydrocarbon production is destined for export, domestic consumption has risen considerably since the middle
of the 1970s.6/ This evolution is reflected in the variations in product elasticity for hydrocarbon consumption, as
well as in the composition of the primary energy destined
for domestic consumption and in the increases in the growth
rate of domestic demand. In fact, the elasticity rose from
1.2 to 1.7 from the first to the second half of the 1970s,
and the share of hydrocarbons in domestic primary energy
consumption grew from 87.8% in 1970 to 89.3% in 1976 and to
92.9% in 1982.

Mexico's growing dependency on hydrocarbons was also
apparent in other areas. The share of hydrocarbons in domestic energy production went from 87.8% in 1970 to more than

95% in the first few years of the 1980s. Following this
trend, oil products and natural gas similarly increased
their share of domestic end use. The phenomenon is even
more acute in the generation of electricity. While in 1970
hydrocarbons were responsible for 43.1% of the gross electric power generated, the percentage grew to 62% in 1975
and to more than 65% toward the end of the 1970s and the beginning of the 1980s (see Tables 2.2, 2.3 and 2.4).7/

The boom in the domestic production of crude oil and
its derivatives had strong repercussions in foreign trade.
In 1983 revenue from their sale made up 74.8% of the income
received from exports of goods; in 1976 the percentage was
only 15.4%.8/

It can then be argued that since the beginning of the
mid 1970s, hydrocarbons have been not only the main source
of foreign exchange for Mexico but also the most important
form of energy consumed domestically. This situation is
reason for concern, given that hydrocarbons are a nonrenewable resource. This concern is magnified further when one
reviews the dynamics of energy consumption and contrasts it
with the dynamics of other macroeconomic variables and with
the growth processes experienced by other countries.

Total energy consumption by sectors (see Figure 2.1) is
characterized basically by a strong increase in the energy
sector's share of domestic consumption during the oil boom.
This share went from 33.4% in 1976 to 46.4% in 1982. This
trend is in line with information given in the annual energy balances, published by the Energy Commission, which relate the percentage of loss in the energy sector to the
gross domestic supply. This projection was 20.4% in 1970
and 18.4% in 1975, and it grew considerably in 1980 and
1982 to 25.2% and 28.5%, respectively.

These results indicate an increase in the inefficiency
of end-use energy production. The energy consumption by energy-producing companies increased, while there were losses
in processing, transportation, distribution, and storage.
In fact, the share held by the energy-producing companies,
which remained around 32% of the sector's total consumption
in 1970 and 1976, climbed to 46.4% in 1982. The losses in
transportation, distribution, and storage were reduced pro-
portionately, while losses in processing remained steady
(see Figure 2.1).

Of the two state-owned energy producers, Petróleos
Mexicanos (PEMEX) and the Comisión Federal de Electricidad
(CFE), PEMEX has shown as increase in energy consumption in
the last decade. Its production of petroleum products in-

creased at a rate of 8.1% annually from 1970 to 1980, while self-consumption increased at a rate of 12.4%. That is, in 1980 PEMEX consumed 218.4 thousand barrels of daily crude oil equivalent (tbdce), which were used to produce 1,689 tbdce of petroleum products. In 1970 self-consumption was 68 tbdce for a production of 774 tbdce. The difference between barrels processed and barrels produced amounted to 8.8% of the latter in 1970 and 12.9% in 1980. Thus, there was a 47% drop in PEMEX's overall efficiency of energy use.

In the field of electric power production, self-consumption trends were different. Thermoelectric generating efficiency from the CFE as a whole rose from 26.6% to 30% in the 1970s. Nevertheless, no attempt was made to diversify sources of generation, especially renewable sources such as hydraulic energy.9/

In spite of the problems posed by not having the information necessary to analyze Mexico's inefficient use of energy on a macro level, one can mention certain factors that help explain the marked increase in energy use in the last few years, especially in the case of end-use sectors. These factors, which induced a consumption pattern characterized by a squandering of energy and financial resources, can be grouped into three closely related areas: technical, economic, and political.

TECHNICAL FACTORS

Under analysis here are the factors that affected the type of technology Mexico used or did not use and the speed with which this technology was introduced into the country's productive processes. Developing countries, including those in transition, like Mexico, must develop their production (of energy, in particular) at an accelerated pace, given the pressures of multiple social problems. Moreover, because these countries are often not capable of generating the technology they require, they must buy it directly or acquire it via the imported equipment.

During the 1970s, with the exception of 1976 to 1977, Mexico's industrialization proceeded at a relatively rapid and sustained rate. With the appearance of oil surpluses and recourse to foreign debt as a source of financing, Mexico's industrialization became even more intense. Electrification increased, within this framework, as a result of the growing economic activity. It expanded, however, at a

faster rate than the economy itself. A similar phenomenon
took place in almost all other energy uses. This phenomenon is explained, in part, by the way in which Mexico's accelerated industrialization occurred.

According to survey data from the business sector,
private investment grew at an amazing rate during this period. Growth was concentrated in the large companies and,
in particular, in those business enterprises that were big
consumers of energy. The substitution of energy for labor
became more acute, with the latter acting as a complement
to capital. Also important were the substitution of mecha-
nized techniques for handcrafted methods used in family
and small units and a more than proportional increase in
the sales of durable consumer goods such as refrigerators,
television sets, stoves, and cars and trucks, all of which
are energy consumers.

Energy demands underwent an important increase as a
consequence of the growth in the number of units operating.
This was favored by the technology incorporated into the
equipment, from industrial motors to gas stoves. This
equipment was neither the most modern equipment nor was it
oriented toward energy efficiency.

Past experience has shown that the transfer of technology to countries that have not consolidated their own technological development is neither automatic nor rapid. New
energy-efficient technology, even when incorporated into
some of the new machinery imported, is not used extensively
in Mexico.

In the oil industry's case, these phenomena were accentuated by the speed with which the boom in production occurred. This led to energy waste, which, when added to
strong demand in other sectors, caused the relationship between energy consumption and product growth to increase far
above previous values. Examples of such waste are the burning off of gas from Campeche Bay and the Huimanguillo
fields because of a lack of processing equipment; the concentration of electric power production in thermoelectric
plants in order to satisfy short-term demand; the use of
distillation processes that require huge amounts of energy;
and, above all, the lack of investments and outlay for improvements and equipment maintenance that would have resulted in energy savings. Because of the low domestic cost
of energy, such expenditures were not feasible during the
time of Mexico's euphoria over its abundant energy and financial resources.

ECONOMIC FACTORS

The most obvious reason for Mexico's exaggerated consumption of energy in the last few years was, as has been
pointed out, the relatively low cost of energy compared to
other goods, especially industrial goods. For example, the
average real price of electricity dropped almost 50% between 1970 and 1981.

Moreover, a relative price structure was not used as a
mechanism for channeling demand toward a rational substitution based on domestic availability, production costs,
consumer trends, and policies promoting particular productive activities. This situation gave rise to an inadequate and inefficient use of energy that affected the conservation of the country's resources, as was the case with
natural gas. Low prices and their distorted structure al-
lowed existing waste to fit, paradoxically, within the
strict logic of economics.

The country underwent a drastic change after new reserves were discovered. Until 1975 one of the main tasks
of the Comisión de Energéticos was to increase overall efficiency in the oil industry or, at any rate, to limit imports, given the productive and financial crisis the country underwent during the mid-1960s. With this enormous increase in hydrocarbon reserves, these worries were put to
one side in practice, although not necessarily in rhetoric:

> The large amount of primary energy sources avail-
> able, together with the dynamic growth of the economy
> and low energy costs, produced an unprecedented growth
> in consumption in all economic sectors, a situation
> from which not even the energy sector itself escaped.14/

There were other economic factors motivating inefficient energy use. The low cost of railroad transportation
impeded financing the necessary expansion of services and
also forced goods and passengers to depend on highway transportation. But neither was highway transportation of goods
very expensive, when diesel and gasoline fuel and even
trucks were so cheap. Just as it had supported industrialization in the 1960s, the state created the conditions for
establishing and later developing the automobile industry,
subsidizing it indirectly through gasoline prices. The con-
tradictions of this development policy clearly surfaced, in
part, during the 1970s and, especially, at the beginning of
the 1980s when the energy system was at the center of the

country's production and financial crisis.

POLITICAL FACTORS

The Mexican state, just as its counterparts in late-industrializing countries, has played a direct and substantial role in promoting growth. A permanent characteristic of its intervention has been the production of goods and services and their sale at "subsidized" prices and tariffs. The fundamental goals of this subsidization were to support industrialization and to provide the urban population with access to basic goods and services. This is in keeping with the state's policy of counteracting the imbalance existing in the domestic income distribution, in which the basic needs of the largest sectors of the population have not yet been met. It also guarantees that the political stability of the system will be maintained, without retarding the expanded reproduction of capital.

The Mexican state's activities as an energy producer and supplier did not escape this logic. This is clearly what happened during the petroleum boom. The López Portillo administration's goal of using hydrocarbons as the pivot and pillar for the accelerated growth and industrialization of the country was in keeping with the view that Mexico had great amounts of these resources. Selling the energy obtained from them at low prices was not, therefore, inconsistent, given this view. Abundant energy resources, the need to recover its growth, and the interest in converting Mexico into an industrial nation meant priority was to be given to economic activity, rather than to protecting the country's nonrenewable resources.

INTERNATIONAL COMPARISONS

International comparisons are one way to approach the study of Mexico's tendency to use energy at an ever-increasing rate. Here, emphasis is on comparing the dynamics of Mexico's macroeconomic variables with those of countries that experienced similar economic development.

Notorious disparities exist between the growth, industrialization, and energy consumption in Mexico and those in other countries. This provides a comparative basis for determining whether Mexico is to be considered, on an international scale, a country making comparatively inefficient use of its energy.

It should be made clear that the results of this comparative study are to be taken as hypotheses, subject to more detailed analysis. The principal limitations in this type of study are the scarcity of information, as is frequently the case in developing countries, and the difficulties in making measurements, implicit in international comparisons.15/ These comparisons, therefore, are based on trends, rather than on absolute figures.

GROWTH AND ENERGY CONSUMPTION: INTERNATIONAL EXPERIENCE

Statistical information from international organizations shows a marked difference between the economic growth and energy consumption trends of developing countries in Southeast Asia and Latin America, including Mexico, and those of the industrialized countries in the West and the Pacific. In particular, there are differences between these two groups in the historical trends of their per capita gross national product (GNP) growth and energy consumption.

During the 1960s, both variables experienced high rates of growth in the industrialized countries of the Pacific as well as in the most dynamic economies of the developing world. In contrast, during the following decade, the rate of growth decreased in the industrialized countries, while the opposite happened in the developing countries.

The AAGR of per capita energy consumption in the industrialized countries of the Pacific declined more drastically during the 1960s than did the AAGR of their per capita GDPs. During the same period, the majority of the south Asian and Latin American countries that were studied recorded larger increases in the AAGR of per capita energy consumption than they did in the AAGR of per capita GDPs (see Tables 2.5, 2.6, and 2.7).16/ The western European countries evolved just as the Pacific industrialized countries did: The relationship between primary energy and GNP moved downward during the 1960s and even more so during the 1970s (see Table 2.8).

Another difference between the advanced industrial countries and the south Asian and Latin American countries is the latter's dependence on hydrocarbons. This structural difference was accentuated during the 1970s when developed countries began diversifying their energy sources (see Tables 2.9, 2.10, and 2.11).

These two groups of countries also differ in how energy consumption is distributed sectorially. Almost all the developing countries studied channel a larger percentage of their energy into transportation than into industry; the inverse was true for the advanced industrial countries (see Tables 2.12, 2.13, and 2.14).

Besides all their differences, Third World countries have similar economic, political, and social structures and share many of the same problems. Another common trait can be added: the process of industrialization sustained in Mexico and in the most dynamic of the developing countries during the 1960s and 1970s. Comparisons between these countries can help identify energy consumption patterns and trends in Mexico with a great deal more precision than is possible using industrialized countries as a reference point. Moreover, such a comparative study would provide a basis for examining the validity of the argument that Mexico's rapid growth and industrialization during the early 1980s is the key to its marked energy consumption.

GROWTH AND ENERGY CONSUMPTION IN MEXICO AND OTHER LATIN AMERICAN AND SOUTH ASIAN COUNTRIES

The available figures (from the 1960s on) on growth and energy consumption in Mexico and other Latin American and south Asian countries reveal certain differences among the countries (see Tables 2.5 and 2.6). During the 1960s the patterns of per capita end-use energy in countries with accelerated growth in per capita GDP are similar. Countries with per capita GDP growth rates higher than Mexico's also showed higher increases in their per capita energy consumption. This was the case with the so-called newly industrialized countries (NICs) of Southeast Asia: South Korea, Singapore, and Thailand.

Any similarity between Mexico's per capita GDP growth and energy consumption and those of the other NICs changed during the 1970s. The latter countries, to which the Philippines and Malaysia could be added, recorded increases in their per capita GDP growth rates but decreases in their per capita commercial end-use energy. In Mexico the trends were exactly the opposite.17/

After the 1973 oil crisis, the differences became even greater. South Asian countries, with the exception of South Korea, reduced the rates of growth of their energy consumption even more. Even when the growth of the per capita GDP went down in some of these countries, it was still higher than Mexico's.

Indonesia's case contrasts with that of the other dynamic south Asian countries, however, and can well be compared to Mexico because both export hydrocarbons. During the 1960s, Indonesia showed a more marked increase in per capita energy consumption than any other country, be it south Asian or Latin American. This agrees with the indicators given by the energy/GDP ratio (see Table 2.15): Mexico and Indonesia were the countries with the lowest ratio in 1973; that is, the ratio increased in both these countries after the first oil crisis.18/

Moreover, although the energy/GDP ratio was lower in the majority of south Asian countries during the second half of the 1970s than during the first half, it increased in Mexico and Indonesia. The increase was greater than in the Philippines and Singapore, the only other countries evolving in the same direction.19/

If Mexico's experience is compared with that of other Latin American countries, the data suggest that Mexico was not a strong energy consumer during the 1960s. In fact, it had the highest rate of growth in per capita GDP, even though its per capita energy consumption grew similarly to the rest of Latin America (see Table 2.6).

Even if this pattern was not maintained during the 1970s, other countries in the region shared Mexico's over-consumption of energy, including Bolivia, Ecuador, Venezuela, and, to a certain degree, Brazil. (Brazil had a higher economic growth rate and per capita energy consumption.) The changes occurring from 1960 to 1979 in the ratio of hydrocarbon and electricity consumption per unit of GDP in those countries confirm this (see Table 2.16).

What was previously said about the different trends in energy consumption in the countries from the two regions studied is confirmed by the way in which they income elasticities evolved. In fact, in the majority of south Asian countries the income elasticity of energy consumption dropped during the period following 1973. India and Pakistan, countries that depended little on hydrocarbons, were exceptions (see Table 2.17).

Just as in the case of Indonesia, product elasticity estimates for energy consumption in the Mexican manufacturing industry indicate that it increased from 1973 to 1979, as compared with the period from 1965 to 1973.20/ In some

Latin American countries--Bolivia, Peru, and Venezuela--the
product elasticity showed an increase during the 1970s as
compared to the previous decade. If we take the first half
of the 1970s as a point of reference, the ratio increased
in the second half of the decade in Argentina, Bolivia,
Brazil, Ecuador, Mexico, and Venezuela (see Table 2.18).21/

If we exclude the stagnant Latin American countries
(Argentina, Chile, Peru, and Uruguay)22/ and take into account that Bolivia, Ecuador, and Venezuela, like Mexico and
Indonesia, export hydrocarbons, we can arrive at a preliminary conclusion: During the decade of the two oil cri-
ses, dynamic Latin American countries (plus Indonesia) that
exported energy were the only ones maintaining a marked
tendency toward increased energy consumption.

We have seen that Mexico, like other hydrocarbon-exporting countries, used more of its nonrenewable energy
forms than other countries undergoing the same sustained industrialization. Additional macro variables exist that
further explain the differences between Mexico and the
other countries that underwent sustained industrialization,
that is, the so-called NICs: South Korea, Brazil, the
Philippines, Singapore, and Thailand. In the following discussion of these variables, we also refer to other dynamic
exporting countries (Ecuador, Indonesia, and Venezuela) and,
to a lesser degree, Colombia and Bolivia.23/

ENERGY CONSUMPTION AND INDUSTRIALIZATION PROCESSES

In the preceding sections we showed that south Asian
countries had higher per capita GDP growth rates than did
Latin American countries, including Mexico, during the second half of the 1970s, notwithstanding the decreases in the
growth of energy consumption. In fact, south Asian countries, as a whole, showed higher GDP growth rates and lower
end-use energy growth rates than did the Latin American
countries importing energy. Differences are greater for
those countries from either region that are net hydrocarbon
exporters. This is valid for both per capita and absolute
rates, and the differences increase after 1973 (see Table
2.19).24/

The AAGRs for the economies of the south Asian countries fluctuated between 6% (the Philippines) and 7.5%
(South Korea), and their end-use energy rates of growth
fluctuated between 3.3% (the Philippines) and 8.9% (South
Korea), in the period from 1973 to 1980. The AAGRs of the

Latin American economies fluctuated between 6.9% (Ecuador) and 3.6% (Bolivia), and their end-use energy consumption was between 6.4% (Colombia) and 14.3% (Ecuador), in the period from 1973 to 1979.

Per capita variables also reflected these disparities. During the period 1973-1980, the GDP for each inhabitant in newly industrialized south Asian countries fluctuated between 3.4% (the Philippines) and 6.1% (Singapore); the AAGR of per capita energy consumption was 0.6% for the Philippines and 4.8% for Singapore. For Colombia and Brazil during the same time frame, the GDP rates were 3.6% and 3.9%, respectively, and end-use energy rates were 1.8% and 7%.

It could be argued that those countries with a clear trend toward increasing their rates of energy consumption were those undergoing marked industrialization. However, experience in the countries studied shows such arguments to be unfounded. The newly industrialized south Asian countries, net energy importers, were those showing the greatest growth in production without showing the greatest increase in energy consumption.

The AAGR for the South Korean manufacturing industry was 12.4% from 1973 to 1980, and the AAGR of its end-use energy was 8.9%. These rates were 9.5% and 5.8% for Thailand, 6.3% and 3.3% for the Philippines, and 5.1% and 6.2% for Singapore. In contrast, the corresponding rates for Latin American countries that were net hydrocarbon exporters were 11.5% and 14.3% for Ecuador, 6.3% and 8.6% for Mexico, 5.7% and 9.5% for Venezuela, and 5.4% and 9.9% for Bolivia. Brazil recorded considerable growth in both manufacturing and energy consumption: 6.9% and 10.2%, respectively.25/

It can then be argued that except for Brazil and, to a lesser degree, Singapore, the manufacturing industry of net energy-importing countries grew at a higher rate than the energy consumption of these countries, whereas the opposite was true for energy exporters.

If we consider that the agricultural sector's growth and, in a certain sense, the transportation sector's growth were similar for the countries studied during the same period of time, we can state that the south Asian NICs were the most dynamic. Their manufacturing sectors had growth rates higher than Mexico's, and they tended to have lower energy consumptions.26/ This result would be even stronger if the economic structure of these countries were similar.

Available information (see Tables 2.20 and 2.21) shows that the participation of industry and the manufacturing

sector in the GDP is similar for all the NICs. The percentages were higher for Mexico and Brazil in 1970, and
they were similar for the NICs as a whole in 1980. In 1980
the industrial sector's contribution in Mexico, the Philippines, and Singapore to the respective GDPs fluctuated between 35% and 37%. It was 39% in South Korea and 29% in
Thailand.27/

The increase in industrial growth in Asian countries
in the 1970s might have been accompanied by a more dynamic
production of goods that were not energy-intensive and by
the adoption of more energy-efficient technology. However,
this does not contradict the conclusion that Mexico's increased energy requirements during that period cannot be
explained exclusively by the industrialization it had undergone during the 1970s.

Before we present arguments that would explain, in
general, the observed differences between the growth of energy consumption in Mexico and in the rest of the NICs, we
will comment briefly on the dynamics of one of the sectors
that consumes the most energy: transportation. Even if one
argues that the average growth in transportation was similar for the countries studied (see Table 2.19), there are
differences in the percentage of energy each country dedicated to it.

In Mexico transportation has the highest end use of
all sectors, including industry. This situation, already
notable in 1970, became more critical in 1980 and contrasts
with that in the rest of the countries analyzed (see Tables
2.12, 2.13, and 2.14). The energy used for transportation
in Mexico rose from 28.7% in 1970 to 35.2% in 1980, according to the Organización Latinoamericana de Energía
(OLADE). It rose from 37.3% to 39.4%, according to BDE,
and from 39.2% to 44.4%, according to the Programa Nacional
de Energía de 1984 (PNE). In contrast, energy use by industry dropped from 28.7% to 26.7% (OLADE) and from 38.0%
to 33.1% (BDE) for the same time period and dropped from
43.1% to 36.2% for the period 1970 to 1982 (PNE).

Brazil had a different experience. The percentage of
energy used in transportion showed practically no change between 1970 and 1982 (29.8% and 29.2%), and the percentage
used in industry rose from 36% to almost 40%.

The information available on south Asian countries suggests that the NICs of this region had experiences similar
to that of Brazil, in contrast to Mexico. The percentage
of end-use energy for transportation is lower than that for
industry. South Korea used only 12.6% of its end-use ener-

gy for transportation and 44.3% for industry. Thailand showed 31.9% and 37.3%, respectively; Singapore, 33% and 38%; and the Philippines, 35.2% and 41.3%.28/

To these differences we can add others that surfaced when we reviewed transportation and manufacturing sector growth rates (see Table 2.19). The use of energy in transportation in Mexico grew faster than it did in manufacturing from 1970 to 1979. The opposite was true for South Korea from 1970 to 1980 and for Thailand from 1973 to 1980. In Brazil the growth rates for both sectors were similar from 1970 to 1980. Transportation grew more than the manufacturing sector in the Philippines, but the difference was smaller than Mexico's. The opposite applies to Singapore.29/

Given the heavy energy requirements of a transportation sector such as Mexico's (which is based on automobile and highway transportation and which, consequently, is overwhelmingly dependent on petroleum products), results so far indicate that the sector's dynamic nature can partially explain Mexico's tendency toward an ever-increasing consumption of energy.30/ The increases in these requirements do not support the hypothesis that industrial growth is the explanatory variable. It seems more viable to propose a hypothesis that Mexico's type of industrialization, characterized, among other things, by a bias toward automobile production, can explain its marked tendency toward the consumption of nonrenewable forms of energy.31/

In fact, the automobile industry has been one of Mexico's most dynamic manufacturing branches since the 1960s. From 1960 to 1981, the industry grew more than the manufacturing and overall GDPs did. Moreover, automobile production is the manufacturing industry's most important sector.32/ In terms of units produced, automobile end production has evolved more rapidly than truck and bus production. From 1970 to 1980, the percentage of automobiles rose from 68.9% to 73% of the total units produced, while the percentage of trucks and buses diminished.33/

PRICES AND POLICIES FOR THE CONSERVATION AND EFFICIENT USE OF ENERGY

The differences in domestic energy prices and the presence or absence of national policies geared toward conservation and efficient energy use further add to the disparity in energy consumption between Mexico and other Latin American and Asian nations.

Using existing information, we analyzed trends in the marked growth in energy consumption in Mexico and other hydrocarbon-exporting countries for a possible link with the low domestic prices and the absence of regulatory measures. We found that during the 1970s the countries with low energy prices were the same ones undergoing notable increases in energy end use. Net hydrocarbon-exporting countries—Bolivia, Ecuador, Indonesia, Mexico, and Venezuela—were in this situation. Domestic prices for oil and gas derivatives were and are kept low, compared to those in the rest of the industrializing countries.

Thomas Sterner's study on gasoline prices in the LDCs, conducted in November 1983, gives information on the price changes, in 1970 dollars, of some petroleum products. If biases produced by devaluations are ignored, the disparities in the 1970 prices of kerosene, bunker oil, and regular gasoline in the two sets of countries increased during the 1970s.34/

Within the first group, Venezuela's prices for those derivatives were the lowest in 1980 and 1981. Indonesia and Mexico followed, in the case of kerosene and bunker oil, and Mexico and Indonesia followed, in the case of regular gasoline. In contrast, prices for these derivatives were considerably higher in Thailand, Brazil, and the Philippines.35/

Domestic kerosene prices were the same in Mexico and Venezuela in 1970, slightly higher in Indonesia and the Philippines, double in Thailand, and almost triple in Brazil. In 1981 Venezuela had the lowest price for that derivative. Indonesia's and Mexico's kerosene prices were double that price; it was more than triple in Thailand, almost four times more in Brazil, and more than five times greater in the Philippines.

A similar situation occurred with bunker oil prices, although to a lesser degree. Even though prices rose in Venezuela, Indonesia, and Mexico from 1970 to 1978, the increases were much less than in the rest of the countries, with the exception of Thailand. In 1978 Venezuela had the lowest price, followed by Indonesia and Mexico, respectively. The price was slightly higher in Thailand and Brazil, and it was approximately 40% higher in the Philippines than it was in Mexico.

Regular gasoline prices followed a similar pattern. However, the difference between the prices current in the exporting countries and those in the net energy importers grew considerably. Prices went down in Venezuela in 1981, relative to 1960. They stayed at the same level in Mexico,

Indonesia, and Ecuador during that period and went up considerably in Brazil and Thailand, especially after the first oil crisis.

Energy Detente provides additional information about the 1983 prices of other derivatives. The current dollar values of the domestic currency are used as a reference currency. Mexico's diesel prices in 1983 were among the lowest, although Venezuela's prices were still lower. In Indonesia prices were 1.7 times higher than Mexico's, and Brazil's prices were 3.6 times higher.

Information on natural and liquefied gas price increases shows the differences between Brazil and some Latin American hydrocarbon exporters to be even more marked. Natural gas prices were similar in Mexico and Bolivia. They were much lower than Venezuela's, and Brazil's were six times higher than Mexico's. Liquefied gas prices in Mexico were the lowest of a wide range of countries. Bolivia's prices, for example, were twice as high; Venezuela's, 1.5 times; and Brazil's, four times.36/

It is necessary to also compare the evolution of prices in Mexico and the newly industrialized Asian countries. The information presented here relates to the changes in the domestic prices of some petroleum derivatives at the end of the 1970s and the beginning of the 1980s, using 1973 as the base year (see Tables 2.22 and 2.23).

Increases in the domestic prices of regular gasoline in 1975, 1977, and 1981 were lower in Singapore and Indonesia than in Mexico, South Korea, and Thailand. Price increases in Mexico and Korea were similar to those in Thailand. Prices in the Philippines were much higher and showed the largest increase. In 1981 the Philippines had much higher prices than any other country.

Discrepancies in the increase rates of domestic gasoline prices in different countries coincide somewhat with the trends observed in the preceding section in respect to the relative growth of the transportation sector.37/ The fact that Singapore's transportation sector grew more than Mexico's coincided with smaller increases in gasoline prices in that country, as compared to Mexico. The same relationship exists between Mexico and Thailand. Like Singapore, Thailand experienced larger increases in gasoline prices and lower growth rates in transportation. In the case of South Korea, slight increases in gasoline prices were linked to higher growth rates in the transportation sector.

The Philippines is the exception. While it was recording large increases in gasoline prices, its transportation sector was undergoing a high growth rate. An explanation might be that the large increase in gasoline prices occurred from 1979 to 1981, and the information available on transportation only covers the period to 1980. As a consequence, the impact on the sector's growth rate is not apparent in the figures used.

The figures in Tables 2.22 and 2.23 give additional information on the changes occurring in the prices of two other petroleum derivatives: kerosene and bunker oil. Price increases for kerosene were smaller in Indonesia, South Korea, and, especially, Singapore, as compared to Mexico and Thailand. The Philippines is, again, the country with the largest increase. In the case of domestic bunker oil prices, Mexico showed the smallest increase. The increment was greater in South Korea and Indonesia, while it was even more pronounced in the Philippines, Singapore, and Thailand.

The results from the price changes in the main petroleum products broaden the information on Mexico's end use energy in an international context. Just as the other dynamic oil countries did during the 1970s and part of the 1980s, Mexico kept end use energy prices below those of industrializing countries.

This, however, did not result in an increased economic growth rate, as compared to the other NICs. It seems that low energy prices favored the individual transportation sectors and definitely had an influence on transportation's trend in end use. As a consequence, Mexico, like the other net energy-exporting developing countries, had larger increases in the growth rate of its end use energy.

An additional factor should be considered. The larger price increases of derivatives occurring in the most dynamic of the south Asian countries were part of a broader policy of efficient energy use and conservation.38/ The Asian NICs took steps toward efficient energy use and conservation just before the end of the 1970s. In contrast, the Indonesian government did not show any official interest in the problem until 1982.

In 1977 South Korea decided to increase energy prices to put them in line with world market prices and to reflect "real costs." Singapore adopted a policy of "realistic prices." Thailand decided to adjust domestic energy prices slowly to those prevailing on the international market, while the Philippines increased them notably.

In addition to adjusting energy prices to conform to the world market, these countries adopted other measures directed toward a more efficient use of energy. Among them are fiscal and financial incentives; regulatory automobile use; standards for energy use in industry, commerce, and residential sectors; information campaigns; and some attempts at research on developing alternative energy sources.39/

There is no doubt that when the south Asian NICs took steps toward efficient energy use and conservation, they experienced repercussions: The growth rates of their energy consumption were reduced, without slowing down the process of economic growth and industrialization.

In contrast, with the exception of Brazil, Latin American countries (Mexico, in particular) as well as other hydrocarbon-exporting countries (Indonesia), showed no official interest in efficient energy use and conservation until the end of the 1970s or even the beginning of the 1980s.40/ In Mexico the official interest shown during the first few years of the 1970s did not resurface until 1980, with the new energy program. It is, therefore, not exaggerated to state that Mexico's pronounced increases in energy consumption can be explained by the absence of measures toward conservation and efficient use of energy and the absence of price policies tending to regulate demand.

Contrasting Mexico's experiences with those of other countries undergoing a pronounced process of industrialization, we can argue that Mexico's experience in industrialization does not, of itself, explain the notable growth of energy end use during the 1970s. Rather, these increases were the consequence of the speed at which the transportation sector grew, the bias in industrialization toward producing goods that are heavily dependent on hydrocarbons (automobiles, in particular), the existence and continuance of low energy prices, and the postponement of measures directed toward conservation and the efficient use of energy.

NOTES

1. Nacional Financiera, S.A. (NAFINSA), La economía mexicana en cifras (Mexico, 1981).

2. A further word is needed on the problem of information. Including the 1960s in this analysis of energy consumption trends in Mexico and given the fact that even the information from the most complete sources available (PEMEX, SEPAFIN-SEMIP, and SPP) will necessitate consulting

other sources. Such is the case with NAFINSA's publication, La economía mexicana en cifras. The information on energy includes only oil and electricity. To this resulting bias, one could add the differences between this information and that from other sources in measuring the growth rates of the GNP and the population. However, as can be seen later in this book, NAFINSA's figures can be used to detect general changes in energy consumption from 1970 to 1979, as compared to the previous decade.

3. NAFINSA's figures (Cf. column f of the same table) show the opposite tendency, the result of the bias produced by the absence of information on natural gas consumption. The evaluation is based on the information supplied in Table 2.3 and indicates a decrease in the natural gas share of end use energy from 1970 to 1975 and an increase in the following five-year period. By not including natural gas consumption, NAFINSA's figures are high for the first half of the 1970s and low for the second half, compared to the information given by the México: Balance de energía and information bulletins from the energy sector.

4. Secretaría de Patrimonio y Fomento Industrial (SEPAFIN), Balance de energía (Mexico, 1975-1981); and NAFINSA, Economía mexicana.

5. Cf. SEPAFIN, Programa de energía: Metas a 1990 y proyecciones al año 2000 (Resumen y conclusiones) (Mexico, 1980); SEPAFIN, Balance de energía; NAFINSA, Economía mexicana.

6. Mexico went from a net importer of hydrocarbons, including oil, in 1970 to a net exporter in 1975. In 1975 13% of the domestic crude produced was exported; this number rose to 42.8% in 1980 and to 54.3% in 1982. Natural gas exports ceased in 1973 to 1974 but were begun again in small volumes in 1980, reaching 7% of domestic production. Cf. Secretaría de Energía y Minas e Industria Paraestatal (SEMIP), Programa nacional de energéticos 1984-1988 (Mexico, August 1984), pp.148 and 151.

7. SEMIP, Programa nacional, p.48; Petróleos Mexicanos (PEMEX), México: Balance de energía, 1982 (Mexico: Subdirección de Planeación y Coordinación, 1983), p.13.

8. SEMIP, Programa nacional, p.41.

9. Raúl Gastelum and Oscar M. Guzmán, "Posibilidades de ahorro de energía en el sector energético de México (Versión preliminar)," mimeograph (Mexico, November 1982).

10. According to the energy balances, end use includes the following sectors: residential, commercial, and public; transportation; farming; industrial; and unidentified. End

use is divided into energy use and non-energy use.

11. It should be pointed out that these figures do not coincide with those obtained from the energy commission. However, both sources show a trend toward an increasing share for the transportation sector and a decreasing share for the industrial sector. Cf. Jaime Mario Willars, "Evolución del sector de hidrocarburos en México: Efectos macroeconómicos, elementos de política y perspectivas," mimeograph (Mexico, November 1983), p.27.

12. This is analyzed in the second part of the chapter.

13. Cf. Gastelum and Guzmán, "Posibilidades," for PEMEX and Santiago Levy, "Sobre el patrón de uso de energía en la economía mexicana," mimeograph (Mexico, Oficina de Asesores del C. Presidente, September 1982), for the non energy industry.

14. Gastelum and Guzmán, "Posibilidades," p.1.

15. Corazón Morales Siddayao, "Energy Conservation Policies in the Asia-Pacific Region: Economic Evaluation," mimeograph (Manila, January 1982).

16. The exceptions are Australia, among the industrialized countries of the Pacific, and the Philippines, Colombia and, to a certain extent, Malaysia, among the most dynamic underdeveloped countries (see Tables 2.5, 2.6, and 2.7).

17. According to PEMEX, México: Balance, the AAGR of per capita energy consumption is higher than what is indicated in Table 2.6: 6.5% from 1975 to 1980, compared to 5.1% from 1975 to 1979.

18. We should point out again that the figures for Mexico underestimate its trend in consumption for 1974 to 1979 because they include only oil and electricity. Cf. notes 2 and 3, this chapter.

19. India is a case apart because it is not very dependent on fossil fuels. Cf. Table 2.9.

20. Alejandro Villagómez, "Crecimiento económico y consumo de energía en el sector manufacturero, 1965-1979," Economía Mexicana 5 (1983).

21. Comparisons of the changes in product elasticity for energy consumption between the countries of both regions only indicate trends, given the discrepancies in calculating the elasticities.

22. It is very difficult to apply the experience of these countries, given all the difficulties they had during the 1970s. These events had repercussions in their rates of growth and energy consumption.

23. There are problems in including these two countries in the study. Colombia ceased to be a net energy exporter during the 1960s (see Table 2.10), and information on Bolivia does not seem very reliable.

24. Although we are certain about the general validity of such conclusions, differences in information could produce bias. Figures for Latin American consumptions include only fossil fuels and electricity, and the most recent information for this group of countries is from 1979, and that for south Asian countries is from 1980.

25. Siddayao, the source for information on the south Asian countries, does not give figures for the manufacturing industry's growth in Indonesia.

26. The estimate is independent of the drop in growth rates of the former countries after the first oil crisis. Mexico's rate is still the lowest.

27. For these same countries, the manufacturing sector's share in the GDP was 23%, 26%, 28%, 28%, and 20%, respectively. It was 30% for Brazil.

28. Discrepancies in sectorial energy use are even more notable in the rest of the Latin American energy-exporting countries: Bolivia applies 40.5% of its end use energy to industry and 49.1% to transportation. In Ecuador the respective percentages are 23% and 42.8% and in Venezuela, 44.7% and 47.5%. Information available does not permit including Indonesia in the comparisons (see Tables 2.20 and 2.21).

29. From 1970 to 1979, the transportation industry grew more than the manufacturing industry in Venezuela. The opposite was true in Bolivia and Ecuador.

30. It is possible that something similar happened in the other net fossil fuel-exporting countries: Ecuador, Indonesia, and Venezuela. The figures in the tables showing their manufacturing and transportation growth suggest this. A more detailed comparative study is needed, however, given their industrialization is more recent and less marked than Mexico's.

31. It has not been possible to compare this experience with that of the rest of the NICs, something necessary to test the validity of this hypothesis.

32. During the period 1970 to 1981, AAGRs for total automobile, terminal automobile, and car parts branches were 11.1%, 12.3%, and 9.4%, respectively. The AAGRs for the manufacturing GDP and the overall GDP were 7.2% and 6.7%, in that order. Cf. Secretaría de Programación y Presupuesto (SPP), Análisis y expectativas de la industria

automotriz en México: 1982-1986 (Mexico, October 1982), chart 2.6, p.17.

33. SPP, Análisis y expectativas, chart 1.3, p.10.

34. The same type of comparison is made later, using a different procedure to avoid the biases mentioned. Comparisons of changes in domestic energy prices among countries use 1973 domestic prices as the basis. This was possible only for Mexico and the south Asian countries.

35. Sterner does not give information for the other countries studied.

36. Cf. Willars, "Evolución," pp.40-47.

37. It should be explained that data referring to the transportation sector include other activities, such as communications (see Table 2.19). This, plus the fact that not all the sector's energy consumption is gasoline, leads to an unavoidable bias. Conclusions made to that effect should be taken as hypotheses, subject to additional study.

38. Siddayao's study on energy conservation policies documents this.

39. The Philippines' effort to substitute gas-alcohol for gasoline is worthy of note. Cf. Siddayao, "Energy Conservation," charts 2 and 3.

40. SEPAFIN, Seminario de economías de energía (Eficiencia y ahorro de energéticos) (Mexico, August 1978 and March 1979).

TABLE 2.1
Domestic Production of Energy in Mexico: Total Consumption and End Use, 1960–1982

Years	Average Annual Growth Rate					
	(a) Domestic Production	(b) Oil Production	(c) Gas Production	(d) Total Consumption	(e) End Use	(f) Total Consumption of Oil and Electricity
1960–1965	—	—	—	—	—	3.4
1965–1970	—	—	—	—	—	7.0
1970–1975	7.4	10.8	3.4	7.2	7.9	9.4
1975–1979	15.4	19.7	7.9	9.4	8.5	7.6
1975–1980	17.9	22.0	10.5	10.1	8.8	—
1981–1982	14.5	18.8	14.5	7.1	3.3	—
1975–1982	17.5	21.2	10.2	9.7	8.8	—
1960–1970	—	—	—	—	—	5.1
1970–1979	10.9	14.7	5.4	8.2	8.2	8.6
1970–1980	12.5	16.3	6.9	8.7	8.4	—

Sources: Columns a, d, and e: Comisión de Energéticos, Energéticos: Boletín Informativo del Sector
Energético (November 19, 1981), p. 1, and Petróleos Mexicanos, México: Balance de energía, 1982 (1982),
columns b and c: Secretaría de Energía, Minas e Industria Paraestatal, Programa nacional de energía
1984–1988 (1982), p. 148; column f: Nacional Financiera, S.A., La economía mexicana en cifras (1981).

TABLE 2.2
Domestic Production of Primary Energy in Mexico, 1970-1982
(in percentages)

Year	Coal	Oil	Natural Gas	Hydro-energy	Geo-energy
1970	2.1	55.2	32.6	10.1	0.2
1975	2.5	62.7	27.6	7.0	0.2
1976	2.0	65.3	25.3	7.2	0.2
1977	2.0	69.5	21.5	6.8	0.2
1978	1.8	70.2	23.2	4.6	0.2
1979	1.5	71.5	22.5	4.3	0.2
1980	1.1	75.1	20.5	3.1	0.2
1981	1.0	70.1	24.9	3.8	0.2
1982	1.0	70.8	25.0	3.0	0.2

Sources: Secretaría de Patrimonio y Fomento Industrial and Secretaría de Energía, Minas e Industria Paraestatal energy balances for 1970 and 1975-1981; Petróleos Mexicanos, México: Balance de energía, 1982 (1983).

TABLE 2.3
Structure of Energy End Use in Mexico, 1970-1982 (in percentages)

Year	Total	Solid Fuels	Petroleum Products	Natural Gas	Electricity
1970	100.0	4.3	67.0	21.8	6.9
1975	100.0	3.7	71.0	17.9	7.4
1976	100.0	3.5	72.2	16.7	7.6
1977	100.0	4.3	71.1	16.0	8.0
1978	100.0	4.2	70.1	17.9	7.8
1979	100.0	3.8	70.2	18.2	7.8
1980	100.0	3.4	69.9	19.2	7.5
1981	100.0	3.1	70.6	18.8	7.5
1982	100.0	2.4	67.3	22.8	7.5

Sources: Secretaría de Patrimonio y Fomento Industrial and Secretaría de Energía, Minas e Industria Paraestatal energy balances for 1970 and 1975-1981; Petróleos Mexicanos, México: Balances de energía, 1982 (1983).

TABLE 2.4
Structure of Gross Generation of Electric Power in Mexico
(in percentages)

Year	Hydroelectricity	Hydrocarbons	Geothermal	Coal
1970	56.9	43.1	—	n.s.
1975	36.7	62.0	1.3	n.s.
1976	38.3	60.4	1.3	n.s.
1977	38.9	59.9	1.2	n.s.
1978	30.3	68.0	1.1	—
1979	30.7	67.5	1.8	—
1980	27.1	71.4	1.5	—
1981	36.0	62.6	1.4	—
1982	31.0	65.7	1.8	1.5
1983a/	27.5	67.5	1.8	3.2

Source: Secretaría de Energía, Minas e Industria Paraestatal,
Programa nacional de energéticos 1984–1988 (1984), p. 146.

n.s. = not significant

a/ Preliminary results.

FIGURE 2.1
Domestic Energy Consumption in Mexico, Equivalent to Millions of Barrels of Crude Oil (in percentages)

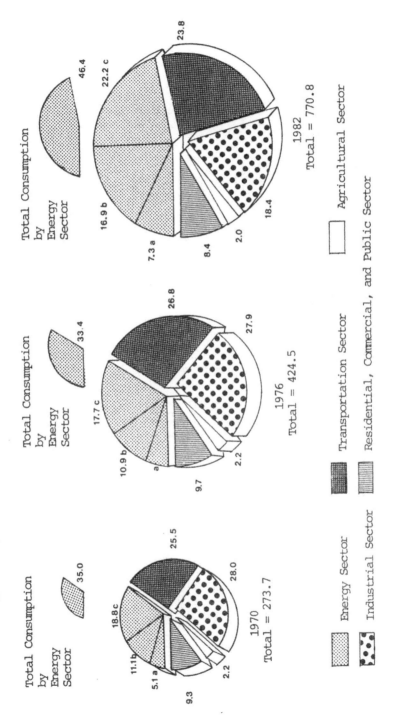

32

TABLE 2.5
Gross Domestic Product and Per Capita Energy Consumption in Selected Countries in Asia (in growth rate percentages)

Country	Per Capita GDP 1960-70	1970-80	1973-80	Per Capita Energy Consumption 1960-70	1970-80	1973-80
South Asia						
Bangladesh	1.16	2.16	3.63	—	8.13[a]	3.64
India	1.65[b]	1.25	2.07	2.32	0.52	2.82
Pakistan	3.31[b]	7.65	2.04	5.22	9.78	4.00
Sri Lanka	2.50	2.94	3.77	3.59	-1.42	-2.14
East-Southeast Asia						
South Korea	5.66	6.57	5.89	11.19	6.99	7.28
The Philippines	2.14	3.42	3.39	7.39	0.86	0.61
Singapore	6.51	7.20	6.05	13.30	7.39	4.84
Thailand	4.39	4.57	4.66	13.40	3.93	3.31
Producers						
Burma	0.77	2.19	3.30	0.95	1.02	3.02
Malaysia	5.01	5.10	4.66	7.76	4.27	2.81
Indonesia	1.26	4.99	4.55	0.94	8.95	10.79

Source: Siddayao, Corazón Morales, "Energy Conservation Policies in the Asia-Pacific Region: Economic Evaluation," mimeograph (Manila, 1982), p. 90.

a/ 1971-1980.
b/ 1961-1970.

TABLE 2.6
Gross Domestic Product and Per Capita Energy Consumption in Selected Countries in Latin America,
1960-1979 (in growth rate percentages)

| Country | Per Capita GDP | | | Per Capita Energy Consumption | | | a/ |
	1960-70	1970-75	1975-79	1970-79	1960-70	1970-75	1975-79	1970-79
Argentina	2.9	2.5	0.75	2.0	4.9	0.2	3.7	1.7
Bolivia	3.2	3.2	1.0	2.2	3.4	7.7	8.3	8.0
Brazil	3.1	8.0	3.9	6.2	3.7	6.4	7.0	6.7
Colombia	2.2	3.8	3.6	3.7	4.3	3.3	1.8	2.6
Chile	2.3	-2.9	5.7	0.8	5.6	-2.7	2.9	-0.25
Mexico	3.6	2.3	2.1	2.2	4.2	3.4	5.1	4.2
Peru	2.1	1.8	-1.5	0.3	4.1	2.4	-1.3	0.7
Uruguay	0.4	0.6	4.0	2.1	1.7	1.6	1.8	1.7
Venezuela	2.2	1.2	1.2	1.2	2.7	2.8	6.4	4.4
Ecuador	2.2	5.4	3.7	4.7	5.2	7.8	10.1	7.9

Source: United Nations, Anuario estadístico de América Latina   (Santiago, 1981), pp. 114, 125, 127.

a/ Hydrocarbons and electricity.

TABLE 2.7
Gross Domestic Product and Per Capita Energy Consumption in Industrialized
Countries of the Pacific (in growth rate percentages)

Country	Per Capita GDP			Per Capita Energy Consumption		
	1960-70	1970-80	1973-80	1960-70	1970-80	1973-80
Australia	3.12	1.46	1.09	2.80	1.64	1.15
Canada	3.35	2.81	1.72	4.23	1.54	0.57
Japan	9.64	3.58	2.65	10.1	1.47	0.96
New Zealand	2.06	1.04	2.68	2.04	2.12	0.83
United States	2.60	1.97	1.30	13.29	-0.43	-1.32

Source: Siddayao, Corazón Morales, "Energy Conservation Policies in
the Asia-Pacific Region: Economic Evaluation," mimeograph (Manila, 1982).

TABLE 2.8
Growth Rates of Total Primary Energy (TPE) Consumption and Gross Domestic
Product (GDP) in Industrialized Countries

Country	1978 International Energy Association Study	1982 International Energy Association Study		
	1960	1973	1980	1981
Austria				
Rate of TPE/GDP (%)	1.37	0.67	0.61	0.59
TPE Per Capita (Kcal x 10^7)[a]	1.76	3.2	3.6	3.5
Elasticity TPE/GDP	1.02	0.54	3.1	—
Annual Growth Rate GDP	—	3.0	0.0	—
Belgium				
Rate of TPE/GDP (%)	1.60	0.78	0.65	0.62
TPE Per Capita (Kcal x 10^7)	2.8	4.80	4.75	4.42
Elasticity TPE/GDP	0.95	0.00	3.9	—
Annual Growth Rate GDP	—	2.5	-1.8	—
Canada				
Rate of TPE/GDP (%)	1.93	1.21	1.19	1.13
TPE Per Capita (Kcal x 10^7)	5.37	8.6	9.5	9.7
Elasticity TPE/GDP	0.98	0.9	-0.4	—
Annual Growth Rate GDP	—	2.9	3.8	—
Denmark				
Rate of TPE/GDP (%)	0.93	0.51	0.45	0.40
TPE Per Capita (Kcal x 10^7)	1.96	3.89	3.75	3.38
Elasticity TPE/GDP	1.38	-0.13	-142.2	—
Annual Growth Rate GDP	—	1.6	0.1	—
Germany				
Rate of TPE/GDP (%)	1.25	0.63	0.55	0.53
TPE Per Capita (Kcal x 10^7)	2.63	4.4	4.5	4.3
Elasticity TPE/GDP	1.04	0.11	-20.48	—
Annual Growth Rate GDP	—	2.2	0.2	—
Italy				
Rate of TPE/GDP (%)	0.9	0.69	0.61	0.60
TPE Per Capita (Kcal x 10^7)	1.0	2.4	2.5	2.4
Elasticity TPE/GDP	1.51	0.35	—	—
Annual Growth Rate GDP	—	2.8	-0.15	—

(continued)

TABLE 2.8 (continued)
Growth Rates of Total Primary Energy (TPE) Consumption and Gross Domestic
Product (GDP) in Industrialized Countries

Country	1978 International Energy Association Study 1960	1982 International Energy Association Study 1973	1980	1981
Ireland				
Rate of TPE/GDP (%)	1.62	0.96	0.86	0.85
TPE Per Capita (Kcal x 10^7)	1.5	2.41	2.54	2.52
Elasticity TPE/GDP	1.08	0.6	0.21	—
Annual Growth Rate GDP	—	3.7	-1.2	—
The Netherlands				
Rate of TPE/GDP (%)	1.16	0.73	0.66	0.63
TPE Per Capita (Kcal x 10^7)	1.91	4.6	4.6	4.3
Elasticity TPE/GDP	1.61	0.37	5.0	—
Annual Growth Rate GDP	—	2.3	-1.2	—
Norway				
Rate of TPE/GDP (%)	1.31	0.75	0.66	0.67
TPE Per Capita (Kcal x 10^7)	2.50	4.9	5.9	5.9
Elasticity TPE/GDP	1.26	0.63	0.80	—
Annual Growth Rate GDP	—	4.8	0.8	—
Spain				
Rate of TPE/GDP (%)	1.27	0.59	0.66	0.66
TPE Per Capita (Kcal x 10^7)	0.65	1.66	2.05	2.02
Elasticity TPE/GDP	1.13	1.73	1.39	—
Annual Growth Rate GDP	—	2.36	0.34	—
Sweden				
Rate of TPE/GDP (%)	1.30	0.70	0.63	0.65
TPE Per Capita (Kcal x 10^7)	3.6	5.9	5.9	6.0
Elasticity TPE/GDP	1.08	0.16	-4.76	—
Annual Growth Rate GDP	—	1.9	-0.65	—
Switzerland				
Rate of TPE/GDP (%)	0.87	0.4	0.4	0.4
TPE Per Capita (Kcal x 10^7)	2.18	3.7	3.9	3.9
Elasticity TPE/GDP	1.28	1.95	-0.43	—
Annual Growth Rate GDP	—	0.3	1.9	—
Great Britain				
Rate of TPE/GDP (%)	1.85	0.99	0.81	0.79
TPE Per Capita (Kcal x 10^7)	3.26	4.2	3.6	3.5
Elasticity TPE/GDP	0.71	-2.2	2.1	—
Annual Growth Rate GDP	—	0.9	-2.0	—
United States				
Rate of TPE/GDP (%)	1.51	0.82	0.79	0.79
TPE Per Capita (Kcal x 10^7)	5.61	0.65	0.73	0.75
Elasticity TPE/GDP	1.05	0.86	1.21	—
Annual Growth Rate GDP	—	4.44	4.41	—

Sources: International Energy Agency, Energy Policies and Programmes of IEA
Countries (Paris, 1982). International Energy Agency, Energy Policies and
Programmes of IEA Countries Paris, 1978. Column 1 represents the 1978 study;
columns 2, 3, 4 represent the 1982 study.

a/ In the source, the data are in MTOE (metric tons of oil-equivalent); 1 MTOE = 10 cal.

TABLE 2.9
Fossil Fuel Consumption in Pacific Asian Countries (in percentages)

Country	1970			1980			Net Energy Imports as % of Total Consumption
	Coal	Oil	Natural Gas	Coal	Oil	Natural Gas	
South Asia							
Bangladesh	9	53	36	4	52	42	68
India	74	22	1	65	29	1	26
Nepal	6	90	0	6	80	0	88
Pakistan	12	48	37	9	34	50	48
Sri Lanka	1	94	0	0	88	0	100
East and South-east Asia							
Brunei	25	---	75	0	9	91	---
Burma	15	81	1	11	65	18	7
China	92	7	---	74	21	3	---
Indonesia	1	69	29	1	82	16	---
South Korea	48	52	0	38	60	0	77
Malaysia	1	95	1	0	76	22	---
The Philippines	1	97	0	3	93	0	90
Singapore	---	100	0	0	100	0	100
Thailand	2	96	0	3	94	0	94
Industrialized Countries	26	49	22	24	48	24	29
Developing Countries	21	62	14	15	64	16	---
World Total	35	43	20	31	43	22	0

Source: Siddayao, Corazón Morales, "Energy Conservation Policies in the Asia-Pacific Region: Economic Evaluation," mimeograph (Manila, 1982), p.86.

TABLE 2.10
Primary Energy by Source in Selected Countries in Latin America (in percentage of total gross domestic supply)

Country	Exports Relative to Gross Domestic Supply	Imports Relative to Gross Domestic Supply	Coal	Fuelwood and other vegetable and animal fuels	Crude Oil	Natural Gas	Associated Gas	Hydro-energy	Geo-energy	Coke
Argentina										
1970	—	9.53	2.7	7.2	69.3	17.1	—	0.6	—	0.03
1978	—	12.41	2.5	4.9	65.2	17.5	—	2.2	—	0.4
Bolivia										
1970	61.9	—	0.02	24.7	60.9	—	3.6	18.2	—	0.03
1979	86.38	—	0.01	18.5	70.1	—	14.4	13.8	—	0.01
Brazil										
1976	—	42.73	3.6	30.0	48.1	0.7	—	8.5	—	0.1
1980	—	41.08	4.9	38.4	45.5	1.0	—	10.7	—	0.3
Colombia										
1970	49.25	—	12.8	24.6	57.2	7.5	7.7	5.6	—	0.02
1979	—	6.03	17.7	13.6	42.1	16.5	6.1	7.8	—	0.02
Chile										
1970	—	31.21	3.3	13.7	37.6	24.8	—	3.5	—	0.07
1978	—	31.56	9.2	13.1	44.8	27.8	—	5.6	—	0.6
Ecuador										
1970	—	40.40	—	44.8	49.1	—	4.3	1.5	—	—
1978	160.99	—	—	21.4	96.0	—	0.9	1.7	—	—
Mexico										
1970	4.43	—	2.2	18.0	47.8	23.3	3.0	10.6	—	0.5
1980	44.43	—	2.1	11.4	54.8	9.7	21.5	4.3	0.2	0.1
Peru										
1970	—	12.62	0.5	38.5	44.4	—	5.1	4.5	—	0.4
1979	28.92	—	0.5	31.7	62.6	—	5.3	6.3	—	0.9
Uruguay										
1970	—	77.01	0.7	19.8	74.9	—	—	5.3	—	0.1
1980	—	69.24	0.1	19.5	69.9	—	—	12.0	—	0.02
Venezuela a/										
1970	807.34	—	0.5	0.02	86.7	—	12.8	0.4	—	0.2
1979	318.32	—	0.5	0.02	75.3	—	23.0	0.2	—	0.3

Source: Organización Latinoamericana de Energía, Balances energéticos de América Latina, Quito, Ecuador.

a/ The gross domestic supply of primary energy was used for Venezuela's percentage.

TABLE 2.11
Energy Consumption by Source in Pacific Industrialized Countries (in percentages)

Country	1970			1980			Net Energy Imports as % of Total Consumption
	Coal	Oil	Natural Gas	Coal	Oil	Natural Gas	
Australia	49	46	3	42	43	13	--
Canada	13	53	23	12	48	27	--
Japan	27	68	2	19	68	8	102
New Zealand	24	55	2	18	48	14	52
United States	21	42	36	23	42	31	18

Source: Siddayao, Corazón Morales, "Energy Conservation Policies in the Asia-Pacific Region: Economic Evaluation," mimeograph (Manila, 1982), p.89.

TABLE 2.12
Sectorial Energy Consumption in Developing Countries in Asia (in percentages)

Energy Type, Country, and Year	Industry	Transportation	Generation of Electricity	Agriculture	Residential, Commercial, Public
OIL					
South Asia					
Bangladesh (1978/79)	20.1	30.9	13.4	5.4	30.0
Natural Gas	(60.0)	—	(29.7)	—	(1.3)
India (1978)	28.7	39.5	8.1	19.1	19.1
Pakistan (1978/79)	5.2	57.2	a	6.0	31.2
Southeast Asia					
Indonesia (1978)	24.5	29.5	7.7	———38.3———	
The Philippines (1981)	41.2	28.2	24.2	n.a.	6.8
Thailand (1978)	17.0	44.4	23.3	8.9	6.4
COMMERCIAL ENERGY					
South Asia					
Bangladesh (1978/79)	61.1	17.5	a	3.0	18.5
Pakistan (1978/79)	34.0	22.0	a	20.0	16.0
Sri Lanka (1980)	36.6	35.9	a	—	27.5
Southeast Asia					
The Philippines (1981)	41.3	35.1	a	n.a.	25.9
Indonesia (1977)	32.8	29.7	6.5	———31.0———	
Thailand (1977)	37.3	31.9	a	1.5	15.1
Korea (1979)	44.3	12.6	a	n.a.	43.1
Singapore (1980)	38.0	33.0	a	—	28.6

Source: Siddayao, Corazón Morales, "Energy Conservation Policies in the Asia-Pacific Region: Economic Evaluation," mimeograph (Manila, 1982).

a/ Distributed in other sectors.

TABLE 2.13
Structure of End-Use Energy in Selected Countries in Latin America, 1970 and 1978 or 1979 (in percentages)

Country	Year	Residential, Commercial, Public	Transportation	Agriculture	Industry	Unidentified	Total
Argentina	1970	19.46	38.23	3.87	36.24	2.17	100.0
	1978	24.43	37.60	4.27	24.27	1.5	100.0
Bolivia	1970	36.29	40.46	4.05	19.16	—	100.0
	1979	29.42	49.09	2.89	18.58	—	100.0
Brazil	1976	27.73	29.79	6.40	36.07	—	100.0
	1980	24.34	29.19	6.72	39.66	0.06	100.0
Colombia	1970	38.76	24.63	2.5	32.74	0.31	100.0
	1979	34.75	30.57	2.23	31.59	0.84	100.0
Chile	1970	31.90	33.02	—	35.06	—	100.0
	1978	30.37	30.23	—	39.39	—	100.0
Ecuador	1970	58.22	23.04	4.03	14.60	0.10	100.0
	1978	35.75	42.82	4.47	16.46	0.48	100.0
Mexico	1970	37.47	28.18	1.92	28.74	3.66	100.0
	1980	30.96	35.16	2.49	26.70	4.69	100.0
Peru	1970	44.38	21.76	7.63	26.23	—	100.0
	1979	45.61	22.41	4.27	27.70	—	100.0
Uruguay	1970	40.71	28.18	—	30.74	0.37	100.0
	1980	37.53	29.52	—	32.47	0.49	100.0
Venezuela	1970	16.79	44.71	0.16	37.45	0.64	100.0
	1979	12.51	47.48	0.07	39.82	0.12	100.0

Source: Organización Latinoamericana de Energía, Balances energéticos de América Latina (Quito, Ecuador, 1981).

TABLE 2.14
Sectorial Energy Consumption in Pacific Industrialized Countries (in percentages)

Country (Year)	Industry	Transportation	Electricity	Residential, Commercial, Public
Australia (1979)	28.7	22.6	35.0	13.9
Japan (1979)	54.3	18.9	a	24.3
New Zealand (1979)	38.1	36.5	a	25.4
United States (1981)	39.2	26.0	a	34.8
United States (1979)	41.1	25.9	a	33.0

Source: Siddayao, Corazón Morales, "Energy Conservation Policies in the Asia-Pacific Region: Economic Evaluation," mimeograph (Manila, 1982), p.93.

a/ Distributed in other sectors.

TABLE 2.15
Ratio of Commercial Energy to Gross Domestic Product in Selected Countries in Asia, Industrialized Countries, and Mexico, 1960–1980

Country	1973	1980	Lowest Point (year)	Lowest Point (value)	Growth Rate (60-65)	(65-70)	(71-75)	(75-80)
South Asia								
Bangladesh	0.234	0.290	1978	0.234		—		10.78[a]
India	1.129	1.190	1973	1.129		4.9	-9.08	-6.2
Pakistan	1.064	1.200	1978	1.024		17.07	-9.46	-5.23
Sri Lanka	0.518	0.356	1980	0.356		8.86	-20.5	-22.44
Nepal	0.106	0.085	1976	0.084		102.04	3.03	-13.73
South Korea	1.851	2.041	1976	1.704		24.38	5.93	-1.24
The Philippines	0.901	0.741	1980	0.741		28.76	2.5	0.67
Singapore	0.860	0.790	1974	0.754		32.77	2.18	3.64
Thailand	0.892	0.812	1978	0.788		54.50	32.14	-8.71
Producers								
Burma	0.454	0.446	1975	0.439		3.07	3.83	-4.5
Indonesia	0.651	1.008	1973	0.651		-10.24	-0.28	43.78
Malaysia	0.880	0.773	1980	0.773		23.24	11.31	-4.09
Mexico[b]	0.925	1.066[c]	1973	0.925		-10.36	13.28	12.92[d]
Industrialized Countries								
Australia	0.855	0.890	1978	0.880		0.97	-4.39	0.22
Canada	1.381	1.27	1980	1.274		5.65	1.73	-7.11
Japan	0.761	0.677	1980	0.677		1.14	-0.25	-0.25
New Zealand	0.732	0.762	1975	0.700		0.45	5.36	5.35
United States	1.554	1.294	1980	1.294		0.06	-0.06	-11.19

Sources: Siddayao, Corazón Morales, "Energy Conservation Policies in the Asia-Pacific Region: Economic Evaluation," mimeograph (Manila, 1982), pp.96-97; Nacional Financiera, S.A. La economía mexicana en cifras, for Mexico (Mexico, 1981).

a/ Data from 1972-1975.
b/ These data have their bias because Mexico's information includes only oil and electricity.
c/ 1979.
d/ 1975-1979.

TABLE 2.16

Per Capita Hydrocarbon and Electric Power Consumption Per Unit of Per Capita GDP, 1960-1979 (in annual average growth rate)

Country	1960-65	1965-70	1970-75	1975-79	1960-70	1970-79
Argentina	2.18	1.71	-2.27	2.36	1.95	-0.24
Bolivia	3.67	-3.32	4.51	7.28	0.12	5.73
Brazil	0.31	0.86	-1.5	2.97	0.58	0.46
Colombia	1.97	2.31	-0.51	-1.70	2.14	-1.04
Chile	2.27	4.35	0.23	-2.61	3.31	-1.04
Ecuador	37.43	4.96	2.17	6.12	20.10	3.91
Mexico	-0.06	1.30	1.07	2.99	0.62	1.92
Peru	1.86	1.99	0.59	0.19	1.92	0.41
Uruguay	4.0	-1.56	1.05	-2.19	1.18	-0.40
Venezuela	-0.54	1.42	1.55	5.11	0.44	3.12

Source: United Nations, Anuario estadístico de América Latina (Santiago, 1981), pp.125, 127, 194 and 195.

TABLE 2.17
Income Elasticity of Energy Demand in Developing Countries in Asia

Country	Period	Income Elasticity	Country	Period	Income Elasticity
South Asia			East and Southeast Asia (Continued)		
Bangladesh	1972-80	1.45	Thailand	1960-80	2.57
	1973-80	1.55		1960-73	2.84
India	1960-80	0.93		1973-80	0.97
	1960-73	0.81	Producers		
	1973-80	0.89	Burma	1960-80	0.31
Pakistan	1961-80	0.95		1961-73	0.67
	1961-73	1.12		1973-80	0.56
	1973-80	1.14	Indonesia	1960-80	1.30
Sri Lanka	1960-80	0.80		1960-73	0.34
	1960-73	0.82		1973-80	2.46
	1973-80	0.79	Malaysia	1960-80	1.55
				1960-73	1.77
East and Southeast Asia				1973-80	0.51
South Korea	1960-80	1.32			
	1960-73	1.52			
	1973-80	1.00			
The Philippines	1960-80	1.89			
	1960-73	2.71			
	1973-80	0.86			
Singapore	1960-73	1.47			
	1960-73	1.50			
	1973-80	1.11			

Source: Siddayao, Corazón Morales, "Energy Conservation Policies in the Asia-Pacific Region: Economic Evaluation," mimeograph (Manila, 1982), pp.37-39.

TABLE 2.18
Product Elasticity of Per Capita Energy Consumption in Selected Countries in Latin America, 1960-1979a,b/

Country	Growth Rate					
	1960-65	1965-70	1970-75	1975-79	1960-70	1970-79
Argentina	1.80	1.60	0.40	2.89	1.70	0.88
Bolivia	2.36	0.06	2.45	8.69	1.05	3.68
Brazil	1.20	1.19	0.80	1.78	1.19	1.08
Colombia	2.20	1.84	0.86	0.51	1.96	0.70
Chile	1.88	3.31	0.92	0.51	2.48	-0.31
Ecuador	1.57	3.13	1.42	2.72	2.41	1.87
Mexico	0.98	1.38	1.48	2.52	1.18	1.91
Peru	1.64	3.03	1.31	0.86	1.92	2.29
Uruguay	-8.92	0.14	2.61	0.45	3.80	0.80
Venezuela	0.83	2.15	2.33	5.79	1.20	3.79

Source: United Nations, Anuario estadístico de América Latina (Santiago, 1981), pp.125, 127, 194, 195.

a/ Product Elasticity = Annual Average Growth Rate of Energy Consumption / Annual Average Growth Rate of Gross Domestic Product.

b/ Hydrocarbons and electricity.

TABLE 2.19
Average Annual Growth Rate of Some Economic Indicators, 1970-1979 and 1980

Period	Country	Gross Domestic Product	Energy Consumption	Per Capita Gross Domestic Product	Per Capita Energy Consumption	Population	Agriculture	Manufacturing	Construction	Transportation
1970-80	The Philippines	6.0	3.6	3.4	0.9	2.7	4.8	7.0	13.9	8.5
	Thailand	7.1	6.5	4.6	3.9	2.6	4.5	10.5	5.8	6.9
	South Korea	8.2	8.7	6.6	7.0	1.7	1.4	14.3	9.5	12.8
	Singapore	8.7	8.5	7.2	7.4	1.5	2.7	9.7	7.0	13.4
	Malaysia	—	—	5.1	4.3	—	—	—	—	—
	Indonesia	—	—	5.0	9.0	—	—	—	—	—
1970-79	Brazil	8.9 (12.8)[a]	10.4	6.2	6.7	2.5	5.1 (6.4)[a]	9.5 (13.9)[a]	(17.6)[a]	(14.0)[a]
	Colombia	5.9	7.0	3.7	2.6	2.2	4.8	6.8	—	8.7[a]
	Bolivia	4.8	9.2	2.2	8.0	2.5	3.1	5.7	—	3.1
	Venezuela	4.8	—	1.2	4.4	3.6	3.6	5.4	—	7.1
	Mexico	5.4 (8.1)	6.1 (8.4)	2.2	4.2	3.2 (3.1)	2.1 (1.2)	6.1 (7.1)	(10.1)	9.0
	Ecuador	7.8	12.6	4.7	7.9	3.0	4.2	10.2	—	8.1[a]
1973-80	The Philippines	6.0	3.3	3.4	0.6	2.7	4.7	6.3	15.0	8.5
	Thailand	7.1	5.8	4.7	3.3	2.5	4.0	9.5	11.0	7.3
	South Korea	7.5	8.9	5.9	7.3	1.6	0.2	12.4	10.4	12.0
	Singapore	7.4	6.2	6.1	4.8	1.4	1.8	5.1	7.3	10.9
	Malaysia	—	—	4.7	2.8	—	—	—	—	—
	Indonesia	—	—	4.6	10.8	—	—	—	—	—
1976-79	Brazil	6.5	10.2	3.9	7.0	2.4	3.8	6.9	—	(12.0)[b]
	Colombia	5.7	6.4	3.6	1.8	2.2	4.3	6.1	—	16.0[a]
	Bolivia	3.6	9.9	1.0	8.3	2.6	0.2	5.4	—	0.7
	Venezuela	4.9	9.5	1.2	6.4	3.6	2.6	5.7	—	4.9
	Mexico	5.1	8.6	2.1	5.1	3.0	2.6	6.3	—	8.9
	Ecuador	6.9	14.3	3.7	10.1	3.1	2.8	11.5	—	7.3[b]

Sources: Siddayao, Corazón Morales, "Energy Conservation Policies in the Asia-Pacific Region: Economic Evaluation," mimeograph (Manila, 1982), pp.90, 91; Nacional Financiera, S.A., La economía mexicana en cifras, 1981; United Nations, Anuario estadístico de América Latina (Santiago (CEPAL), 1981), pp.114, 125, 127.

Notes: Figures for Latin America are for oil and electric power consumption.
Figures in parentheses for Mexico are from NAFINSA, La economía mexicana en cifras.
Figures in parentheses for Brazil take real production indexes into account, with 1970 as a base.

a/ 1970-1978.
b/ 1976-1978.

TABLE 2.20
Industrial Indicators in Mexico and Selected Countries in Asia (in percentage of gross domestic product)

Country	Industry			Manufacturing		
	1960	1970	1980	1960	1970	1980
South Asia						
Bangladesh	7	10	13	5	7	7
India	20	22	26	14	14	18
Pakistan	16	23	25	12	16	16
Sri Lanka	20	20	30	15	12	18
East and Southeast Asia						
South Korea	20	27	39	14	18	28
The Philippines	28	30	37	20	23	26
Singapore	18	30	37	12	20	28
Thailand	19	25	29	13[b]	16[b]	20[b]
Mexico	29	31	35	19[b]	21[b]	23[b]
Poor Countries[a]	18	20	35	12	12	15
Intermediate Countries	32	35	37	23	22	25
Industrial Countries	40	40	37	30	29	27

Sources: Siddayao, Corazón Morales, "Energy Conservation Policies in the Asian-Pacific Region: Economic Policies," mimeograph (Manila, 1982), p.86; Nacional Financiera, S.A., La economía mexicana en cifras (Mexico, 1977). pp.29-34.

a/ Includes oil producers such as China and Indonesia.
b/ Excludes mining, oil, coal, electricity, and construction.

48

TABLE 2.21
Manufacturing Industry's Percentage in Generating Product in Selected
Countries in Latin America

Country	1960	1970	1975	1979
Argentina	26.3	30.2	32.0	30.1
Bolivia	11.4	14.3	14.9	15.9
Brazil	25.8	28.4	29.7	30.3
Colombia	16.4	17.5	18.4	18.7
Chile	24.9	27.2	22.9	23.7
Ecuador	15.1	16.8	17.1	20.2
Mexico	19.2	23.2	23.6	24.7
Peru	18.7	20.7	21.6	20.3
Uruguay	22.8	23.0	23.7	25.5
Venezuela	12.9	15.0	15.1	15.5

Source: United Nations, Anuario estadístico de América Latina (Santiago (CEPAL), 1981).

Note: GDP percentages at constant 1970 prices.

TABLE 2.22
Consumer Price Indexes for Refined Products in South and Southeast Asian Countries

Country	Year	Regular Gasoline	Kerosene	Bunker Oil
Indonesia (Jakarta)	1975	139	139	254
	1977	171	156	295
	1979	163	143	--
	1981	243	219	401
South Korea (Seoul)	1975	116	110	213
	1977	141	81	177
	1979	203	103	259
	1980	252	144	365
The Philippines (Manila)	1975	361	312	350
	1977	471	338	404
	1979	589	438	406
	1981	1,306	869	451
Singapore	1975	118	50	259
	1977	122	57	260
	1979	147	113	268
	1981	194	155	620
Thailand (Bangkok)	1975	164	125	225
	1977	188	139	250
	1979	354	217	448
	1981	546	317	694

Source: Siddayao, Corazón Morales, "Energy Conservation Policies in the Asia-Pacific Region: Economic Evaluation," mimeograph (Manila, 1982).

TABLE 2.23
Prices to the Public in the Federal District in Mexico

Energy Type	Pesos Per Unit	1973	1975	1977	1979	1980	1981	1982	Price Increases (%) 73-75	73-77	73-79	73-80	73-81
Natural Gas[a]	meter^3	0.14	0.44	0.51	0.74[b]	0.78[b]	0.83[b]	1.26[b]	214.28	264.28	428.57	457.14	492.85
Liquefied Gas	kilogram	0.85	2.98	2.40	2.40	2.50[c]	3.15[b]	4.72[b]	144.70	182.35	182.35	194.11	270.58
Reg. Gasoline	liter	1.40	2.10	2.80	2.80	2.80	6.00[d]	20.00	50.0	100.0	100.0	100.0	328.57
Extra	liter	2.00	3.00	4.00	4.00	7.00[c]	10.00[d]	30.00[d]	50.0	100.0	100.0	250.0	400.0
Kerosene[a]	liter	0.45	0.70	0.94	0.94	0.97	1.21[e]	9.12[d]	56.5	108.8	108.8	215.5	168.8
Diesel	liter[3e]	0.32	0.50	0.65	1.00[d]	1.00[b]	2.50[d]	10.00[b]	56.3	103.1	212.5	212.5	681.3
Bunker Oil[a]	meter^3	126.47	215.00	280.00	306.08[b]	370.83[b]	483.04[b]	796.86[b]	70.0	121.4	142.01	193.21	281.9

Source: Petróleos Mexicanos, Anuario estadístico 1982, pp.129-132.

a/ Average for all types.
b/ Yearly average.
c/ Beginning November 21.
d/ Beginning December.
e/ Beginning June.

3

An Overview of
Sectoral Energy Consumption
in Mexico

The general study in Chapter 2 pointed out some basic
characteristics of the dynamics of energy consumption in
Mexico during recent years (1970-1982). Factors shaping the
development of Mexico's energy consumption patterns were
examined and compared with the experiences of other developing countries, demonstrating a clear trend toward inefficient energy use and a marked tendency toward wasting the
country's resources. However, a general treatment of the
topic has clear limitations in that it does not allow for
the formulation of concrete proposals for defining policy
guidelines related to the conservation and the efficient
use of energy. To overcome such limitations, an analysis
by sectors is required. Likewise, the specific characteristic of each sector, and even intersectorial differences,
should be defined. This will lead to a better understanding of the factors determining how efficiently energy has
been used in Mexico.
   The energy content of a product or service can be attributed to technological choices as well as social and
economic options. Interpreting the evolution of partial energy consumption levels, particularly in industry and transportation, requires determining the interaction between
those technological and economic options that are possible
and those that are actually used. Here, the main emphasis
is on the technical aspects that shaped the development of
energy use into the early 1980s, but this should not be
seen as indicating a viewpoint that separates the technological from the socioeconomic and political fields. The
fact that the socioeconomic and political aspects are not
emphasized must be made explicit because it makes us aware
of the need and desirability of studying the evolution of

energy consumption levels in more depth.

The problem of obtaining adequate information is an important restriction in an analysis of energy consumption in Mexico. If the inconsistencies in the physical data, either in general or by source, for energy consumption are significant or even irreconcilable, they are even more so for the economic variables. This applies to existing information, which, in and of itself, is not sufficient to cover the wide range of needs of a study of this type.

We present here a macroanalysis of the evolution of energy use in Mexico, as well as a detailed study of consumption patterns and the efficient use of energy. We examine the relevant indicators for the variables considered for each economic sector and its components. These include the energy sector (hydrocarbons and electricity); the transportation sector; the industrial sector; the residential, commercial, and public (RCP) sector; and the rural sector.

The energy sector is made up of two large state-owned companies: Petróleos Mexicanos (PEMEX: Mexican Petroleum Company) and the Comisión Federal de Electricidad (CFE: Federal Commission of Electricity). PEMEX has a monopoly on extracting hydrocarbons and producing derivatives for energy and non-energy uses. CFE produces and distributes the country's electricity. The energy sector is not classified as an end-use consumer in the energy balances. However, it is of paramount importance to consider the energy sector in any study on the conservation and efficient use of Mexico's energy resources.

The rural sector is included separately because of the particular nature of this sector in underdeveloped countries such as Mexico, where the contrast between "rural" and "urban" is extremely sharp. The fact that large portions of the population inhabiting rural areas have limited access to the benefits of development--commercial energy, in particular--makes it necessary to analyze energy problems in these areas separately.1/

The sectorial analyses cover three basic aspects: (1) patterns of consumption and the efficient use of energy and their evolution, (2) measures for the conservation and efficient use of energy, and (3) potential energy savings. The sectors are examined in the order of importance of their estimated energy losses. These estimates are based on the amount of energy consumed by each sector and on the different transformation efficiencies. This allows us to predetermine the direction that efforts should take to conserve and use energy more rationally. Sectorial losses are calculated by size, as indicated in the country's 1975, 1980, 1981, and 1982 energy balances.

Although energy sector losses can be obtained directly from the balances, the same is not true of end-use sector losses. As a way of approximating, rough estimates are made supposing that losses are 75% of consumption in the transportation and rural sectors2/ and 25% in the industrial and RCP sectors (see Table 3.1).3/

From the results of these loss studies, one can infer the following:

1. The energy sector accounts for more than half of the energy losses since the mid-1970s. Moreover, losses grew considerably from 1975 to 1982.
2. Transportation losses follow in importance and account for close to 30% of the total.
3. Industrial sector losses are lower than energy and transportation losses, between 8% and 10% of total losses.
4. The RCP and rural sectors have the lowest losses. They represent only about 4% and 2%, respectively, of the total. However, estimates of the rural sector's losses tend to be low because information on the sector's energy consumption does not include noncommercial energy.

Before the results of the sectorial studies are presented, the part played by the producers (PEMEX and CFE) in energy sector losses should be noted. The following trends were seen in the evolution of the losses by these two companies from 1970 to 1982 (see Table 3.2): In obtaining and producing hydrocarbons, derivatives, and basic petrochemicals, losses grew at a rate of 10.4% annually. The losses corresponding to electricity were on the order of 6.4% annually. As a consequence, PEMEX's share of the energy sector's total losses increased from 48.4% in 1970 to 61.8% in 1982, and CFE's share decreased from 44% to 36.1%.

In the second half of the 1970s, however, hydrocarbon subsector losses began to rise at an accelerated rate. The average growth rate rose from 2.7% annually during the first half of the 1970s to 16.3% during the seven years that followed.

Such results confirm an observation made in the preceding chapter: The dynamics of the hydrocarbon subsector since the mid-1970s explain a good deal of the increase in energy consumption in the Mexican economy as a whole.

NOTES

1. One of the subsectors included in the rural sector is the "campesino" or peasant subsector, consisting of production units that likewise are domestic consumption units. This characteristic might have led us to include peasants in the RCP sector. We did, however, because many of them do not have access to commercial energy, which is destined mainly for urban areas.

2. The Balances de energía do not include the noncommercial energy consumption that exists in rural areas in particular.

3. These estimates, as approximate as they are, are still useful for the purposes of our study. Given the magnitude of sectorial energy consumption, any modification of the percentages, within reasonable limits, would not affect the order the sectors are in.

TABLE 3.1
Distribution of Energy Losses in Energy and End-Use Sectors in Mexico, 1975 and 1980-1982

Sectors	1975		1980		1981		1982	
	Kcal x 10^{12}	%	Kcal x 10^{12}	%	Kcal x 10^{12}	%	Kcal x 10^{12}	%
Energy	176.38	51.52	330.77	56.26	371.90	56.04	409.76	56.27
Hydrocarbons	77.15	—	196.67	—	226.46	—	253.22	—
Electricity	92.74	—	130.18	—	143.36	—	147.98	—
Other	6.49	—	3.92	—	2.08	—	8.56	—
Transportation[a]	109.65	32.03	176.88	30.24	202.08	30.45	203.49	27.95
Industrial[b]	35.75	10.44	44.77	7.66	51.25	7.72	74.29	10.20
Residential, Commercial, Public[b]	17.40	5.08	19.68	3.40	22.30	3.36	24.04	3.30
Agricultural[a]	3.18	0.93	12.50	2.14	16.14	2.43	16.57	2.28
TOTAL	342.36	100.00	584.78	100.00	663.67	100.00	728.15	100.00

Sources: National energy balances for the respective years. For the information on losses, see
Fernando, Schutz E., Uso eficiente de la energía en México, pp.17-28.

a/ Loss estimates suppose that the energy used in the sector is 25% of its total energy consumption.
b/ Loss estimates suppose that the energy used in the sector is 75% of its total energy consumption.

TABLE 3.2
Amount and Distribution of Energy Sector Losses in Mexico

Energy Type	1970 By Branch (Kcal X 10^{12})	1970 Part of Total Losses (%)	1975 By Branch (Kcal X 10^{12})	1975 Part of Total Losses (%)	1980 By Branch (Kcal X 10^{12})	1980 Part of Total Losses (%)	1981 By Branch (Kcal X 10^{12})	1981 Part of Total Losses (%)	1982 By Branch (Kcal X 10^{12})	1982 Part of Total Losses (%)
Hydrocarbons	77.09	48.37	87.87	46.96	196.67	59.46	226.46	60.89	253.22	61.80
Electricity	69.97	43.91	92.74	49.57	130.18	39.36	143.36	38.55	147.98	36.11
Other Losses	12.30	7.72	6.49	3.47	3.92	1.19	2.08	0.56	8.56	2.09
Total Losses	159.36	100.00	187.10	100.00	330.77	100.00	371.90	100.00	409.76	100.00

Sources: National energy balances, according to Organización Latinoamericana de Energía.

Notes: Includes transportation, distribution, and storage losses. The row "Other Losses" refers to coke, coal, and non-energy products. Losses are treated in detail in the analyses or the two main energy sectors.

4

Petróleos Mexicanos

In 1982 and 1983, energy consumption by the oil and
electricity sectors was the single most important component
of total domestic energy consumption. These sectors used
42% of the net domestic energy consumed during the years under consideration. PEMEX, in particular, used 29.9% of that
energy, while CFE used approximately 12.0% (see Figure 4.1).

Basic petrochemicals, which form an integral part of
PEMEX's activities, made up a larger percent of the company's total consumption. This increase was due mainly to
expanded production, which implied not only that larger
amounts of fuel and raw materials would be needed but also
that other areas of the oil industry had been making better
use of energy sources during the last two years.

The remaining sectors' share of domestic energy consumption, 58%, was an indication of the enormous needs of
the energy sector and, in particular, PEMEX own needs. A
clear knowledge of the levels and conditions in which energy is used by the energy sector itself, including petrochemicals is an indispensable basis for formulating energy policies, especially those related to savings and conservation.

Given the great complexity of oil industry operations,
there are a large number of factors and options that enter
into energy use. The majority of the industry's processes
are energy-intensive. Because of the size of its operations, the oil industry requires large amounts of fuel and
materials in its different stages: extracting, collecting,
transporting by oil pipelines and tankers, processing in refineries and petrochemical plants, distributing and the final commercializing, and so forth. PEMEX is, therefore energy-intensive in its different stages. Given the size of
its operations, it is the major energy user in the country.

A detailed analysis of the oil industry's energy requirements would allow us to quantify the specific energy
consumption for each unit of production for each area and
would make it easier to estimate the potential energy
savings for a certain level of production. It would permit
us to compare the economic and energy efficiencies associated with specific processes and products. Such an analysis, however, presupposes the existence of a large volume
of information. Due to limitations in the data presently
available, this objective cannot be met.

Nonetheless, we propose, at least, to present an overall view of energy consumption in the oil industry based on
information contained in the energy balances for Mexico and
on figures published in widely circulated documents. Therefore, the values we present on the magnitude of consumption
do not necessarily come from direct data, but may be derived, in part, from the overall sense of the energy balances.

ENERGY CONSUMPTION AND LOSSES

Given the nature of its operations, PEMEX consumes significant amounts of natural gas. It generates and is a
large-scale consumer of electrical energy and uses bunker
oil, gasoline, diesel, naphtha, and liquefied gas. Its use
of energy shows the following main characteristics:

1. A large percentage of its hydrocarbon and natural gas requirements is used as fuel to provide the caloric energy
   for production, the generation of steam and electricity,
   the operation of drilling equipment, transportation,
   and so on.
2. Some hydrocarbons and derivatives are also used as raw
   materials for the petrochemical industry. The type of
   production process and the yields from these processes
   form the chemical reactions that use these energy
   sources. Raw materials put precise limitations on the
   amount of input for each unit produced.
3. In the energy balances, the statistics for losses
   shrinkage, and unutilized energy reflect, in part, the
   serious difficulties the company has in efficiently
   using the energy sources at its disposal.

Table 4.1 is a summary of PEMEX's energy consumption

for 1982 and 1983. The table is divided into four categories: crude oil, natural gas, other fossil fuels, and raw
materials for basic petrochemicals. PEMEX consumes hydrocarbons for both energy and non-energy ends and also as a
raw material for the petroleum industry. Such is also the
case with ethane, petrochemical naphthas, industrial lubri-
cants, and greases (the latter on a smaller scale in areas
not connected with petrochemicals). The use of hydrocarbons added about 15% to the oil industry's oil consumption
in 1982 and 1983. There was an estimated 8.9% decrease in
energy uses by PEMEX in 1983, a significant decline.

The average for these two years shows that the amount
of hydrocarbons consumed as a source of energy was 33%
higher than the amount used as raw materials... The percentage used as raw materials is important because hydrocarbons
represented about 63% of basic petrochemical requirements
in 1982.

The use of liquefied gas, gasoline, diesel, kerosene,
and bunker oil as sources of energy increased from 25 to
60 tbdce between 1970 and 1980, according to the energy balances. Bunker oil and diesel represented 80% of consumption, on the average. Even though bunker oil was the most
widely used fuel in the industry after natural gas (57% in
1980), diesel has gradually replaced it as such (14% in
1970 and 23% in 1980).

The transportation sector, particularly the transportation of products, uses a significant portion of the hydrocarbons consumed as fuel. In 1980 gasoline, diesel, aviation fuel, and turbosine represented about 14% of PEMEX's
total consumption. However, the most intensive area of consumption was in primary production, especially industrial
production such as refining.

Natural gas, just as some hydrocarbons, is used both
as a fuel and as a raw material in PEMEX's petrochemical
production. It represented from 9% to 10% of the company's
total gas consumption in 1982 and 1983, 34.5% of the raw materials required for basic petrochemicals during those
years, and 14.5% of the oil sector's 1982 consumption.

PEMEX's energy losses increased notably once hydrocarbon production was accelerated during the latter part of
the 1970s and the beginning of the 1980s. Into this category falls 48% of the energy sector's total losses for 1970,
47% for 1975, and close to 60% for 1980-1982 (see Table 4.2
and 4.3).

All areas showing losses in the production of hydrocarbons and their derivatives experienced a marked increase in

such losses during the oil-boom years: Oil and gas transformation losses fluctuated around 14 X 10^{12} Kcal in 1970 and 1975 and over 100 X 10^{12} Kcal in 1982. Transportation, distribution, and storage losses went from 16.2 X 10^{12} Kcal in 1970 to 20.9 X 10^{12} in 1975 and to 68.6 X 10^{12} Kcal in 1982. Losses from unutilized energy, fluctuating around 50 X 10^{12} Kcal in 1970 and 1975, grew to 83.7 X 10^{12} in 1982 (see Table 4.2).

In the extraction and handling of primary energy (crude oil, liquids, and natural gas), that is, before transformation, two areas experienced important losses: unutilized energy (the burning off of the associated gas that is present, especially when exploiting marine deposits) and crude losses and shrinkage that occurred somewhere between the case head and the refinery.

Since the middle of the 1970s, as a result of the oil boom and the marked underdevelopment in the infrastructure needed to collect, transport, and distribute the gas associated with crude oil, an increasing amount of the gas has been burned off in the air, with no benefit derived from its use. Unutilized energy from natural gas was of the order of over 75 X 10^{12} Kcal in 1981 and 1982, respectively (see Table 4.2).

Crude oil losses between the case head and the refinery occur in separating the crude from the other substances mixed with it (principally water). Losses also occur in transporting and storing the fuel. These losses began to rise in 1975, with an AAGR of 26.2% until 1982 (see Table 4.2).

In the phase of industrially transforming hydrocarbons, where the hydrocarbons are changed into secondary energy sources and basic petrochemical products, one can observe the following:

1. A difference exists between the energy content of primary hydrocarbons and their derived products. In 1980 this difference translated into an energy content loss of 6.4% for refineries and 10.7% for gas plants.
2. There are considerable losses incurred in transporting, distributing, and storing hydrocarbons. As the energy balances show, these losses especially concern diesel, gas, and bunker oil.
3. Because of the very nature of the processes, basic petrochemical production losses are relatively smaller than refining losses, so that the margins for using energy more efficiently are also smaller. However, significant improvements can be made.

It is worthwhile to consider the changes in the a-
mounts of PEMEX's losses during the last few years. Losses
occurring during hydrocarbon production went down in absolute terms between 1980 and 1983, from 94 tbdce in the
first year to 91 tbdce in 1982 and to 83 tbdce in 1983 (see
Table 4.1). Comparing the figures for the years cited, one
can see notable improvements. Differences in the data re-
ported for spillage and evaporation losses of crude oil can
be attributed, in part, to probable deficiencies in measuring systems.1/

In the last few years, associated gas has been an important aspect in PEMEX's improved use of hydrocarbons.
The amount of gas released into the air has been reduced in
both absolute and relative terms, from a high of 665 millions of daily cubic feet (mdcf) in 1981, representing more
than 16% of gross production, to 434 mdcf in 1984, just
10.7% of gross production.

Better utilization is expected to be assured once the
policies for the integral exploitation of natural gas go
into effect in 1984 or 1985. This will mean that more than
96% (with 4% losses) will be utilized, making additional a-
mounts of gas available for domestic consumption in strategic and priority sectors of the economy. According to the
Energy Program 1984-1985, it is hoped that the gas burned
off will be reduced to 2% of production, which is the technical limit.2/

The integral exploitation of natural gas, which is
within grasp, has required PEMEX to install equipment for
treating and transporting the gas, as well as equipment for
compressing and processing the wet and sour gas. Such development projects have required long periods of maturation,
as well as large-scale investments. These investments have
been, on occasion, very difficult to make because of budget-
ary restrictions.

When all these goals are finally reached, close to 18%
of the energy consumed by PEMEX will be utilized (see Table
4.1). This is the equivalent of 100 tbdce, or 60% of the
nonassociated gas produced in the entire system. Such an
amount will more than justify the investments made.

CONSUMPTION AND THE EFFICIENT USE OF ENERGY

PEMEX is an organization with a highly vertical method
of handling oil and gas. Its activities encompass exploring,

exploiting, refining, transporting, and distributing these energy sources. Among these activities, exploration and exploitation belong to the extraction industry, refining is a transformation industry, and transportation and distribution are services. Studying the efficient use of energy has different implications, therefore, according to whether extraction, transformation, or transportation is being considered.

We can approach the analysis of the general behavior of transformation efficiency in the oil industry during the course of the 1970s using Table 4.3. By contrasting the figures in the table with those that define the relationship between highly refined derivatives and less refined derivatives (see Table 4.4), one can conclude that (1) the transformation efficiency of petroleum products has decreased progressively, from 86.0% in 1970 to 82.2% in 1981, and (2) the ratio of highly refined products to less refined products does not directly explain the decrease in transformation energy efficiency.

Two factors, among others, have had an effect on energy waste in industrial transformation. One is the design of equipment and processing plants. Traditionally, they have been designed with low hydrocarbon prices and ample availability in mind. Most designs tend, therefore, to be energy inefficient. One can add to this Mexico's basic dependence on U.S. technology and equipment, which are notorious for using fuel inefficiently. As a consequence, Mexico has adopted these same energy deficiencies into its technical activities.

It is extremely difficult to make a precise estimate of the savings possible from improving energy use in Mexico's oil industry because of inadequate knowledge of the amounts and locations of the inefficiencies in energy use in the entire productive chain. However, we can evaluate the margin for improving energy yields by comparing the efficiencies of the country's industries with those at an international level. To that end, we present two case studies on refining and a third on ammonia production in the field of basic petrochemicals. In the first two studies, even when comparisons are used, different levels of detail are also used to evaluate the energy requirements of the refineries and to compose the reference consumption pattern.

CASE 1

It is estimated that the present average transformation efficiency in refineries internationally is between
90% and 92%.3/ Comparing this with Mexico's 80.2% operating
efficiency in 1981, a potential savings of 13% can be made
if international norms are followed. Under such conditions
and with the same input, savings would be equivalent to
about 288 tbdoe, or 155 millions of barrels of crude equivalent (mboe) a year.

The importance of improvements in efficiency can clearly be seen if one considers the specific consumption associated with different levels of efficiency (see Table 4.5).
For each point efficiency improves, there is a 12,800 Kcal/
barrel reduction in specific consumption. Thus, there is a
potential savings of 60% when consumption goes from 256,000
Kcal/barrel to 102,400 Kcal/barrel, that is, when efficiency increases from 80% to 92%.

CASE 2

The consumption patterns treated here refer to the
self-consumption of fuel in European refineries at the end
of the 1970s. These installations had capacities between
100 and 200 thousands of barrels daily (tbd) if electricity
bought from the network is not taken into account. The complexity of these refineries is closer to that of Mexican refineries than to their U.S. counterparts (see Table 4.6).
The indexes allow for the different types of plants in each
refinery complex, as is the custom in Europe. Percentages
give special weight to the makeup of the different types of
installations.

Judging Mexican refineries according to European consumption patterns allows one to evaluate the percentage of
self-consumption for 1980, both overall and for each refinery, taking the structure and type of plant in each center
into account (see Table 4.7). These estimates give the average energy required for each barrel that is used to operate
each system examined, which was 5.7% of the volume. This
implies that 62.6 tbdoe were consumed in refineries in 1980,
according to European standards.

Considering that PEMEX actually consumed 79.0 tbdoe of
bunker oil in 1980, this leaves a difference of approximately 16.5 tbdoe. Refinery consumption, therefore, is 26.4%
above the European pattern. The difference is equivalent to

more than three times the total amount of premium gasoline sold in Mexico or to earnings of 105 million dollars a year, if that amount of premium gasoline were exported.

These figures clearly show that at the beginning of the 1980s, Mexico's refinery system did not operate as efficiently as possible, according to the international standards at the time. There is, therefore, sufficient room for planning and implementing a program for saving energy in this area of production.

CASE 3

In the case of basic petrochemicals, the analysis involves ammonia, the product with the largest volume of production in Mexico. Ammonia is used as a raw material for solid nitrogen fertilizers and can be applied directly to the soil as a fertilizer. It is, therefore, strategic for programs of food production. The production of ammonia accounted in the early 1980s for more than 20% of all the basic petrochemicals produced. Ninety-six percent of the ammonia consumed in the last several years was a fertilizer.

The analysis of how the energy was used in manufacturing ammonia is based on 1980 operating figures. As is well known, Mexico uses natural gas both as a fuel and as a raw material in ammonia production. As a point of reference for how efficiently energy is used in ammonia production we used the optimal international norm. From this, we can determine the possible margins for savings. Because of design specifications, modern plants producing 445 thousand tons a year require approximately 5.5×10^6 Kcal of methane per ton of ammonia for use as a raw material and between 2.5 and 3.0×10^6 Kcal per ton for use as fuel.

Because comparisons of the specific consumptions of raw materials in Mexican plants are based on rough estimates, it is normal for the plants in operation not to be too far from the norm (see Table 4.8). However, there are significant deviations in fuel requirements. Fuel can obviously be used more efficiently because even the unit that wastes the least fuel in the country consumes 44.0% more than the norm. The Cosoleacaque, Veracruz, complex could achieve overall energy savings of 73%, considering that in some cases the differences were more than 300%. The Salamanca-Guanajuato complex, whose efficiency in fuel use comes close to the statistical European norm, could save almost 40%. More precise estimates require knowing the caloric value of the gas used in each installation and the direct quantification of input. Nevertheless, differences from the norm are so large that they show the advantages of using the natural gas more efficiently as fuel in the production of ammonia.

PEMEX has two 445,600 ton/year plants on the drawing board: one in Camargo, Chihuahua, and another in Salina Cruz, Oaxaca. This would add an additional 890,000 tons/year to the 2,963,000 already being produced (see Table 4.9). Improvements in fuel efficiency would allow saving important amounts of energy, given the large amounts at stake. This would increase the natural gas available for other sectors and contribute to conserving a nonrenewable resource.

ELABORATING A PROGRAM FOR EFFICIENT ENERGY USE

Before defining the types of procedures conducive to efficient energy use in industry and, even more importantly, before defining goals in this area, we have to know the specific energy consumptions for each of PEMEX's plants and installations. How the energy was consumed should be made explicit for each production or transportation system, pointing out those areas and phases of production where there are losses and inefficient energy use. The procedure followed in defining a program to use energy more efficiently should include several steps, described in the following sections.

STEP 1

The first indispensable step is to develop energy accounting procedures in the oil sector. At the same time, energy enterprises should continue with measures to identify losses and waste and then reduce them to a minimum.

The proposed study should be done by the best specialists in these areas, who would be sensitive to and knowledgeable about the problems existing in the utilization of energy. The external energy-accounting procedures could be done at the following groups of installations, ranked in increasing order of consumption:

1. Gas plants and refineries
2. Petrochemical plants: energy and raw materials
3. Transportation: pipelines, compression and pumping systems, tankers, and tank cars and trucks
4. Production: oil, gas (associated, nonassociated), and secondary recuperation

Advantage should be taken of the experience acquired in obtaining data for the 1982 survey on energy consumption in industry. With some minor adjustments, the questionnaire used in that study could be used for industrial manufacturing plants.4/ It would likewise have to be adapted for studying the transportation and the production of gas and oil as well as the collecting and handling of these resources on their way to transformation centers or points of export.

An analysis of this information, together with comparisons of domestic and international patterns of energy use, will allow us to make a precise estimate of PEMEX's potential savings and to point out those areas requiring the most urgent attention.

STEP 2

As a second step, detailed evaluations of the potential savings should be made in situ. Not only would processes be analyzed for the sole purpose of equipping installations with energy-saving devices, but special attention would also be given to maintenance levels, the conditions of the insulation, and the presence of possible leaks. The operating conditions of each piece of equipment would be an additional topic for study. These evaluations would serve as a basis for determining what action should be taken.

STEP 3

The next step would be the preparation of a catalog on energy-saving measures. During this phase of research and as a function of the data provided by the field studies, technical-economic analyses could be done on the different energy-saving options. These studies should include a cost-benefit analysis of the different measures at both domestic and international energy prices. The study should

keep in mind that measures can be grouped into three categories:

1. The first category is those measures that increase
the use of existing equipment but do not require any investments. This category includes all maintenance measures,
such as stopping leaks and making precise adjustments in
equipment, and, generally speaking, all those measures in
which energy is saved simply through using equipment better
and more carefully.

2. The second category is investments to make existing
equipment more efficient. This includes all investments
that improve the energy efficiency of an existing process
by installing additional equipment

3. The third category is investments in equipment that
utilize more efficient technology. This includes equipment
that from its very conception was planned with energy-efficient criteria. Generally speaking, these measures should
be included when expanding the productive plant rather than
when modifying existing equipment. Once the different measures have been evaluated as to how much energy they consume,
they can be listed in order of importance for each plant,
as a function of the unit of investment needed for each
unit of energy savings.

MEASURES TO EFFECT EFFICIENT ENERGY USE

Even if people are clearly aware that formulating a
set of measures to improve energy efficiency in the different production phases in the oil industry is a positive
step, a precondition for implementing those measures is a
detailed study of the energy flow and the technical characteristics and conditions of the processes. If one knows
that specific aspects of the industry are functioning inefficiently and has recourse to the experiences of other
countries in this field, one can point out the advantages
of adopting measures to promote energy savings.

The first measures to be proposed are aimed at reducing exploitation losses (point 1, below), and transportation, distribution, and storage losses (points 2 to 5).
The other measures (points 6 to 12) concern industrial
transformation and are those with the greatest potential
for savings in the oil industry.

1. Follow through with the reduction of energy losses
from the burning off of gas, which occurs mainly in off-
shore deposits.

2. Reduce losses from dehydration and water drainage. This would require maintaining the correct balance in the materials and introducing more precise measuring systems. The goal is to avoid losing part of the oil when getting rid of the salt water mixed with the crude.

3. Substitute pipelines for rolling stock. Where more than 5,000 barrels a day are produced, pipelines are recommended instead of rolling stock.

4. Optimize the system for transporting products. This should should include combining the difference means available, while keeping in mind the costs associated with each.

5. Reduce evaporation losses from storage tanks. This can be achieved through vapor recuperation systems, using tanks with floating roofs, etc.

6. Make improvements in generating and using steam, including the following:

a. Optimize the steam system. Steam is needed as process heat and to do mechanical work. Designing a steam system that makes maximum use of available energy at the different pressures and temperatures required in the plant is usually very complicated. A boiler produces steam at maximum pressure. As steam is sent to consumption points, the pressure drops gradually, creating different levels. Unless steam pressure is correctly balanced according to supply and demand, a great deal of steam is wasted. Optimizing a steam system can produce savings of up to 40%.5/

b. Generate steam and electricity at the same time (cogeneration). (This is examined more fully in Chapter 5.) The main problem is the plants' electrical and steam needs. Since PEMEX generates large amounts of steam and electricity without combining them, significant potential savings can be made with cogeneration.

7. Use air preheaters to recuperate residual heat from smokestacks. The fuel used in the process heaters accounts for the major part of the energy consumed in a refinery. Exhaust gases leaving the heaters have temperatures between 250°C and 660°C.6/ These gases result in an important loss in the combustion process.

Today, air preheaters that utilize stack gases are regularly installed in new furnaces. Even though this equipment is sometimes difficult to install in existing refineries, it is estimated that such equipment can improve operating efficiency by 10% to 15%.

8. Use energy-efficient insulation in refineries to minimize equipment losses. Selecting the type and thickness

of insulation is an economic problem: better insulation is needed as energy costs increase. Radiation and convection losses are currently about 75 Kcal/kg.

9. Use effective instrumentation and control.[7] There has been some experience with computers monitoring and controlling the complex system of units operating in refineries, in particular, catalytic reformers, desulfurization units, crude distillation, lubricant plants, and hidrodisintegration. Better control is usually reflected in better utilization of input, including energy.

10. Adopt general administrative measures. Due to the varying complexity of different processes in different refineries, preventive and corrective maintenance measures have a strong impact on the rational use of energy. The procedures adopted should apply mainly toward the following:

a. Eliminating losses from steam, water, air, and fuel leaks
b. Controlling air in furnaces and boilers
c. Maintaining and reevaluating insulation
d. Cleaning surfaces and optimizing heat transfer systems
e. Permanently controlling the specific consumptions of the products manufactured
f. Repairing steam condenser recuperation systems.

11. Improving overall fuel use which should take into account the efficiency of internal combustion engines as well as the refining of oil to produce motor fuel.

12. Make predictions of the changes oil products might undergo in a changing (domestic and foreign) market, including their impact on refineries and the energy consumption in these refineries.

In the medium and long terms, energy consumption could be reduced by researching, developing, and incorporating new technology, such as using a combined cycle for turbines, with a binary cycle to utilize low-temperature gases and residual heat, and developing heaters to substitute the inefficient direct-flame heaters used in distillation.

Measures such as these are presently being considered by PEMEX as an integral part of the design and implementation of a program for using energy efficiently.

PEMEX'S PROGRAM FOR CONSERVATION AND ENERGY SAVINGS

For some time now, various parts of PEMEX and other public agencies throughout Mexico have been aware of how inefficiently energy is used in the oil industry. However, it was not until recently that PEMEX began to develop its own program for conserving and saving energy.8/ This program follows the guidelines set forth by the national energy policy in the energy program for the period 1984-1988.9/

PEMEX suggests a three-stage program, with each step associated with possible levels of energy savings (see Figure 4.2):

1. The first stage, during the first two years, is one of corrective maintenance and operational adjustments, with savings of 3% to 7%.
2. The second stage, during the third and fourth years, includes substituting equipment and materials, with potential savings of 5% to 10%.
3. The third stage, beginning in the fourth year, is to modify processes, with a margin of savings estimated at 5% to 10%.

Each stage would be implemented by key personnel at different and increasing hierarchical levels: by department heads in the first stage, area superintendents in the second, and high-level executives in the final stage.

PEMEX calculates that if the proposed measures were to be implemented, there would be an average potential savings of 20%. The substitution of obsolete production systems with other more modern and efficient ones would increase savings an additional 15% to 25%.

Using these figures and those from PEMEX's Preliminary Operational Plan (see Figures 4.3 and 4.4), we can calculate PEMEX's potential energy savings for 1990 and 2000. The calculations suppose the same rate of self-consumption as in 1983, that is, 556.2 tbdce (see Table 4.10), and continual improvements in efficiency beginning in 1984. In particular, an 18% reduction in self-consumption is expected by 1990 and 35% by the year 2000.

Reaching these levels would mean a savings of 36.5 mbce for the first year and 71.1 mbce for the second. In cumulative terms, the figures would be 139 mbce for 1984-1990 and 513 mbce for 1991-2000. At current average prices for Mexican crude (27.5 dollars a barrel), the savings would be equivalent to 3,822.5 million and 14,107.5 million dollars, respectively. This would mean a total cumulative savings of almost 18,000 million dollars.

If the PEMEX energy-savings program were to be broadened and implemented, there could be a substantial improvement in the country's use of energy. This would mean modifying the energy consumption patterns of one of the country's most inefficient sectors in energy use. Moreover, the experience acquired by PEMEX could be passed on to other areas of the economy, principally manufacturing, with the similar goal of increased energy savings.

The economic crisis affecting the country and the realization of the need to move toward improving transformation efficiencies and, therefore, overall productivity, as well as the search for a reasonable consercation of nonrenewable resources, were some of the factors PEMEX considered when formulating this program. However, a precise definition of the means and effects of such a program, estimating its costs and impact on welfare and its implications, is still to be made.

NOTES

1. Apparently, more careful records were kept in 1983. This assured more precise and congruous information. Such record keeping should continue to be improved in the near future, so as to offer the necessary data base for reducing losses to a minimum.

2. Secretaría de Energía, Minas e Industria Paraestatal (SEMIP), Programa nacional de energéticos 1984-1988 (Mexico, 1983).

3. Cf. Lazanidis Gyftopoulos and Witmar Gyftopoulos, Potential Fuel Effectiveness in Industry (1978), p.57.

4. Cf. annex to Chapter 4.

5. Cf. Gordian Associates, An Energy Conservation Target for Industry (New York, 1976), pp.iv-10.

6. Cf. Federal Energy Administration, "The Political for Energy Conservation in Nine Selected Industries," Petroleum Refining 2:219.

7. Cf. Gordian Associates, An Energy Conservation, pp.28-32.

8. Cf. Petróleos Mexicanos (PEMEX), Programa de conservación y ahorro de energía (Mexico, 1984).

9. SEMIP, Programa nacional.

FIGURE 4.1
Structure of Net Energy Consumption in Mexico, 1982 and 1983 (in percentage of total gross domestic supply)

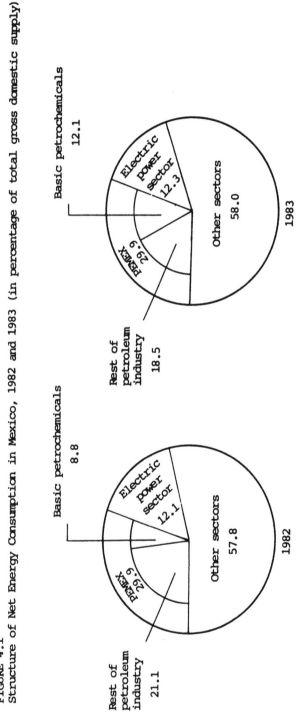

Source: Petróleos Mexicanos, México: Balance de energía, 1983 (México, 1984).

TABLE 4.1
Energy Consumption in Petróleos Mexicanos, 1982–1983

Energy Type	Thousands of Barrels of Daily Crude Oil Equivalent		Variation in Percentage	Percentage	
	1982	1983		1982	1983
Crude Oil	91.146	-3.337	-103.7	14.43	-0.60
Accidental spills	0.041	0.060	46.3	n.s.	0.01
Evaporation losses	27.464	13.301	-51.6	4.35	2.39
Eliminating impurities	23.544	—	—	3.73	—
Differences in measurement	40.097	-16.698	-141.6	6.36	-3.00
Natural Gas	356.651	367.155	2.9	56.47	66.01
Losses and shrinkage	—	20.533	—	—	3.69
Associated gas not used	154.362a/	97.796	-6.5	24.44a/	17.58
Associated gas consumed	—	25.973	—	—	4.67
Residual gas used	109.399	125.018	14.3	17.32	22.48
Other Fossil Fuels	91.482	83.376	-8.9	14.48	14.99
Total	539.279	447.194	-17.1	85.38	80.40
Basic Petrochemicals (raw materials)	92.349	109.019	18.1	14.62	19.60
Natural gas	34.243	35.298	3.1	5.42	6.35
Fossil fuels	58.106	73.721	27.1	9.20	13.25
Grand Total	631.628	556.213	-11.9	100.00	100.00

Sources: National energy balances for 1982–1983; Petróleos Mexicanos, Memoria de labores (Mexico, 1982), Petróleos Mexicanos, Memoria de labores (Mexico, 1983).

a/ Includes losses and shrinkage, associated gas not used, and associated gas consumed.
n.s. Not specified.

TABLE 4.2
Amount of Losses in Oil Industry in Mexico (Kcal x 10^{12})

Sector	1970	1975	1980	1981	1982
Transformation					
Refineries	10.93	11.05	57.76	38.95	32.38
Gas Plants	2.43	3.07	28.86	49.95	68.61
Total	13.36	14.12	86.62	89.90	100.99
Transportation, Distribution, and Storage					
Crude	1.89	9.59	43.87	44.11	48.95
Refined Oil	10.25	4.52	13.32	21.40	9.09
Gas and liquefied Gas	4.11	6.76	4.96	6.10	10.53
Total	16.25	20.87	62.15	71.61	68.57
Unutilized Energy	47.48	52.88	47.90	74.95	83.66
Grand Total	77.09	87.87	196.67	226.46	253.22

Source: National energy balances according to Organización Latinoamericana de Energía.

TABLE 4.3
Evolution of Transformation Efficiency in Oil Industry, 1970–1981

Year	Input to Be Transformed (Kcal X 10^{12})			Energy Consumed in Transformation (Kcal X 10^{12})	Product Transformed (Kcal X 10^{12})	Efficiency[a] (%)
	Crude	Gas	Total			
1970	237.404	131.610	369.014	44.367	355.630	86.03
1975	326.847	169.822	496.669	64.851	482.556	85.94
1977	411.439	185.496	596.935	79.323	562.549	83.18
1979	467.245	286.721	753.966	109.219	689.565	79.89
1981	608.508	382.347	990.855	145.430	910.953	80.17

Sources: Petróleos Mexicanos, Anuario estadístico 1983 (Mexico, 1984); Petróleos Mexicanos, Memoria de labores.

a/ Efficiency is calculated from the following formula:

$$\text{Efficiency} = \frac{\text{Product Transformed X 100}}{\text{Input to Be Transformed + Energy Consumed}}$$

TABLE 4.4
Evolution of Highly Refined and Less Refined Products

Year	Highly Refined Products (Kcal × 10^{12})			Less Refined Products (Kcal × 10^{12})	Ratio (1)/(2)
	(1)			(2)	
	Gasoline	Diesel	Total	Bunker Oil	
1970	66.318	44.038	110.356	75.891	1.45
1975	89.088	82.483	171.571	106.905	1.60
1977	109.420	96.280	205.700	135.598	1.51
1979	134.818	113.918	248.736	168.088	1.48
1981	170.684	141.525	312.209	201.777	1.54

Source: Based on unpublished data of Petróleos Mexicanos.

TABLE 4.5
Relationship Between Efficiency and Specific Consumption

Efficiency (%)	Specific Consumption (Kcal/barrel)
92	102,400
90	128,000
88	153,600
86	179,200
84	204,800
82	230,400
80	256,000

Source: Based on unpublished data of Petróleos Mexicanos.

TABLE 4.6

Energy Requirements for European Refineries in 1970 (in percentage of tons of crude equivalent/unit of charge)

Installation	Norm
General Needs	0.5
Primary Distillation	1.5
Vaccum Distillation	1.5
Catalytic Cracking	6.0
Viscosity Breaking	2.0
Cracking	8.0
Hydrodesulfurization	1.5
Deasphalting	5.0
Alkylation	5.0

Source: Based on unpublished data of Petróleos Mexicanos.

TABLE 4.7
Probable Fuel Consumption in Refinery System According to European Norms (in barrels per day)

Refinery	Crude and Liquids Processed (Annual Average)	Self-Consumption (%)	Self-Consumption (Crude Oil)
Azcapotzalco	102,228	4.5	4,600.3
Cadereyta	100,619	3.9	3,924.1
Madero	163,484	6.9	11,280.4
Minatitlán	259,724	5.1	13,245.9
Poza Rica	27,318	3.2	874.2
Reynosa	10,540	2.6	274.0
Salamanca	168,781	8.3	14,000.5
Salina Cruz	130,194	3.4	4,426.6
Tula	134,280	7.4	9,936.7
Total	1,097,036	5.7	62,562.8

Source: Based on unpublished data of Petróleos Mexicanos.

TABLE 4.8
Unitarian Consumptions of Natural Gas in Different Complexes in Mexico and Current Norms of Consumption, 1980

Complex	Raw Materials ($*C_1 10^9$ Joule/ton.NH_3) a,b,c/	Fuel ($C_1 10^9$ Joule/ton.NH_3)	Total ($C_1 10^9$ Joule/ton.NH_3)	Difference from the Optimum Norm: Raw Materials (%)	Difference from the Optimum Norm: Fuel (%)	Difference from the Optimum Norm: Total (%)
Cosoleacaque I	27.9	48.4	76.3	21.8	317.2	121.2
Cosoleacaque II	34.4	28.6	63.0	50.2	146.6	82.6
Cosoleacaque III	22.9	18.3	41.2	0.0	57.8	19.4
Cosoleacaque IV	23.1	16.7	39.8	0.9	44.0	15.4
Cosoleacaque V	23.9	17.5	41.4	4.4	50.9	20.0
Total	23.7	20.1	43.8	3.5	73.3	27.0
Camargo	23.0	16.7	39.7	0.4	44.0	15.1
Salamanca I	15.3	13.5	28.8	-33.2	16.4	-16.5
Salamanca II	35.8	16.7	52.5	56.3	44.0	52.2
Total	31.0	16.0	47.0	35.4	37.9	36.2
Optimum Norm	22.9	11.6	35.5	—	—	—
Statistical European Norm	23.0	15.9	38.9	0.4	37.1	12.8

Source: Based on unpublished data of Petróleos Mexicanos.

a/ C_1 = Methane.
b/ Methanecaloric content: 53.1 x 10^6 Joules/Kg.
c/ C_1 Joule = 0.24 cal.

TABLE 4.9
Supply, Consumption, and Capacity of Ammonia

Year	Production	Imports	Exports	Consumption	Variation (%)	Ton/Year Installed Capacity	Percent Utilized	First Year Production Capacity
1962						151,000		Cosoleacaque I and Salamanca I (60,000 and 91,000 t/year)
1963	101,782	n.a.	—	n.a.	n.a.	151,000	67.4	
1964	130,955	n.a.	—	n.a.	n.a.	151,000	86.7	
1965	121,111	111,460	—	232,571	n.a.	151,000	80.2	
1966	139,823	152,817	—	292,640	25.8	151,000	92.6	
1967	132,370	200,004	—	332,374	13.6	283,000	46.8	Camargo (132,000 t/year)
1968	163,170	212,068	—	375,238	12.9	583,000	8.0	Cosoleacaque II (300,000 t/year)
1969	390,658	109,966	984	499,640	33.2	583,000	67.0	
1970	453,955	74,246	—	528,201	5.7	583,000	77.9	
1971	459,952	115,643	325	575,270	8.9	583,000	78.9	
1972	504,664	205,691	5,626	704,729	22.5	583,000	86.6	
1973	529,808	247,238	3,271	773,775	9.8	583,000	90.8	
1974	525,428	246,968	498	771,898	-0.2	883,000	59.9	Cosoleacaque III (300,000 t/year)
1975	801,235	102,517	37,827	865,925	12.2	883,000	90.7	
1976	864,765	—	—	864,449	-0.2	883,000	97.9	
1977	943,791	—	30,211	913,580	5.7	1,328,000	71.1	Cosoleacaque IV (445,000 t/year)
1978	1,579,243	—	670,000	909,243	-0.5	2,073,000	76.2	Cosoleacaque V and Salamanca II (445 and 300,000 t/year)
1979	1,632,729	—	647,254	1,005,475	10.6	2,073,000	79.7	
1980	1,883,176	—	710,100	1,173,076	16.7	2,073,000	90.8	
1981	2,540,000	—	1,198,514	1,341,486	14.4	2,963,000	85.7	Cosoleacaque VI and VIII (445,000 t/year each)
1982	2,469,336	—	834,634	1,634,702	21.9	2,963,000	83.3	

Source: Based on unpublished data of Petróleos Mexicanos.

FIGURE 4.2
Potential Fuel Savings in the Energy Sector

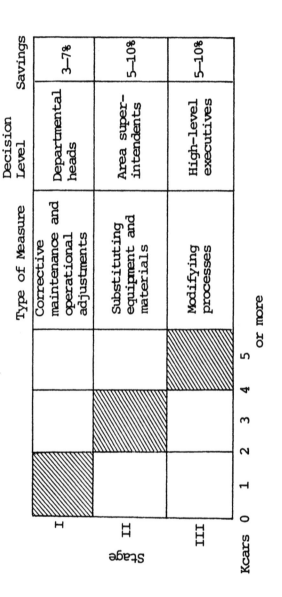

Stage	Kcars 0 1 2 3 4 5 or more	Type of Measure	Decision Level	Savings
I		Corrective maintenance and operational adjustments	Departmental heads	3–7%
II		Substituting equipment and materials	Area super-intendents	5–10%
III		Modifying processes	High-level executives	5–10%

Source: Petróleos Mexicanos, Programa de conservación y ahorro de energía (México, 1984).

FIGURE 4.3
Potential Savings in Petróleos Mexicanos

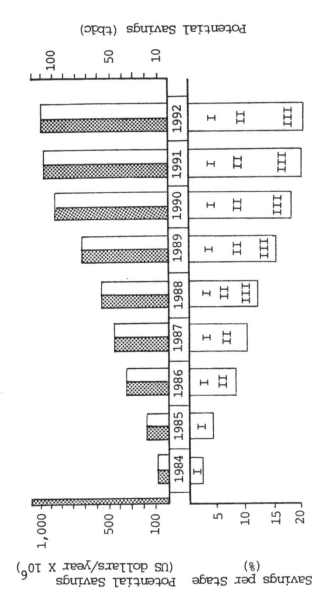

Source: Petróleos Mexicanos, Programa de conservación y ahorro de energía (México, 1984).

84

FIGURE 4.4
Cumulative Potential Savings in Petróleos Mexicanos

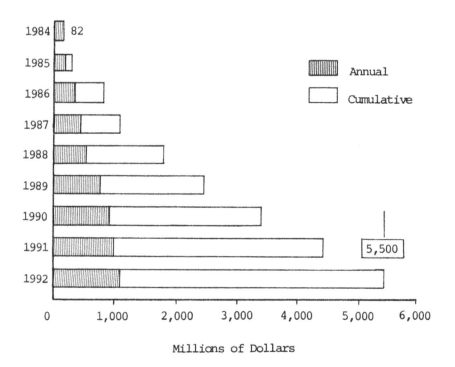

Millions of Dollars

Source: Petróleos Mexicanos, Programa de conservación y ahorro de energía (Mexico, 1984).

TABLE 4.10
Potential Energy Savings in Petróleos Mexicanos, 1984-2000

Year	Percentage[a]	Daily Savings (tbdoe)[b]	Annual Savings Kcal X 10^{12}	mboe	U.S. Dollars (millions)
1983	--	--	--	--	--
1984	1.5	8.2	--	--	--
1985	4.0	22.2	--	--	--
1986	8.0	44.5	--	--	--
1987	10.0	55.6	--	--	--
1988	12.0	66.7	--	--	--
1989	15.0	83.4	--	--	--
1990	18.0	100.1	46.8	36.5	1003.8
1991	19.0	105.0	--	--	--
1992	20.0	110.0	--	--	--
1993	21.0	116.8	--	--	--
1994	22.0	122.4	--	--	--
1995	23.0	127.9	--	--	--
1996	25.0	139.1	--	--	--
1997	27.0	150.2	--	--	--
1998	29.0	161.3	--	--	--
1999	32.0	178.0	--	--	--
2000	35.0	194.7	91.2	71.1	1954.3
1984/1990	--	380.7	178.2	139.0	3822.5
1991/2000	--	1405.4	657.7	513.0	14107.5
1984/2000	--	1786.1	835.9	652.0	17930.0

Sources: Tables 4.3 and 4.4 and estimates made by the authors.

a/ The saving percentages are applied to 1983 self-consumption (Cf. Table 4.1).
b/ tbdoe = Thousands of barrels of daily crude equivalent.

5

Comisión Federal de Electricidad

The electric power consumed commercially in Mexico is produced by the state-owned company Comisión Federal de Electricidad (CFE:- Federal Electricity Commission) with synchronous generators. Transmission and distribution networks deliver the electric power to the customers. The synchronous generators are driven by different mechanisms, mainly turbines and internal combustion engines. They get their energy from the following sources: bunker oil, gas, coal, diesel, steam from geothermic sources, and hydraulic installations.

The principal characteristics of the Mexican electric industry in 1982 were as follows:

```
Installed capacity (power)...................18,390    MW
Annual generating capacity (energy)...........161.10  TWh
Effective generation in 1982 (energy)..........73.2   TWh
Utilization factor.............................43.3%1/
Growth of electric power generated
     1971-1982....................................9.0%
     1975-1982....................................8.8%2/
```

From 1960 to 1980, the Mexican electric power industry showed constant expansion of its installed capacity at a cumulative AAGR of 9.7%, one of the highest growth rates among developing countries. The growth in the infrastructure of production, transportation, and distribution brought electric power to wider sectors of the urban and rural population, in spite of the rapid demographic growth the country recorded during the same period.

In 1970 hydroelectric plants provided some 57% of the gross amount of electricity generated, while thermic units

provided some 43%. This distribution reflects the relatively balanced development of overall production between
both types of generation during the decade following the
industry's nationalization (1962). However, during the
1970s, decisions made in the area of equipment modified the
situation that had prevailed in previous years. Policies
favored developing thermoelectric options, and, consequently, 65% of the country's 18.4 TW of installed capacity in
1982 came from thermal plants, although these plants represented only 47% of the 6.0-TW total installed power in
1970 (see Tables 5.1 and 5.2).

Because of the development of the electric power
schema, 69% of the gross electric power production, or 73.2
TWh, in 1982 was generated by fuel combustion. Petroleum
derivatives, especially bunker oil, were what essentially
sustained the growth in generation, while natural gas lost
the relative importance it had in 1970 when its share in
plant fuel consumption dropped from 39% to about 23% in
1980. While gas consumed in producing electricity represented around 10% of the country's total gas needs during
the 1970s, according to the energy balances the consumption
of petroleum derivatives doubled its share in total derivative needs, reaching 19.3% in 1980.

The growing dependence on thermoelectric plants to generate electricity, together with the fact that energy
losses for hydroelectric generation are very low, leads us
to concentrate our analysis of the consumption and the efficient use of energy on thermoelectric plants. Nevertheless,
the prospect of conserving energy sources calls for an
analysis of hydroelectric generation as an alternative energy source.

Within the thermoelectric schema, steam plants are the
most important type of plant as far as generating capacity
is concerned. This is the case even more so when we look
at production. The differences in production capacity percentages reside, of course, in the mode of operation within
these plants. Steam plants generally have a high load factor. The capacity of combined-cycle plants has increased
during the last few years; however, they operate with low
load factors, just as gas, internal combustion, and carbo-
electric turbines do. Geothermal plants have high load factors, but their incidence in the system is reduced, both in
capacity and production. Therefore, energy-saving efforts
are concentrated mainly on steam plants, especially on
those with the largest capacities (see Tables 5.3, 5.4, and
5.5).

The structure of the Mexican thermoelectric system
shows a high concentration of power generation centered
around the system's main units. The following should be
pointed out:

1. The two largest steam plants (Tula, in the state of
   Hidalgo, and Salamanca in the state of Guanajuato) produce close to 25% of the total gross generation.
2. The six largest steam plants produce 52.8% of the total
   gross generation.
3. The twenty-three plants with the largest capacity produce 84.2% of the gross generation, while close to two
   hundred smaller plants produce 15.8%.
4. It is estimated that within a few of years these percentages will change and 90% of the production will be
   provided by the larger plants and only 10% by the smaller plants. This conclusion follows from the fact that
   several plants with 300-MW units did not reach normal
   operational levels in 1981.
5. The 15.8% produced by the smaller plants is virtually
   accounted for by small steam and gas turbine units. Combined-cycle plants are all larger than 100-MW, and internal combustion plants play practically no role at
   all in generation.

PATTERNS OF CONSUMPTION AND EFFICIENT ENERGY USE

A simplified diagram of a typical thermoelectric steam
plant (see Figure 5.1) allows us to visualize the main components and their respective energy flows. These components are:

. Steam generators or boilers
. Steam turbines
. Synchronous-triphasic generators
. Main condensers
. Cycle water heaters
. Cycle water pumps
. Transformers

Major forms of energy loss can likewise be classified.
They can be quantified, if a 38% efficiency is assumed for
the overall system. A comparison of values (see Table 5.6)
shows that the greatest losses are to be found in the condenser (44%) and in the boiler (12%).

A 38% efficiency refers to the energy available after the fuel moved through the transformer, in terms of the energy contained in the fuel fed to the boiler. Expressed another way, 2,263 Kcal/KWh represents this level of efficiency. We call this value the specific consumption, unless there is a need to distinguish between gross and net generation.3/

The ratio between the fuel consumed annually in thermoelectric plants and the net electricity generated makes it possible to calculate the specific consumptions of these plants and, hence, their efficiencies (see Table 5.7). From the trends observed in 1961-1982, we may conclude that net generation grew at a rate of 13.2% annually during this period, while fuel consumption averaged 11.9%. The difference reflects technological improvements, which naturally influence the specific consumptions and efficiencies throughout the two recent decades period. Specific consumption has decreased at an average of 1.08% annually, which is reflected in the 1.09% increase in efficiency (see Figure 5.2).

These findings apply to thermoelectric production as a whole. There is a marked difference between types of plants, so that more detailed analyses of specific consumptions and efficiencies of thermoelectric plants are desirable, especially for those plants with larger capacities (see Table 5.8). Among the large-capacity plants, we might single out steam, combined-cycle, and gas turbine plants, but we should assess the overall performance of the other thermal plants (187 in all) classified as minor. The main conclusions are as follows:

1. If gas turbines are excluded, the efficiency of steam and combined-cycle plants varies between 26% and 33%, as is confirmed in Figure 5.3.
2. The average weighted efficiencies for the different types of plants in 1981 were:

Steam	31.49%
Combined cycle	29.28%
Gas turbine	21.84%
Minor thermal	22.16%
System total	29.36%4/

The significance of the increases in the efficiencies of CFE's thermoelectric plants can be obtained when international comparisons are made. If the efficiency ranges prevailing internationally for steam plants are compared with Mexico's ranges (see Tables 5.5 and 5.8, columns 2 and 4, respectively, versus Table 5.9) or with the weighted averages for steam plant efficiencies in Mexico, it is apparent that the operating efficiencies of these plants are below the international average.

However, international norms indicate that gas turbines used to generate energy during peak-demand hours have an efficiency of 20% to 27%.5/ The average weighted efficiency of Mexican gas turbine plants (21.8%) is only a little above the lower limit for other countries.

Combined-cycle plants utilize the energy of exhaust gases from gas turbines. Generally speaking, the addition of a steam cycle to gas turbines produces a 10% to 12% increase in the gas turbine's efficiency. Efficiencies of 30% to 39% could, therefore, be reached in combined-cycle plants. This means they would operate in a range similar to that of steam plants larger than 100-MW. The average weighted efficiency for Mexican plants of this type (29.28) does not even equal the bottom limit of international figures.

Figure 5.4 shows the evolution of the specific consumptions of thermoelectric plants in some industrialized countries from 1950 to 1976. There is a clear tendency toward a specific consumption of 2,810 Kcal/KWh, equivalent to an efficiency of 35% (see Tables 5.10). The Mexican system of thermoelectric plants, however, reached levels of only about 30% efficiency in 1981 and 1982 (see Tables 5.7 and 5.8).

It is worth pointing out that the figures for the efficiency in generating electric power do not clearly reflect the particular characteristics of Mexico's thermoelectric system. This is due to the rapid development of the system in the last few years. Overall efficiency is influenced by the large plants that have recently been installed (see Figure 5.3). It would be worthwhile, therefore, to make a detailed comparison of the larger Mexican plants and those in selected industrialized countries. The estimated efficiency is 32% for Mexican plants and 38.5% for industrialized countries. This indicates that greater potential savings are possible for Mexico than have been suggested so far by the figures.

MEXICAN THERMOELECTRIC PLANT EFFICIENCIES AND THE
INTERNATIONAL NORM

In this section, we evaluate the implications, in
terms of energy and economics, of the differences between
consumption trends in Mexican thermoelectric plants and
those in plants operating in industrialized countries,
with special emphasis on large plants.

We can see the importance of maintaining a high level
of efficiency in a thermoelectric plant when we calculate
the energy and economic impact a 1% decrease in efficiency
would have in a 300-MW steam unit.6/ A decrease from 38%
to 37% in the efficiency of such a plant means a 7.7% increase in specific fuel consumption and a correspondingly
larger hourly fuel flow.7/

If we consider that a 300-MW unit operates at 78% capacity and at an 80% plant factor, the 1% increase in inefficiency means an additional 9.65×10^6 liters per year
of fuel consumed. Thus, the reduction in efficiency costs
289.5 million pesos annually (1.5 million dollars, at an
exchange rate of 195 pesos per dollar), assuming an international bunker oil price of 30 pesos per liter.

In order to estimate the impact an increase in efficiency would have on Mexican thermoelectric plants, we utilized previous estimates and results from comparisons of
the efficiencies for Mexico and for industrialized countries. On this basis (see Tables 5.5 and 5.8), we found
the following:

1. Steam plants with units larger than 100 MW should have
   at least a 35% efficiency, almost four points more than
   the current level.
2. Combined-cycle plants should also have an efficiency
   close to 35%, instead of the 29.28% attained so far.
3. Gas turbine groups should reach an average efficiency
   of 22% to 23%, and those larger than 100 MW should operate close to 25% efficiency, not the 16.01% or 23.17%
   efficiency of the Jorge Luque and Nonoalco plants, respectively.

To summarize, the main plants in the Mexican thermoelectric system should have 34% to 35% efficiency, instead
of the present 30.4%.

A 1% increase in the efficiency of the system has a
more than proportional effect on the efficiencies of specific consumptions and total fuel consumption, given the

inverse relationship between specific consumption and efficiency. That is, specific consumption is defined by the ratio 860/efficiency.

The importance an improvement in thermoelectric generating efficiency could have for the Mexican energy system is evident when one evaluates the energy savings that result from an increase in efficiency, such as the 30.36% efficiency generated in 1982.8/ In fact, if efficiency had been 36% in 1982 (5.6% greater than it actually was) when producing 48.1 TWh, the savings would have been 21.35 X 10^{12} Kcal. This is equivalent to 16.6 mboe a year or approximately 457 million dollars (see Table 5.11).

MEASURES FOR EFFICIENT ENERGY USE AND CONSERVATION

The nature of electrical energy has permitted the development of a great variety of transformation techniques, making it possible to obtain an electric flow from diverse primary energy sources and conversion devices. Figure 5.5 shows a series of sources from which electrical energy can be obtained, classified as renewable or nonrenewable. The differences between the sources might lead one to consider using only renewable sources for generating electricity as an optimum solution. However, this is hardly feasible because of, among other reasons, the present high cost of some renewable sources compared to nonrenewable ones and the physical limitations of the renewable sources.

The majority of electric power systems in other countries use a mixed variety of renewable and nonrenewable sources to generate electric power. Even though Mexico's electric production structure was balanced at the beginning of the 1970s, it has since become increasingly dependent on hydrocarbons and has reduced the role of renewable sources.

To conserve resources, measures should be implemented to:

1. Keep generating plants in good enough condition to provide the efficiency for which they were designed.
2. Let the plant function at maximum efficiency.
3. Make full use of the fuel's energy potential, considering the following:
 a. Apply full use of the fuel's potential to generating process steam, thereby obtaining electric power in the process. This means using cogeneration in industrial plants that require steam.

b. Make full use of the residual steam in large thermoelectric plants. This means using cogeneration in
   electric companies where steam is a by-product.
c. Improve the conditions for energy conservation with
   technological innovations such as combined-cycle plants.

With regard to point 1 above, we should note that for
a thermoelectric plant to operate as efficiently as expected, one must assure that the design, construction, and
quality of the equipment are compatible. Once in operation,
preventive and corrective maintenance programs should exist
to preserve the plant's efficiency. Such steps, which
translate into energy savings, include the following:

1. Adequate maintenance of the steam condenser, making sure
   heat is transferred correctly. This transfer can be affected by solids in the tubing, tubing in poor condition,
   insufficient water flow, or an improperly functioning
   cooling tower. Steam condenser losses can add an additional 2% to 4% to total conversion process losses.
2. Preventive and corrective maintenance for boilers and
   steam generators. If this is not done, a 2% to 3% decrease in the overall efficiency of the process could
   result.
3. In addition to the previous steps, any program should
   provide control over other equipment, such as heat ex-
   changers, turbines, valves and pumps, compressors, fans,
   speed controls, and electric motors. The main problems
   with equipment that can affect efficiency are exchanger
   deposits, defective insulation, steam leaks, deficient
   instrumentation, excessive vibrations, excessive wear on
   parts, disalignment, and corrosion.

With regard to point 2 on page 92 , the following measures would permit the system to work at maximum efficiency:

1. Transmitting power economically by performing daily hydrothermic coordination. This operation makes it possible to utilize the hydraulic energy available on a particular operating day, minimizing the operating costs of
   the thermoelectric plant complex, while satisfying the
   power demands made on the network at a particular time.
2. Annual hydrothermic coordination. This measure is aimed
   at maximizing the hydraulic resources available year
   round. Generally speaking, this means having the greatest possible power available, without wasting all the energy that dam overflow can provide at any given moment.

Other measures are planned to flatten the demand curve. This means reducing capital costs as well as operational costs by extending "base" plant operations, thereby improving overall efficiency. These measures include the following:

1. Differential tariffs to dissuade consumption during peak-demand hours. This means putting pressure on users through electric power prices that encourage energy consumption outside peak-demand hours.
2. Repumping, allowing the electric company itself to optimize its generation. This entails feeding a hydraulic system with repumping during the low-demand hours in order to give back the energy during the peak-demand hours.
3. Interconnecting networks. Specific consumption can be improved by interconnecting the network. This increases load factors for base plants, thereby improving their levels of energy consumption.
4. Direct load control. This is a medium-term measure that flattens the curve by identifying precisely, whether by magnitude or by hour and duration, when the user has a real power need. Being able to exercise this control depends on perfecting means of communication and connecting the power plants through a computer system.

With regard to point 3a on page 92 —the utilization of the fuel's energy potential—cogeneration should be encouraged in industrial plants. With this system, efficiencies of 55% to 70% are possible. Also, demands on the power network can be reduced, thereby eliminating transmission losses and making it possible, in some circumstances, to send energy back to the network.

The Mexican industries with the potential to generate both steam and electricity are, among others:

. PEMEX: The electric power cogeneration potential of this industry has been calculated from the daily production of the refineries in barrels of crude oil. A study done for PEMEX indicates that cogeneration with gas turbine and recuperation boilers would make 370-MW of electric power available for every 100,000 barrels produced daily.9/ From this estimate, one can conclude that there is an estimated electric potential of 4,400 MW, given the 1,200,000 barrels/day capacity that PEMEX has.
. Steel: It has been estimated that at least one-third of this industry's electric power needs can be satisfied by

the steam already available within the system. These
needs can be met by cogeneration.
. Chemical: The steam requirements for this sector would
  require substituting cogeneration for low-pressure
  boilers. Some 50% of the chemical industry's electric
  power requirements could be covered internally by this
  measure.
. Cellulose and paper: As in the case of the chemical industry, it is estimated that 50% of the electric power
  consumed by this industry could be self-generated.
. Sugar: Process-steam needs suggest that 100% of the industry's electric power requirements could be satisfied
  by cogeneration, and, furthermore, electric power could
  be sent to the network.

In regard to the utilization of steam from thermoelectric plants (point 3b on page 93), the integration of the
existing large-capacity thermoelectric plants (Tula and Salamanca) into future projects should be considered because
these plants are right next to the refineries.

Finally, measures to improve conditions for energy conversion (point 3c on page 93) could be implemented when
the systems are modified. Combined-cycle plants, utilizing
gas turbine gases produced during team-plant operations,
would be able to increase overall efficiency. Efficiencies
of 40% are possible, but figures of from 50% to 55% could
be attained in the near future.

POTENTIAL ENERGY SAVINGS BY 1990 AND 2000

An analysis of potential savings implies predicting
the growth of electric power production. This estimate is
based on the historical trends of electric power generation
(see Table 5.12):

Period	AAGR (%)
1950–1960	9.20
1960–1970	11.45
1971–1981	9.05
1975–1981	8.90
1982	7.80
1983	2.2010/

This trend in AAGRs reflects a slowing of the growth
rate for the electric power sector that began during the

1970s. According for this trend, we will now examine possible future patterns of behavior (see Figure 5.6). Our predictions of future energy consumption patterns in the electric power industry, calculations of potential savings, and studies on the conservation of nonrenewable energy resources are based on CFE projections for electric power generation and the structure of the electric power system in the year 2000 (see Table 5.13). It is on this basis that we have produced figures for the year 1990.

THE GENERATION AND STRUCTURE OF THE ELECTRIC POWER SYSTEM BY 1990 AND BY 2000

Projections are based on the structure and level of electric power generation in 1982 and the CFE's most conservative production estimates (see Table 5.13). The AAGR for the electric power generated for 1982 through 2000 is calculated at 6.6%. In addition, two possible types of diversification policies have been considered: moderate (MD) and high (HD).

Based on the above statistics, it can be said that by the year 2000 with MD, electricity generated from nonrenewable resources will be 178.3 TWh, and from renewable resources, 51.7 TWh (see Table 5.14). With HD, the figures are 1963.8 TWh and 66.2 TWh, respectively. The total electric power generated will be 125 TWh by 1990 and 230 TWh by the year 2000.

With MD, 90.5 TWh generated from nonrenewable energy resources and 34.5 TWh generated from renewable sources will be required by 1990. With HD, the requirements for that same year will be 86 TWh and 39 TWh, respectively.

The diversification of sources leads to greater dependence on nonrenewable resources such as coal and uranium. In 1982, coal's share in the generation of electricity from nonrenewable resources was only 2.7%. By 1990, coal and uranium should reach a total share of 5.2% with MD and 23.8% with HD. The relative importance of both sources would be even greater by the year 2000: 31.6% with MD and 40.8% with HD (see Tables 5.14 and 5.15).

The path proposed for the future leads to a progressive reduction in the share of renewable resources. In fact, although the share of renewable sources was 32.8% in 1982. it would reach 27.6% by 1990 in the moderate case and 31.2% in the high case.11/ This trend will become more acute by the year 2000, when the shares of renewable resources will be 22.5% and 28.8%, respectively.

Future diversification in the direction of renewable resources is, therefore, limited, especially when one considers that the CFE plans to cover any increase in the demand of electric power beyond 230 TWh with power plants that use hydrocarbons.

ENERGY CONSERVATION AND SAVINGS BY 1990 AND 2000

We propose three measures for achieving greater energy conservation and savings in the generation of electric power:

1. Diversification: Using more renewable energy resources and conserving nonrenewable resources
2. Efficiency: Increasing the operating efficiency of thermoelectric plants
3. Cogeneration: Utilizing steam to generate electric power in industry.

Energy Conservation Through Diversification

With regard to diversification, the advantages of HD outweigh those of MD (see Figures 5.7 and 5.8). With a program of HD, by 1990 a savings of 4.5 TWh over that gained using MD would be possible from nonrenewable sources (see Figure 5.7). The difference is equivalent to 3.6% of the total generation projected for that year. If operating efficiency is 32.6%, 11.8 X 10^{12} Kcal, or 9.4 mbce, would be saved.12/

By the year 2000, 14.5 TWh less would be generated from nonrenewable energy sources under HD than under MD (see figure 5.7). This represents 6.3% of the projected generation. In caloric terms and assuming a 32.85% efficiency, 37.96 X 10^{12} Kcal, or 29.6 mbce, of nonrenewable fuel would be saved that year.13/

Cumulative savings during the 18 years amount to 130.8 TWh, the equivalent of 267.11 mbce. The amount saved would be larger if the proposals from the 1980 energy program were followed. The program proposed incorporating two-fifths of the potential hydroelectric power by the year 2000. That is, of the 171.9 TWh of potential hydroelectricity, 68.7 TWh were to be generated that same year. This figure is 25.4 TWh higher than what is required from renewable sources under

HD (see Figure 5.8 and Table 5.14).

These figures indicate that the projections for developing hydroelectric power are presently more limited than they were when the 1980 energy program was formulated by Secretaría de Patrimonio y Fomento Industrial (SEPAFIN). This delay in developing hydroelectric power will put greater pressure on the supply of hydrocarbons. At the same time, it will encourage the alternative, of doubtful justification, of using sources such as coal and nuclear energy. This means that the country not only will increase its use of the nonrenewable sources it needs but also its dependence on foreign markets in the areas of energy, technology, and finances.

Thermoelectric Plant Operating Efficiency

Projections of the amount of energy to be generated by thermoelectric plants are based on the use of three energy sources: hydrocarbons, coal, and uranium. In this area, primary energy demand is defined by what is needed for thermoelectric generation and by the operating efficiency of the plants in the system. Estimates of potential savings for 1990 and 2000 take these needs into account, together with plans for HD and different levels of transformation efficiency (see Tables 5.16 and 5.17).14/

If we contrast two possible trends, one maintaining the current level of efficiency and the other continuing the present rate of improvement (1% increase annually), the following is evident:

. If the current 30% efficiency were maintained and if the assumptions made about growth and generation hold true, an equivalent of 527 mbce and 1,004 tbdce of energy would be required in 1990 and 2000, respectively.
. If efficiency improves at the historical rate, thermoelectric plants will have a 32.75% and 36.18% efficiency in 1990 and 2000.
. At this level of efficiency, thermoelectric plants will require 494 tbdce in 1990. This amount is 33 tbdce less than the amount required for a 30% efficiency, that is, a 6.3% savings. The figures for the year 2000 are 837 tbdce, or 167 tbdce less, a savings of 16.6%.

Increased efficiency and the corresponding energy savings should result, in part, from the maintenance of gen-

erating plants. This maintenance would provide the efficiency the plants were designed for as well as assure that
the system allows the plants to operate at those levels of
efficiency. However, there is an option for accelerating
improvements in system efficiency, thereby increasing potential savings, if we consider that by the year 2000 world
technology will evolve and provide commercial combined-
cycle plants and other plant types with efficiencies of 42%
and that, by then, the Mexican domestic system should have
an overall efficiency of 36%. Given these two considerations, the difference between the 36% and 42% efficiency
levels would mean a 120 tbdoe reduction in fuel consumption. Therefore, if the specific consumption of the
thermoelectric system were to drop by the end of the century to the lowest level mentioned here, the demand for
nonrenewable energy sources would be 28.6% lower than it
would be if the current level of efficiency remained in effect (see Table 5.16).15/

In monetary terms, future fuel savings would be 3.3
million dollars a day in 1990 and 7.9 million dollars a day
in 2000, given a price of 27.5 dollars/barrel.

Savings with Cogeneration

To analyze the possible energy saved with cogeneration
by 1990 and 2000, for a total production of 125.0 TWh and
230.0 TWh, respectively (see Table 5.14), we must consider
the following:

. The industrial sector could generate approximately 7.5%
  of its own electric power needs with cogeneration by 1990
  and some 20% by 2000.16/
. Once transmission and distribution losses (14% of the energy generated) have been discounted, the industrial sector's part in the end consumption of electricity would
  increase to 56.5% in 1990 and would stay at this level
  until the year 2000.
. The transformation efficiency of the electric power industry will be 32.6% by 1990 and 36% by the year 2000.

Using these statistics, we can conclude that a 7.5%
cogeneration by 1990 means that the industrial sector will
require 56.1 TWh from the network, instead of the 60.7 TWh
required if cogeneration were not introduced (see Figure
5.9). These figures also affect transmission losses: The

net power generated by the plants will drop from 125 TWh to 119.7 TWh. This means 5.3 TWh less electric power will have to be generated by the CFE. At 32.68% efficiency, there would be a savings of 13.94 X 10^{12} Kcal (30 tbdce) in fuel or primary energy.

By the year 2000, cogeneration would mean a 22.4 TWh reduction in the industrial sector's demand. As a consequence, CFE's production would decrease by 26.0 TWh, and the net electric power produced for sectorial consumption would drop from 230 TWh to 204 TWh. This is equivalent to a nonrenewable energy savings on the order of 62.11 X 10^{12} Kcal (133 tbdce) (see Figure 5.10).

Estimates for the reduction in the demand of primary energy should take into account the energy consumption needed for cogeneration in industry. A real energy balance requires knowledge of the increase in amounts of hydrocarbons caused by the change from low-pressure boilers generating steam to high-pressure or gas boilers generating electricity and steam.

Taking these consumption levels into account, we can calculate that savings are reduced by 45%, on the average. Thus, effective levels of savings equivalent to 16.5 tbdce and 73.1 tbdce could be achieved by 1990 and 2000, respectively. 17/ In monetary terms, these levels mean 163 million dollars and 724 million dollars, respectively, for the years indicated.

The primary energy needed for cogeneration in 1990 will be 4.6 X 1.5 = 6.9 TWh, or 5.93 X 10^{12} Kcal. The effective savings, therefore, will be

$$13.94 \text{ X } 10^{12} \text{ Kcal} - 5.93 \text{ X } 10^{12} \text{ Kcal} = 8.01 \text{ X } 10^{12} \text{ Kcal.}$$

By the year 2000, 22.4 TWh of primary energy will be needed for cogeneration, or 28.75 X 10^{12} Kcal. Subtracting this value from the previous savings estimate (62.11 − 28.75) gives an effective savings of 33.36 X 10^{12} Kcal.

An idea of the combined impact of the three proposals for the efficient use, savings, and conservation of energy in generating electricity can be formed by adding the previous partial results. The total amount of nonrenewable energy saved by combining diversification, better efficiency, and cogeneration would be 74.8 tbdce by 1990 and 463.3 tbdce by 2000. Such amounts are equivalent to 2.1% and 13.0%, respectively, of the primary energy produced domestically in 1984 and almost double CFE's fuel consumption for 1982 (see Table 5.18). In monetary terms, 750 million and 4,650 million dollars would be saved by 1990 and 2000, respectively, at current prices for Mexican crude.

NOTES

1. The utilization factor is defined here as the effective generation divided by the total generating capacity.

2. Cf. Tables 5.1 and 5.2.

3. Because the heat dissipated for each KWh is equal to 860 Kcal, given a 4% efficiency, the specific consumption in Kcal/KWh is obtained from the ratio 860/x.

4. Cf. Table 5.8. The difference between this figure and that in Table 5.7 (29.94%) is due to the difference in the figures on the net generation of the plants.

5. The preceding efficiency is typical of a machine with an open cycle and straight drive shaft. These units can have a power of 100 MW.

6. H. Hidalgo C., "Aprovechamiento racional de la energía en centrales termoeléctricas," mimeograph (Mexico: CFE, Gerencia de Generación y Transmisión).

7. The calculation assumes a nominal efficiency of 38%, a fuel flow of 68,000 liters/hour, and a specific consumption of 2,263 Kcal/KWh.

8. In Table 5.11 we show the advantages of increasing the efficiency by 1%, based on the 30.36% efficiency obtained in 1982. The chart is designed as follows: Column 1 represents the percentage of efficiency, column 2, the corresponding specific consumption; column 3, the percent savings for the specific consumption; and column 4, the savings in kilocalories for the 48.1 TWh production in 1982 (Cf. Table 5.7).

9. Martiniano Aguilar, Refinación petrolera en México: Desarrollo tecnológico actual (Mexico: Instituto de Investigaciones Eléctricas, 1978).

10. The details of these changes are shown in Figure 5.6.

11. Hydrothermal and geothermal electricity are included in generation from renewable sources.

12. The CFE foresees a 32.68% efficiency during the period 1984 to 1993. Cf. Comisión Federal de Electricidad, "Evolución de la eficiencia de conversión de energía térmica en energía eléctrica," mimeograph (Mexico: Gerencia de Estudios, 1984).

13. CFE, "Evolución de la eficiencia." CFE foresees a 32.85% efficiency by the year 2000.

14. The efficiencies considered range from 30% to 42%.

15. We mentioned previously that the steel industry could generate a third of the electric power it consumes and that the chemical, celloluse, and paper industries could generate up to half their electric power needs. Moreover, PEMEX and the sugar industry have an important generating potential.

16. Some 287 tbdce would not be consumed.

17. Such requirements are calculated assuming the use of turbines and recuperation boilers with a 67% efficiency. This means that to generate 1 Kcal of electricity, a 1.5 Kcal input is needed. Cf. Lazanidis Gyftopoulos and Witmar Gyftopoulos, <u>Potential Fuel Effectiveness in Industry</u> (1978), p.24.

TABLE 5.1
Development of Installed Capacity Operating (MW)

Year	Hydro-electric	Thermoelectric								Total
		Steam	Combined Cycle	Gas Turbine	Geothermal-electric	Internal Combustion	Carbo-electric	Sub-totals	Thermal's Share of Total (%)	
1965	2,149	1,775	—	—	—	241	—	2,016	48.40	4,165
1966	2,482	1,771	—	—	—	262	—	2,033	45.05	4,515
1967	2,511	1,863	—	—	—	268	—	2,131	45.91	4,642
1968	2,509	1,933	—	—	—	354	—	2,287	47.69	4,796
1969	3,229	2,038	—	—	—	391	—	2,429	42.93	5,658
1970	3,228	2,353	—	—	—	487	—	2,840	46.80	6,068
1971	3,227	2,677	—	318	—	276	—	3,271	50.34	6,498
1972	3,228	2,698	—	619	—	368	—	3,685	53.31	6,913
1973	3,446	3,049	—	866	75	290	—	4,280	55.40	7,726
1974	3,521	3,415	130	971	75	259	—	4,850	57.94	8,371
1975	4,044	3,821	610	—	75	251	—	5,786	58.86	9,830
1976	4,541	5,012	610	948	1,029	274	—	6,919	60.38	11,460
1977	4,723	5,061	720	1,266	75	247	—	7,369	60.94	12,092
1978	5,225	6,456	720	1,267	75	249	—	8,767	62.66	13,992
1979	5,219	6,716	720	1,259	150	234	—	9,079	63.50	14,298
1980a/	5,992	6,616	540	1,190	150	137	—	8,633	59.03	14,625
1981	6,550	7,486	1,223	1,539	180	118	300	10,846	62.35	17,396
1982	6,550	8,325	1,223	1,686	205	101	300	11,840	64.38	18,390
AAGR b/	6.78	9.52	10.45	16.37	11.82	-4.99	0	11.70		9.13

Source: Comisión Federal de Electricidad.

a/ Starting with 1980, the real power installed by December 31 is indicated. Previous years report the sum of the plate capacities of the generating units.
b/ AAGR = Average annual growth rate.

TABLE 5.2
Development of Gross Generation

Year	Hydro-electric (GWh)	Thermoelectric (GWh) [a]							Thermal's Share of Total (%)	Total
		Steam	Combined Cycle	Gas Turbine	Geothermal-electric	Internal Combustion	Carbo-electric	Sub-totals		
1965	8,638	5,690	—	—	—	389	—	6,079	41.31	14,717
1966	9,954	5,742	—	—	—	466	—	—	—	16,162
1967	10,855	6,601	—	—	—	479	—	—	—	17,935
1968	12,408	7,078	—	—	—	533	—	—	—	20,019
1969	13,303	8,974	—	—	—	788	—	—	—	23,065
1970	14,085	10,360	—	—	—	865	—	11,225	43.12	26,030
1971	14,269	13,321	—	437	—	456	—	—	—	28,483
1972	15,246	14,780	—	1,060	—	447	—	—	—	31,533
1973	16,081	15,462	—	2,070	161	470	—	—	—	34,244
1974	16,602	17,915	198	2,068	463	762	—	—	—	38,008
1975	15,016	19,562	1,640	3,403	518	734	—	25,863	63.27	40,879
1976	17,087	22,128	1,932	2,366	579	540	—	—	—	44,632
1977	19,035	25,280	2,045	1,537	592	456	—	—	—	48,945
1978	16,066	30,322	2,488	3,027	598	476	—	—	—	52,977
1979	17,839	33,098	2,317	3,343	1,019	454	—	40,231	69.28	58,070
1980 [b]	16,740	37,012	3,267	3,623	915	311	—	45,128	72.94	61,868
1981	24,446	35,527	3,456	3,202	964	251	33	43,451	64.01	67,879
1982	22,729	40,025	5,272	2,438	1,296	187	1,278	50,496	68.96	73,225
AAGR [c]	5.86	12.16	18.09	8.69	13.73	-4.22	—	13.26	—	9.90

Source: Comisión Federal de Electricidad.

a/ GWh = Gigawatts (a million Kwh).
b/ During June, July, and August 1980, there were restrictions of 538 GWh in the supply of energy, due to the electric system's inadequate capacity. This should be taken into account when trying to determine trends.
c/ AAGR = Average annual growth rate.

TABLE 5.3
Percent Variation in Generating Electric Energy in Different Thermoelectric Plants, 1976–1982

Year	Steam	Combined Cycle	Gas Turbine	Geothermal	Internal Combustion	Carbo-electric	Total
1976	80.33	7.02	8.59	2.10	1.96	—	100.00
1977	84.52	6.84	5.14	1.98	1.52	—	100.00
1978	82.15	6.74	8.20	1.62	1.29	—	100.00
1979	82.27	5.76	8.31	2.53	1.13	—	100.00
1980	82.01	7.24	8.03	2.03	0.69	—	100.00
1981	81.80	7.96	7.37	2.22	0.58	—	100.00
1982	79.26	10.44	4.83	2.57	0.37	2.53	100.00

Source: Comisión Federal de Electricidad.

TABLE 5.4
Percent Variation in Different Thermoelectric Plant Capacities, 1976-1982

Year	Steam	Combined Cycle	Gas Turbine	Geothermal	Internal Combustion	Carbo-electric	Total
1976	72.44	8.82	13.70	1.08	3.96	---	100.00
1977	68.68	9.77	17.18	1.02	3.35	---	100.00
1978	73.64	8.21	14.45	0.86	2.84	---	100.00
1979	73.97	7.93	13.87	1.65	2.58	---	100.00
1980	76.63	6.26	13.78	1.74	1.59	---	100.00
1981	69.02	11.28	14.19	1.66	1.08	2.77	100.00
1982	70.31	10.33	14.24	1.73	0.85	2.54	100.00

Source: Table 5.3.

TABLE 5.5
Power and Gross Generation of Domestic Thermoelectric Plants

Thermoelectric	Real Installed Power		Gross Generation		
			GWh	GWh	%
	1980	1981	1980	1981	1981
Steam					
Francisco Pérez Ríos (Tula)	1,200	1,200	7,715	6,402	14.74
Salamanca	860	860	5,061	4,198	9.67
Altamira	820	820	3,673	3,729	8.58
Valle de México	730	730	3,891	3,692	8.50
Monterrey	465	465	2,877	2,514	5.79
Guaymas II	484	484	2,472	2,409	5.55
Mazatlán II	316	616	1,897	2,112	4.86
Francisco Villa	—	415	699	1,807	4.16
Rosarito (Tijuana)	294	287	1,131	1,265	2.91
Jorge Luque	224	224	865	1,239	2.85
Lerma (Campeche II)	150	150	764	788	1.81
San Jerónimo	105	105	732	737	1.70
Poza Rica (Manantial)	117	117	886	666	1.53
Manzanillo	—	300	—	421	0.97
Río Escondido (Carbón)	—	300	—	20	0.05
Total	5,765	7,073	32,663	31,999	73.67
Combined Cycle					
Dos Bocas	360	360	2,181	1,508	3.47
Gómez Palacio	180	180	1,086	914	2.10
Huinalá	—	252	—	780	1.80
Tula	—	278	—	204	0.47
El Sauz	—	153	—	45	0.11
Total	540	1,223	3,267	3,451	7.95
Gas Turbine					
Jorge Luque	132	132	330	130	0.30
Nonoalco	136	136	270	19	0.04
Total	268	268	600	149	0.34
Geothermal					
Cerro Prieto	150	180	915	964	2.22
Total: Major Thermal Plants	6,723	8,744	37,445	36,563	84.18
Minor Thermal Plants	1,910	2,102	7,683	6,870	15.82
Thermal Plants	8,633	10,846	45,128	43,433	100

Source: Comisión Federal de Electricidad, Informe de Operación 1981 (Mexico, 1982, p.29).

108

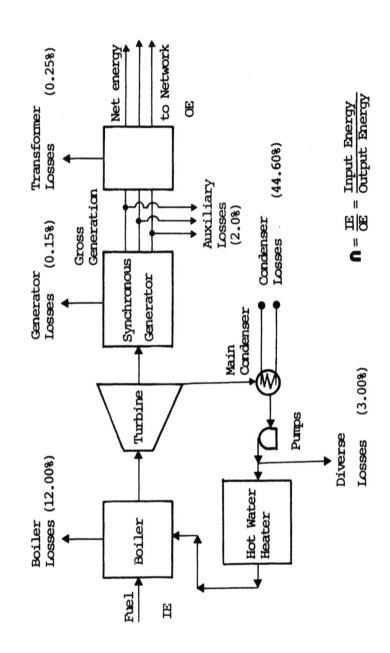

FIGURE 5.1
Diagram for Energy Consumption in Thermoelectric Steam Plants

TABLE 5.6
Energy Consumption in a Thermoelectric Steam Plant
(in percentages)

Plant Areas	Percentages
Boiler	12.00
Condenser	44.60
Diverse Losses	3.00
Auxiliary Services	2.00
Generator	0.15
Transformer	.25
Efficiency (Available Output Energy)	38.00
T o t a l (Input Energy)	100.00

Source: Instituto de Investigaciones Eléctricas (IIE),
Evaluation of Energy Supply and Demand in La Guacamaya,
Mich. Mexico (Mexico, 1983).

TABLE 5.7
Development of the Specific Consumption of the Domestic Thermoelectric System

Year	Net Generation (TWh)	Fuel Consumption (Kcal X 10^{12})	Specific Consumption (Kcal/KWh)	Efficiency (%)
1965	5.866	19.999	3,409.3	25.23
1966	5.992	20.236	3,377.2	25.47
1967	6.830	22.569	3,304.4	26.03
1968	7.376	25.894	3,510.6	24.50
1969	9.437	31.337	3,320.7	25.90
1970	10.866	36.327	3,343.2	25.72
1971	13.772	44.737	3,248.4	26.47
1972	15.753	50.525	3,207.3	26.81
1973	17.556	56.165	3,199.2	26.88
1974	20.669	64.154	3,103.9	27.71
1975	24.928	79.567	3,191.9	26.94
1976	26.478	82.819	3,127.8	27.49
1977	28.717	86.284	3,004.6	28.62
1978	35.392	105.091	2,969.3	28.96
1979	38.589	112.857	2,924.6	29.41
1980	43.107	126.204	2,927.7	29.37
1981	42.169	121.140	2,872.7	29.94
1982	48.134	136.333	2,832.4	30.36
AAGR[a]	13.18	11.95	-1.08	1.09

Source: Comisión Federal de Electricidad, Sector eléctrico nacional: Estadísticas 1965-1982 (Mexico, 1982), p. 79.

Note: Net generation from the first column comes from multiplying the total net generation by the percentage of thermoelectric generation for each year considered.

a/ AAGR = Average annual growth rate.

FIGURE 5.2
Development of Domestic Electric Power System Efficiency

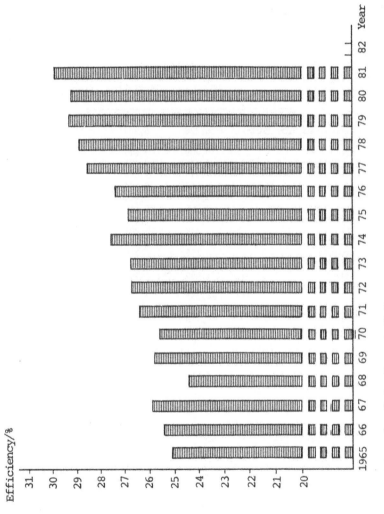

Source: Comisión Federal de Electricidad.

112

TABLE 5.8
Specific Consumptions and Efficiency of Domestic Thermoelectric Plants, 1981

Thermoelectric Plant	Fuel Consumption (Kcal X 10⁹)	Net Generation (GWh)	Specific Consumption (Kcal/KWh)	Efficiency
Steam				
Francisco Pérez Ríos (Tula)	16,226	6,209	2,612.9	32.91
Salamanca	11,236	4,072	2,759.8	31.16
Altamira	9,209	3,617	2,545.9	33.78
Valle de México	9,216	3,581	2,574.4	33.42
Monterrey	7,570	2,591	2,920.8	29.44
Guaymas II	6,093	2,336	2,607.5	32.98
Mazatlán	5,376	2,048	2,624.2	32.77
Francisco Villa	4,765	1,752	2,718.5	31.63
Rosarito (Tijuana)	3,871	1,227	3,154.7	27.26
Jorge Luque	3,848	1,201	3,201.8	26.86
Lerma (Campeche II)	2,230	764	2,917.5	29.48
San Jerónimo	2,155	714	3,014.4	28.53
Poza Rica (Manantial)	1,889	646	2,924.1	29.41
Manzanillo	1,080	408	2,644.7	32.52
Río Escondido[a/]	131	19	—	—
Total	84,897	31,185	2,731.1	31.49
Combined Cycle				
Dos Bocas	4,476	1,462	3,060.0	28.10
Gómez Palacio	2,517	886	2,839.0	30.29
Huinalá	2,167	756	2,864.1	30.03
Tula	521	197	2,632.9	32.66
El Sauz	141	43	3,230.2	26.62
Total	9,822	3,344	2,937.2	29.28
Gas Turbine				
Jorge Luque	468	126	3,711.3	23.17
Nonoalco	99	18	5,371.7	16.01
Total	567	144	3,937.5	21.84
Total: Major Thermal Plants	95,286	34,673	2,748.1	31.29
Minor Thermal Plants	25,853	6,663	3,880.1	22.16
Thermal Plants	121,139	41,336	2,930.6	29.36

Source: Comisión Federal de Electricidad, Informe de operaciones 1981 (Mexico, 1982), p.38.

a/ This plant only operated for a short time in 1982.

FIGURE 5.3
Histogram of Net Energy Efficiency Generation (GWh)

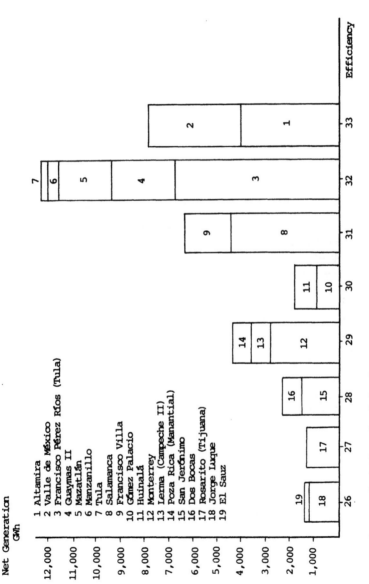

Source: Comisión Federal de Electricidad.

TABLE 5.9
Typical Steam Plant Efficiency Internationally

Power/Unit (MW)			Efficiency Range (%)		
0	–	0.1	7.5	–	11.5
0.1	–	1.0	10.0	–	19.0
1	–	10	17.0	–	24.5
10	–	50	22.0	–	31.0
50	–	100	27.0	–	34.0
100	–	1,000	35.0	–	40.0

Source: United Nations, Small Scale Power Generation
(New York, 1967), p.199.

FIGURE 5.4
Development of Specific Consumption in Thermoelectric Plants in Selected Countries

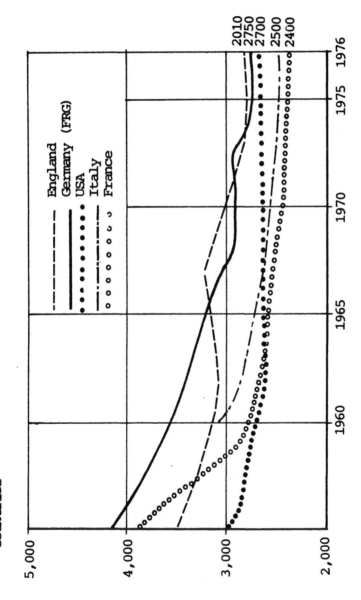

Source: Centro de Estudios de la Energía, Situación energética de la industria, sector eléctrico (Madrid, 1979).

TABLE 5.10

Energy Efficiency and Specific Consumption of Selected Countries, 1976

Country	Specific Consumption (Kcal/KWh)	Efficiency (%)
West Germany	2,750	31.27
United States	2,700	31.85
Italy	2,500	34.40
France	2,400	35.83

Source: Centro de Estudios de la Energía, Situación energética de la Industria, sector eléctrico (Madrid, 1979), p.64.

FIGURE 5.5
Possible Sources of Future Electric Power Generation

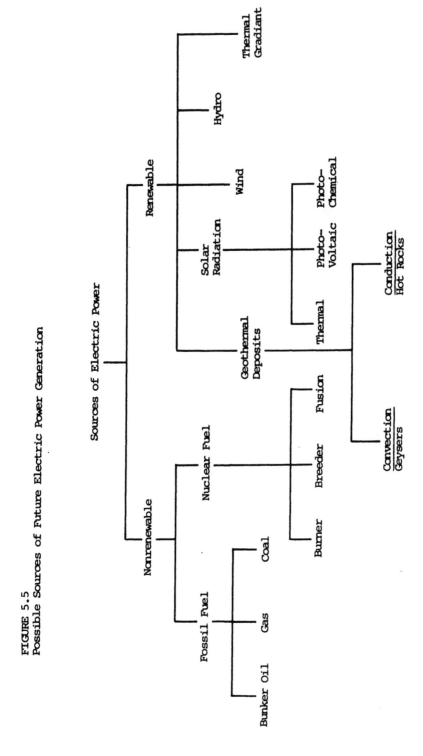

TABLE 5.11
Fuel Savings for a Graduated Variation in Efficiency, 1982

Efficiency	Specific Consumption (Kcal/Kwh)	Improvements in Efficiency of Specific Consumption	Fuel Reduction
30.36	2,832.36	0.0	0.0
31.00	2,774.19	2.05	2.80
32.00	2,687.50	5.11	6.97
33.00	2,606.06	7.99	10.89
34.00	2,529.41	10.70	14.58
35.00	2,457.14	13.25	18.06
36.00	2,388.89	15.66	21.35
37.00	2,324.32	17.94	24.45
38.00	2,263.16	20.10	27.40

Source: Estimate of authors.

TABLE 5.12
Development of Net Generation of Electric Power, 1950-1983 (GWh)

Year	Net Generation[a]	Year	Net Generation[a]
1950	3,549	1967	17,363
1951	3,913	1968	19,425
1952	4,272	1969	22,349
1953	4,595	1970	25,288
1954	5,078	1971	27,672
1955	5,616	1972	30,569
1956	6,543	1973	33,161
1957	6,724	1974	36,664
1958	7,297	1975	39,428
1959	7,680	1976	42,617
1960	8,563	1977	46,873
1961	9,373	1978	51,181
1962	10,070	1979	55,164
1963	11,006	1980	59,100
1964	12,896	1981	65,900
1965	14,232	1982	71,050
1966	15,645	1983	72,650

Source: Comisión Federal de Electricidad.

a/ To obtain an approximate value for gross generation, add 3%.

120

FIGURE 5.6
Development of the Rate of Net Generation of Electric Power, 1951-1983 (in percentages)

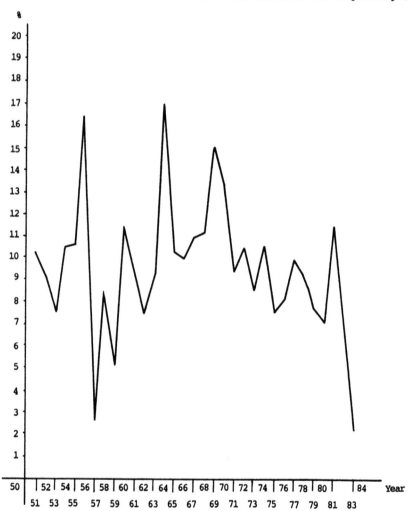

Source: Table 5.12.

TABLE 5.13
Net Production of Electricity, 1982-2000

Year	TWh[a]
1982	73.2
1985	88.7
1990	122.1
1995	168.0
2000	231.3
AAGR[b]	6.6%

Source: Based on Comisión Federal de Electricidad "low projection," CFE "Evolución de la eficiencia de conversión de energía térmica en energía eléctrica (Mexico, 1984), p. 68.

a/ Gross generation is approximately 3% above this value.
b/ AAGR = Average annual growth rate.

TABLE 5.14
Composition of Generating Plants in the Electric Power System, 1982, 1990, and 2000

Plant	1982 Present Structure (TWh)	1990 Diversification		2000 Diversification		2000/1982 AAGR[a]		2000 Installed Capacity	
		Moderate (TWh)	High (TWh)	Moderate (TWh)	High (TWh)	Moderate (%)	High (%)	Moderate (GW)	High (GW)
Hydroelectric	22.7	27.9	30.2	36.2	43.3	2.62	3.65	11.4	14.1
Geothermal	1.3	2.8	3.0	7.0	9.9	9.80	11.90	1.0	1.5
Coal	1.3	5.1	5.5	28.4	32.8	18.70	19.60	5.4	6.8
Nuclear	—	12.4	15.0	27.9	34.0	—	—	5.3	8.3
Hydrocarbons	47.9	73.0	65.5	122.0	97.0	5.30	4.00	27.8	22.1
Cogeneration	—	3.8	5.8	8.5	13.0	—	—	2.0	3.0
Total	73.2	125.0	91.8	230.0	230.0	36.92	39.15	52.9	55.8

Source: Estimate of authors.

a/ AAGR - Average annual growth rate.

TABLE 5.15
Share of Renewable and Nonrenewable Resources in Generating Electric Power, 1982, 1990, and 2000 (in percentages)

	1982	1990 Diversification		2000 Diversification	
		Moderate	High	Moderate	High
Renewable Resources a/	32.8	27.6	31.2	22.5	28.8
Nonrenewable Resources b/	67.2	72.4	68.8	77.5	71.2
Total	100.0	100.0	100.0	100.0	100.0

Source: Table 5.14

a/ Includes coal, nuclear, and hydrocarbons.
b/ Includes hydroelectric, geothermal, and cogeneration.

124

FIGURE 5.7
Nonrenewable Resources Needed to Produce Electricity: Moderate Diversification
and High Diversification

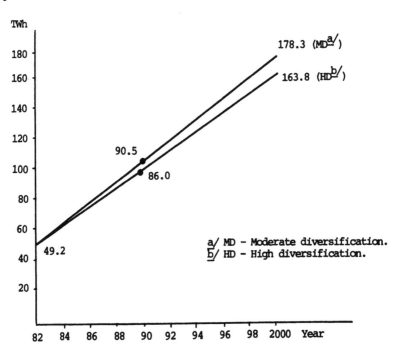

Source: Estimate of authors.

FIGURE 5.8
Renewable Resources Needed to Produce Electricity: Moderate Diversification
and High Diversification

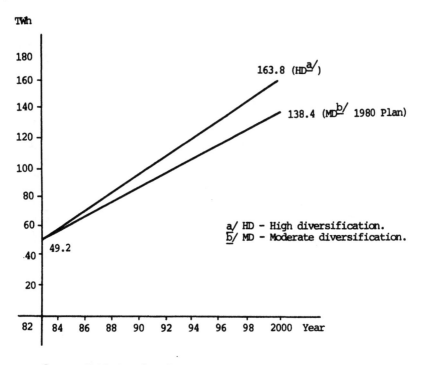

Source: Estimate of authors.

TABLE 5.16
Fuel Needs for Thermal Generation of 86 TWh by 1990 and 163.8 TWh by 2000 for Different Efficiencies

| Efficiency (%) | Nonrenewable Resource Needs[a] | | | | | |
| | Kcal x 10¹² (annual) | | Annual Barrels (millions) | | Daily Barrels (millions) | |
	1990	2000	1990	2000	1990	2000
30	246.56	469.56	192.3	366.8	0.527	1.004
32	231.08	440.21	180.2	343.9	0.494	0.944
34	217.49	414.31	169.6	323.6	0.465	0.886
36	205.45	391.30	160.3	305.7	0.439	0.837
38	194.62	370.70	151.8	289.6	0.416	0.793
40	164.90	352.17	144.2	275.1	0.395	0.753
42	176.13	335.40	137.4	262.0	0.376	0.717

Source: Estimate of authors.

Note: Thermal generating levels corresponding to high diversification are considered here.

a/ As a point of comparison, in 1983 50.3 TWh were generated from thermoelectric sources (excepting coal and geothermal), with approximated 30% efficiency. This implies an equivalent consumption of 309,000 barrels daily.

TABLE 5.17
Improvements in Efficiency According to 1% Historical Rate

Year	Efficiency (%)
1981	29.95
1985	31.16
1990	32.75
1995	34.42
2000	36.18

Source: Estimate of authors.

FIGURE 5.9
Energy Savings in Electric Sector Due to Cogeneration in Industry, 1990

a) <u>Without Cogeneration</u>

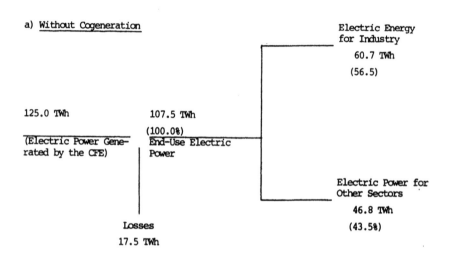

b) <u>With 7.5% (4.6 TWh) Cogeneration in the</u>
   <u>Industrial Sector</u>

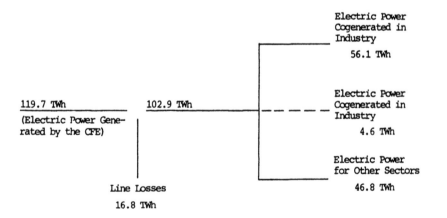

<u>Sources</u>: Table 5.13 and estimates of authors.

FIGURE 5.10
Energy Savings in Electric Sector Due to Cogeneration in Industry, 2000

a) Without Cogeneration

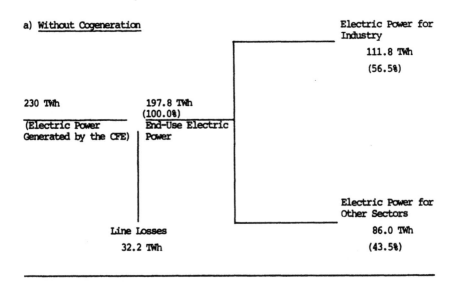

b) With 20% (22.4 TWh) Cogeneration in
   the Industrial Sector

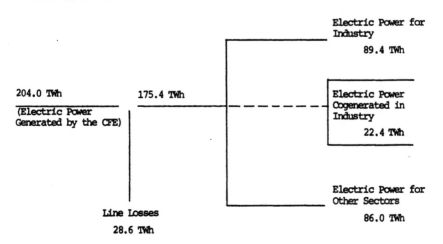

Sources: Table 5.13 and estimates of authors.

TABLE 5.18
Electric Sector: Impact of Measures to Conserve and Use Energy Efficiently, 1990 and 2000

| | | Amount Saved (tbdoe) a/ | |
| | | 2000 | |
	1990	According to 1980 Plan	HD b/
Diversification	25.3	223.2	--
HD	--	81.1	81.1
Energy plan 1980	--	142.1	--
Due to increase in efficiency	33.0	167.0	167.0
Due to net cogeneration	16.5	73.1	73.1
Total	74.8	463.3	321.2
Share of the domestic energy production (1984) c/	2.1%	13.0%	9.0%
Amount saved: Equivalent to billions of dollars d/	2.1	12.7	8.8

Sources: Estimates of authors and Programa nacional de energéticos 1984-1988
         p.155.

a/ tbdoe - Thousands of barrels of daily crude oil equivalent.
b/ HD - High diversification.
c/ 3,579 thousands of daily barrels of hydrocarbons.
d/ For the amount of total savings, we used the current average price for each
   barrel of Isthmus and Maya crude: $29 and $25.5, respectively.

6

Transportation Sector

In Mexico transportation of passengers and freight has
grown rapidly since the 1940s as a consequence of the economic integration of the country's different regions. Since
that time, the state has contributed actively to the creation and improvement of an extensive network of highways.
This infrastructure served as a basis for the development
of highway transportation, which was stimulated in the 1950s
by the installation and growth of the automobile industry
in Mexico. At the same time, the railroad progressively declined in importance as a means of transportation.

The rapid growth of this economic activity during the
1960s was reflected in its macroeconomic variables. The
gross value of production in the transportation sector grew
at an annual rate of 10.3% between 1970 and 1981, increasing
its share in the GDP from 4.2% to 6.0%. Since 1982, however, there has been a considerable decrease in transportation, which corresponds to the difficulties the domestic
economy currently faces.

The structure of Mexico's transportation system is un-
balanced: The various means of transportation have a different share in moving freight and passengers. Domestic transportation of goods is done mainly by highway transportation,
which takes up 67.4% of the freight, compared to 18% for
the railroad and 14.6% for maritime transportation. Air
transportation is not significant in this area (see Tables
6.1, 6.2, and 6.3).

The rapid urbanization of the country and the increasing mobility of the population have caused an accelerated growth in passenger transportation. Here again, highway transportation is the cornerstone of the system, consti-

tuting 97% of public passenger service (see Tables 6.2 and 6.4). During the 1960s, this trend was further reinforced by the decline in the importance of the railroad. At the same time, air transportation grew rapidly, moving a percentage of passengers (1.1%) slightly lower than that moved by the railroad (1.8%).

PATTERNS OF CONSUMPTION AND EFFICIENT ENERGY USE

The structure of the transportation system conditioned the sectorial consumption of energy, and the production of energy, together with low prices, contributed to the reinforcement of this structure. Transportation worldwide is highly dependent on oil for its energy needs. Mexico is no exception; 98% of the energy used for transportation is derived from this primary source. This feature can be attributed to the advantage the sector has in using a liquid fuel with a high-energy density. In Mexico at the same time absolute consumption levels rose, its relative share of overall national consumption also increased.

During the period from 1970 to 1982, the AAGR of end-use energy for the sector was 8.5%, with rates between 11% and 13% from 1979 to 1982. Furthermore, its relative share of national end-use energy rose from 38.2% in 1970 to 39.2% in 1975 and 41.3% in 1982, with a corresponding decrease in the percentage held by other sectors such as industry (see Tables 6.5 and 6.6).1/

Within the structure of the transportation sector, an area deserving special attention is the Mexican petroleum industry. PEMEX is a major user of the railroad and highway transportation networks, as well as port facilities, holding close to 40% of the freight transported nationwide. Thus, PEMEX plays an especially significant role in transportation planning and, in particular, in the efficient use of energy in the sector.

In 1981 the total freight transported by PEMEX totaled 202 million tons, nearly all of which (96%) was crude oil, gas, and derivatives; the remainder was equipment and materials used in the company's operations. Seventy-five percent of this load was transported by pipeline, 12% by ship, and 13% by highway or railroad (2% of the load transported by these last three means consisted of equipment and materials).2/ PEMEX is thus responsible for 8% of the goods transported nationally by highway and 6% of the total freight moved nationally over the rails.

Among the energy sources used by the transportation
sector, gasoline, diesel, liquefied gas, and, to a lesser
extent, natural gas are similar in character because of
their common origin. There are, however, important differences in the role they play in preferential use; their degree of substitutability; the quality of their use; and the
particular capital requirements for their production, distribution, and consumption.

The share of the sector's consumption held by the different secondary energy sources in 1982 shows a high concentration of petroleum derivatives, in particular, gasoline (55.5%) and diesel (37.6%). The list is completed by
turbo and jet fuels (5.5%) and liquefied gas and bunker oil
(1.4% together). Given the consumption level of these
fuels, electricity and natural gas do not play a significant role in consumption patterns.3/

GASOLINE

Gasoline is used exclusively to satisfy transportation
needs, and its use centers around individual transportation
(see Table 6.7). There are two types of automobile gasoline on the market: Nova and Extra. Nova, 83 octane and
leaded, accounts for 95% of the national market. Extra, 91
octane and unleaded, is only marginally consumed, except in
the U.S. border area. There, consumption patterns are distorted by the type of vehicle characteristic of the area as
well as by the influx of foreign cars into Mexico.

In 1982, domestic sales of gasoline totaled 131,736
thousands of barrels (tb), distributed in the following man-
ner: 65% to private automobiles, 21% to trucks, 8% to taxis,
and 6% to buses. The growth in gasoline consumption was
8.0% annually from 1972 to 1982, with a maximum AAGR of 15%
in 1981. This rapid growth in consumption can be attributed, in part, to interurban transportation, but it was
principally due to the growing traffic and congestion in major Mexican cities.

PEMEX has 61 distribution points throughout the country. In 1982, 43% of gasoline sales was concentrated in
four of these areas, which were the most rapidly growing urban centers: Mexico City (the Federal District), Ciudad
Juárez, Guadalajara, and Monterrey. The last two stand out,
in particular because their consumption increased, on an
average, by 10.4% and 9.7%, respectively, from 1972 to 1982.
In the Federal District, which accounted for 26.6% of total

domestic sales in 1982, the demand for gasoline grew at the rate of 5.9% annually during the same period.

This means that automobile transportation, urbanization, and the concentration of economic activities in a few cities combined with vehicle production to significantly affect the rise in gasoline demand. This process was accelerated during the latter half of the 1970s, when economic expansion based on exploiting hydrocarbons was in full swing. This resulted in pressure being placed on the productive structure of the country's major refineries.

DIESEL

There are two types of diesel fuel produced nationally: Diesel Nacional and Diesel Especial. Diesel Nacional has a higher sulphur content than Diesel Especial, which is marketed mainly in those cities where there are high levels of environmental pollution, such as Monterrey, Guadalajara, and the Federal District. Diesel Especial is also used in certain locomotives of Ferrocarriles Nacionales (National Railroad), which require this type of fuel to avoid rapid deterioration of certain engine parts. Diesel Especial represents about 25% of the total diesel marketed and is produced in only three of the nine refineries operated by Petróleos Mexicanos. Diesel Nacional, however, is the type normally used in interurban buses and trucks as well as in the vessels in the merchant and fishing fleets.

In 1982, the diesel fuel used by the transportation sector totaled 77.5% of the national consumption, most of which was used in highway transportation (89%). Less was used for sea (7.6%) and railroad transportation (3.4%) (see Table 6.7).

Diesel is similar to gasoline in the relationship between consumption, urban concentration, and transportation. In 1982, 33.2% of this fuel was marketed through just four areas: Gómez Palacio, Guadalajara, Monterrey, and the Federal District. The Federal District was the major consumption point, accounting for 16% of national sales. Just as in the case of gasoline, the Monterrey and Guadalajara agencies showed the strongest growth from 1972 to 1982. Their sales' AAGRs were 10.6% and 9.3%, respectively. The highly concentrated diesel and gasoline market justifies focusing conservation and efficient-use strategies on the major centers of consumption.

LIQUEFIED GAS

The use of liquefied gas as a fuel for internal combustion engines has been marginal in comparison to its other applications, representing only about 0.5% of total consumption. In the last few years, however, primarily because of the difference in price between this product and gasoline (measured in pesos per Kcal), there has been an increase in its use as a fuel, especially by companies with large fleets of vehicles.

At the present time, the municipal transport systems in at least two major cities (Guadalajara and Ciudad Juárez) use liquefied gas as a fuel. A significant number of private cars have been converted to accommodate this fuel, a relatively simple and economical conversion in terms of the cost of the unit and the savings in fuel consumption (see Table 6.8). The use of liquefied gas as a fuel in heavier machinery has been facilitated by turbocharger technology. It is now possible to adapt the diesel systems in semiheavy machinery, such as farm tractors, to liquefied gas.[4]/

As for the remaining secondary energy sources used in transportation, it should be noted that fuel oil mixed with diesel (in a proportion of 85%/15%) is used in marine engines and in large-scale industrial installations. Its share of sectorial consumption is very low, however, compared to gasoline and diesel.

Electrical energy is used very little in comparison to other energy sources. It is concentrated in urban transportation, that is, in the subway and trolley bus systems. Despite its limited role in sectorial energy consumption, the subway is one of the most important components of the urban transportation system in Mexico City. The subway began operating in 1969 with a single line, 11.5 kilometers long. Today, it operates with a network of over 100 kilometers and has a daily transportation capacity of over four million passengers. It has provided rapid transportation for a growing segment of the population, covering the relatively long distances in the city and lessening congestion and environmental pollution.

The subway is not only the most efficient transportation means in terms of the relationship between energy consumed, passengers transported, and distance covered, it also has continually increased its efficiency. In fact, the electricity consumed went from 246.6 GWh in 1972 to 377.8 GWh in 1980, growing at an annual rate of only 4.4%. Mean-

while, energy consumed for each passenger dropped from
0.634 KWh to 0.415 KWh during the same period. This variation in specific consumption reveals an increase on the
order of 65% in the efficiency of this means of transportation.

FACTORS AFFECTING INEFFICIENT ENERGY USE

The factors affecting the sector's trend toward an inefficient use of energy can be classified in two main
groups. The first group is economic factors, and the second is the structural and organizational techniques of the
transportation system. The distinction between the two is
a formal one, made for the purpose of simplification; in
actuality, both groups are intimately linked.

Given the importance of highway transportation in the
Mexican transportation system, this analysis concentrates
on this component, without implying that the other means
are less important. Potential savings lie in the area of
highway transportation, even though the other means should,
in the future, play a central role in modifying the present
structure, thereby conserving energy.

ECONOMIC FACTORS

The traditional Mexican policy of low energy prices remained in force throughout the 1960s. The 1973 price increases did not represent a substantial change in this policy, but the increases introduced in 1981, together with
the economic crisis, have had an influence on reducing energy demands, particularly for gasoline used in transportation. Keeping fuel prices low for transportation encouraged wasteful practices, above all in the use of automobile
gasoline, but at the same time these low prices helped the
development of transportation services (see Figure 6.15).5/

The relative prices of complementary or substitute
fuels can be instrumental in directing users toward specific types of consumption. In the case of gasoline and
diesel, the prices set for each constituted an incentive
for consuming diesel. In fact, whether we measure in terms
of volume or units of energy, gasoline has been considerably more expensive than diesel. However, this situation
began to change in the second half of the 1960s, the relationship of gasoline prices to diesel prices went from 4.93

in 1973 to 1.76 in 1983 (see Table 6.9). This incentive
to use diesel did not bring about any basic changes in the
type of automobiles used, but it did have an effect on
mass freight transportation.

The price differential existing between alternative
fuels has encouraged consumers to substitute. Such is the
case with liquefied gas, whose low cost and high degree of
substitutability in internal combustion engines has caused
a partial replacement of gasoline (see Table 6.9). The
difference between the price of liquefied gas and the price
of Nova gasoline was 0.41 in 1973 and 0.24 in 1983. The
price drop generated an increased national demand for liquefied gas culminating in the need to import this fuel because of insufficient capacity at the installed production
facilities.

Substituting or complementing energy sources also applies to diesel and kerosene. These products are often
mixed as a substitute for pure diesel, a common practice
among freight transporters, causing inefficient engine performance.

TECHNICAL FACTORS: STRUCTURE AND ORGANIZATION OF THE TRANSPORTATION SYSTEM

Because the Mexican transportation system is based on
highway transportation, with internal combustion engines
that mainly use gasoline, an analysis of the efficiency of
energy conversion in the transportation system is necessary. One also has to consider the different energy efficiencies for Otto-cycle and diesel engines. Using diesel
engines might be an alternative to improving fuel use because they are more efficient and are not commonly used in
Mexico. Operating conditions are just as important, if not
more so, as structural considerations when determining
levels of energy consumption and their evolution.

Transforming fuel energy into mechanical energy in internal combustion engines is characterized by low levels
of conversion. Gasoline and diesel engines are designed
with a maximum efficiency of 26% and 38%, respectively.
Actual performance, however, rarely surpasses 10% for
gasoline engines and 30% for diesel engines.

It has been calculated that fuel energy not utilized
in the engine is dissipated as follows: 45% of caloric energy is lost through high-temperature engine exhaust gases,
20% through cooling air or water, and 5% through friction.

Furthermore, in more modern high-compression machines, only 30% of the useful energy can be converted into work.

In a vehicle, the transformation efficiency of the engine is affected by factors related to vehicle design characteristics. The use of power steering, power brakes, and, in particular, automatic transmissions reduces efficiency and increases energy consumption. In this respect, the relationship between the dead weight and the engine power has significant influence. Vehicle manufacturing has been oriented toward reducing this ratio and achieving more efficient energy use through improvements in the design and materials used.

In operating a vehicle, there are several factors affecting energy consumption, including:

1. Operating speed
2. Passenger load in passenger transportation and freight load in highway transportation of goods
3. Highway characteristics: Differences in energy consumption between travel on level ground and on slopes.6/

With respect to point 1, it should be noted that the specific energy consumption of a vehicle with an internal combustion engine varies according to the operating speed. Technical engine-performance curves show that specific consumption progressively decreases as speed increases until a low point is reached, beyond which consumption starts to increase again. For this reason, continuous traffic flow in urban areas, avoiding frequent stopping, and an average speed that is not too low contribute to a higher efficiency in energy consumption in vehicles and avoid further reductions in already low engine-performance levels. These general aspects are also affected by the characteristics of the engine, whether it is an engine operating on gasoline or on diesel.

Using typically light conditions and a comparable operation basis, a study was conducted to compare the fuel economy of diesel and gasoline engines. Analyzing the distance covered for each unit of fuel consumed showed that diesel engines have a fuel economy approximately 35% higher than gasoline engines.7/ On an energy basis, the advantage is approximately 20%. Generally speaking, a liter of diesel contains 13% more energy than a liter of gasoline. Thus, diesel has the advantage of providing more energy per unit of fuel carried in the vehicle. Furthermore, fuel economy in certain diesel engines can be considerably

greater for vehicles operated in urban areas and in cold
climates. In all operating modes (idling, traffic, cruising,
and accelerating) diesel engines are superior to gasoline
engines (see Figure 6.2).

When evaluating the advantages of using diesel engines
in the mass production of vehicles, it is important to remember that it is still an internal combustion engine and
thus has a low efficiency and that the production of diesel
fuel requires crude oil and additional energy.

In regard to environmental pollution, diesel engines
have both advantages and disadvantages, compared to gasoline engines. Although carbon monoxide and hydrocarbon
emissions are lower in diesel engines, nitrogen oxide and
particle emissions are generally higher.8/ A vehicle's
load capacity, whether passenger or freight (point 2 on
page 138), is also an operating factor affecting the relationship between fuel consumed, load transported, and distance covered. This thus influences the efficiency of the
transportation system in a given environment.

The predominance of private cars in urban areas and
the low number of passengers transported per unit gives
rise to an increasingly inefficient transportation system.
In Mexico, cars carry an average of 1.3 passengers per
vehicle/trip. Under these conditions, a 6-cylinder vehicle
consumes approximately 2 liters of gasoline during a normal
12-kilometer urban trip, that is, about 1.54 liters per
passenger. This example, which is also valid for buses and
trucks, clearly demonstrates that the efficiency of a transportation system can be improved by using the vehicle's
load capacity better. The wider use of public transportation should, therefore, be encouraged.

The infrastructure and organization of the transportation network (point 3 on page 138) have a decisive influence on the amount of energy needed for urban and interurban transportation. These factors also affect the efficiency of the use of resources by society as well as the
quality of people's lives. An inefficient system not only
generates losses by wasting energy but also affects the
overall productivity of the labor force by requiring more
time for travel to production centers and causing a deterioration in living conditions.

The inefficiency of Mexico City's urban network is evident in, among other aspects, the reduced speeds. The main
cause is undoubtedly the traffic congestion caused by the
imbalance between the size of the areas dedicated to traffic
circulation and the number of vehicles in these areas (both

moving and stationary). Apart from the aforementioned
causes related to reduced speeds, inefficiency is also evident in the lack of synchronized traffic lights, driver at-
titudes, discontinuous working hours, and so on. To illustrate this, it is sufficient to mention that rush-hour
traffic in the central area of Mexico City (with four pe-
ripheral roads and other radial and axial roads) only
reaches speeds of 6 kilometers per hour, which means a considerable loss in efficiency.

Excessive gasoline consumption in the Federal District
due to traffic congestion totals nearly 2.6 million liters
per day, 15% of total daily gasoline consumption in the metropolitan area. More than a quarter of national gasoline
sales are concentrated here. If there are traffic congestion problems on at least 200 days a year, total excess
consumption is 520.0 million liters. At the current price
of 40 pesos a liter, this amount represents a waste of
close to 104 million dollars a year.9/ The man-hours lost
due to urban traffic congestion represents a loss on the
order of 1,400 million dollars annually. We should add to
this the cost of environmental pollution damage, which has
not yet been calculated.10/

Greater speed, comfort, and reliability in transportation, low energy costs, government policies encouraging
the expansion of the automobile industry, and investments
directed toward the urban road infrastructure are all factors contributing to the continual decline in the energy
efficiency of transportation. The underdeveloped public
transportation system and the neglect of the railroad had a
marked effect on this process.

Overall, the elements making up the transportation
system affect its energy efficiency. Thus, for transporting passengers, air transportation is less energy efficient
than automobile transportation. Automobiles, in turn, are
less efficient than buses or railroads. For moving freight,
air transportation is again less efficient in terms of energy consumption than truck transportation, and airplanes
are much less efficient than railroads. The most energy efficient means of transporting freight, especially over long
distances, are ships, pipelines, and electric railroad systems with energy regeneration and recuperation.

Moving from the present transportation system in Mexico toward the greater use of a mass transportation system
that is more efficient than the automobile means that a
better use of energy resources and a substantial change in
the quality of people's lives are possible. The extension

of Mexico City's subway network and the construction of
this means of transportation in the country's other major
cities would be important steps toward solving the problems
discussed.

MEASURES FOR EFFICIENT ENERGY USE AND CONSERVATION

The transportation sector, because of its strong influence on the country's energy end use and its characteristic
inefficiency, constitutes an area in which the efficient
use of energy would have a significant impact on the saving
and conservation of energy resources.

Given the limited information at our disposal concerning the composition and operation of the transportation
system, we present a number of measures that can be applied
within the context of our present state of knowledge. Also
included are other measures that require a wider data base
and analysis to be used. These measures can be divided
into two groups: modification of consumption patterns and
technological changes.

MODIFICATION OF CONSUMPTION PATTERNS

Most measures that could be adopted do not imply substantial changes to the existing transportation system. At
most, the measures would require minor structural changes.
Therefore, with relatively simple measures related primarily to the structure and organization of the system, substantial short-term savings could be made in energy consumption:

1. Improve the flow of traffic in large urban centers.
   Given the direct relationship between fuel consumption
   and speed, this variable could be controlled to increase
   efficiency in the sector's energy consumption. The low
   average speed of traffic in the major cities is undoubtedly due to traffic congestion. Among causes for this
   congestion are the following:
   a. Using the same streets and axial roads for both public transportation and private automobiles
   b. Parking on major streets and avenues important to the
   vehicular traffic network
   c. Lacking effective traffic flow control and sufficiently synchronized traffic lights

d. Lack of knowledge by the drivers of the negative effects of mechanical failures in cars and buses and the effects of driving habits on energy consumption.

A high percentage of vehicles are concentrated in the Mexico City metropolitan area. High-consumption rates are partially explained by traffic congestion and the tie-ups suffered by drivers and passengers. Measures should, therefore, be taken to minimize the causes of congestion. Drivers should, moreover, have more information at their disposal on the effect of driving habits on fuel savings. If adopted in the major cities, these measures would affect close to 37% of national gasoline consumption as well as diesel consumption in these same cities.

2. Transfer a part of the trips currently made in private cars to mass public services.

Buses and the subway offer alternatives to the automobile. A 10% transfer of car passengers to public transportation would result in considerable energy savings. However, to be able to achieve this percentage, or an even higher one, the public transportation system must be expanded and improved. This is a long-term consideration that must be examined as part of the changing urban planning system.

3. Increase the number of passengers per car. Energy consumption would be reduced if there were an average of 2.2 passengers per car, instead of the current 1.3 passenger average. This presupposes that the new passengers are already car users, either drivers or passengers, and that vehicles are not used for other ends.

4. Transfer part of the freight currently transported on the highway to the railroad. If 50% of this freight were transferred, there would be important energy savings. At the same time, the highways would be freed of traffic. Savings would be on the order of 30 X 10^{12} Kcal per year, that is, 3,246 million liters of diesel. In financial terms, this represents nearly 88,000 million pesos at the current domestic diesel price, and, supposing that an equivalent amount of crude oil could then be exported, the amount would total 650 million dollars. Present railroad capacity could be an obstacle, which should be taken into account to guarantee the viability of this solution.

In the longer term, two additional measures could contribute to energy savings: (1) Reduction in the size of en-

gines produced nationally: This measure, already legislated
in Mexico, is designed to regulate fuel consumption by restricting the sale of vehicles with large engines. The objective will be reached when the manufacture of engines
above a certain size is banned.11/ (2) Conversion of a part
of the vehicle engines produced domestically from gasoline
to diesel: Converting 10% of the vehicle engines produced
from one fuel to the other would save close to 244 million
liters of gasoline, approximately 50 million dollars annually.

TECHNOLOGICAL CHANGES

There are numerous technological improvements that
could be made in engines and mechanisms so that they use energy more efficiently. These improvements range from adapt-
ing certain parts or making minor modifications in design
and construction to more profound transformations of this
type. It is also possible, however, to reduce conventional
fuel consumption by using the substitutes or complements
already known in the energy markets of some of the industrialized and developing countries.

Improvements in Vehicle Efficiency

Current automobile industry programs stress reducing
the average size and veight of the vehicles produced. More
use of lightweight materials, such as aluminum, plastics,
and highly resistant steel alloys, will further diminish
vehicle weight. Such trends in production will facilitate
a more efficient use of fuel. Improvements in the transmission and drive shaft and lower power requirements for ac-
cessories will also produce greater fuel economy. The use
of electronic controls for fuel flow and ignition will allow
the engine to function efficiently, reducing the frequency
of tune-ups.

In the longer term, research and development are directed toward a more efficient use of energy, in keeping
with trends in the industrialized countries. Incorporating
the innovations made in this field into the country's vehicle production will be conditioned by the well-known lag in
transferring technology from industrialized to developing
countries. However, this process might be stimulated by
passing an adequate series of norms that would force industry to accelerate such transfer.

Alternatives to conventional fuels

Liquid fuel is easier to use, store, and distribute than solid fuel, gas, or electricity. It is, therefore, especially well suited to the automobile, in which the energy storage space should ideally be small and light. Liquid hydrocarbons meet these requirements because they have a very high energy density and good combustion characteristics.

By virtue of the advantages mentioned, alternative fuels for transportation, especially for highway and air transportation, will probably continue to be liquid. The smaller the technical changes required to incorporate alternative fuels into consumption, the more acceptable they will be to the user.

Alcohols (such as methanol, ethanol, and methyletherbutilic ether   MTBE) are presently used in their own right among gasoline substitutes.

Methanol and ethanol, the two types of alcohol that have attracted the most attention as fuel, are well known chemicals and have the advantage, especially for LDCs, of being biomass products. Another chemical family of a similar nature is ether. MTBE, in particular, has possibilities for highway transportation. However, ether will probably only be used to improve the octane rating of gasoline and not as an integral substitute for it.

Other substitutes have been on the fuel market for many years. Liquefied petroleum gas has made modest inroads in some countries as a fuel in highway transportation. It is estimated that in 1981 it accounted for close to one percent of worldwide consumption in this area, excluding socialist countries. Apart from the industrial energy sources already well known, vegetable oils, another biomass product, can be transformed into diesel fuel.

The spectrum of potential gasoline substitutes is as wide as the availability of crude oil for gasoline production. The development of these substitutes will thus depend on future trends in the international hydrocarbon market.

POTENTIAL ENERGY SAVINGS BY 1990 AND 2000

Quantitative predictions of energy needs in the transportation sector imply evaluating the interaction of a set of complex variables that go beyond the sector itself. In Table 6.10, we use an estimate of future energy consumption based on the model designed by the University of Wisconsin and the International Institute for Applied Systems Analysis (IIASA). The main factors considered in making the estimate were:

1. The rate and structure of economic growth, which determine the volume and type of products to be transported
2. The geographic distribution of the economic activity and the population centers, which determines the distances that goods have to be transported
3. Expected technological changes that might affect the different means of transportation

Estimates do not cover the transportation system as a whole but are limited to three main forms of transportation that have an obvious effect on the sector's energy consumption: automobile, highway freight, and air. To evaluate the potential energy savings in these three areas, two possible scenarios are included from a common projection base. For the first scenario, it is supposed that there will be no change in consumption patterns. The second scenario assumes that a more efficient use of energy and a progressive modification of the structure of the transportation system will be introduced (see Tables 6.10 and 6.11).

Results indicate that for the years 1990 and 2000 energy savings on the order of 42×10^{12} Kcal and 60×10^{12} Kcal, respectively, could be reached. This means 33.8 mboe and 46.8 mboe for the years indicated. In monetary terms and if these amounts could be exported, approximately 930 and 1,300 million dollars would be saved in 1990 and 2000. The cumulative total potential savings by the year 2000 would be close to 13,000 million dollars.

NOTES

1. Figures obtained from other sources differ. However, all indicate that consumption rose during the 1960s. Cf. Chapter 2.

2. Petróleos Mexicanos.

3. Grupo Intersectorial de Transporte, Consumo de energéticos por productos del sector transporte (Mexico, 1981).

4. It has already been practically demonstrated that it is possible to operate diesel locomotives using the complementary fuels. In such operations, the primary fuel is liquefied gas, but a small quantity of diesel is also injected into the engine to create the compression ignition

necessary for operating the engine. In some parts of the United States, where prices favored liquefied gas, it was substituted for diesel in locomotives.

5. Cf. Chapter 2, "International Comparisons."

6. The friction of the tires against the pavement, according to each vehicle's characteristics, and air resistance are additional factors that reduce a vehicle's original efficiency.

7. The diesel engine is used in trucks and buses in the United States. In Europe it has also been adapted to smaller vehicles such as delivery vans, taxis, and passenger cars. In the case of passenger cars, however, it has not enjoyed great popularity, even in Europe, because it is noisy and responds slower than gasoline vehicles of the same weight.

8. An additional point of criticism concerns the generation of 3,4-benzopyrine, which is suspected of being a carcinogen. There are, however, test results that demonstrate that under the appropriate operating conditions this compound is not found in exhaust gases.

9. This level of consumption was based on normal traffic figures and applies exclusively to the metropolitan area.

10. The calculation of man-hours lost was based on a standard trip of 28 kilometers a day, two passengers to a vehicle, at the national wage rate for a man-hour.

11. Eight-cylinder engines are no longer manufactured in Mexico.

TABLE 6.1
Basic Indicators for Transportation Sector, 1982

Number of People Employed (thousands)		
Highway Transportation		602,862
Railroad Transportation		103,507
Maritime Transportation		16,556
Air Transportation		29,028
Total		751,943
Length of Network (kilometers)		
Main Highways		213,316
Secondary Highways (including unpaved)		
Railroad		25,500
Total		238,816
Number of Vehicles	Registered	Circulating a/
Cars	4,889,100	2,453,400
Buses	98,600	88,740
Trucks	1,991,600	1,310,600

Source: Secretaría de Comunicaciones y Transportes.
Programa 1984–1989.

a/ Estimate based on DIEMEX-Wharton, Proyecto automotriz (Mexico, 1983),
p.68.

TABLE 6.2
Passenger and Freight Movement by Transportation Means, 1982

Transportation Means	Freight		Passengers	
	10³ Tons	Ton/km (millions)	(millions)	Pass./km (millions)
Highway	281,640	91,760	—	—
Buses	—	—	1,267	169
Cars	—	—	—	—
Railroad	68,340	45	23	5.4
Maritime	150,900	—	1.4	—
Air	205	—	16	9.9
Total	501,085	91,805	1,307.4	104.3

Source: Secretaría de Comunicaciones y Transportes.
Programa 1984-1989.

TABLE 6.3
Freight Transported by Transportation Means

Year	Freight Transported (thousands of tons)	Transportation Means				Total (%)
		Highway (%)	Railroad (%)	Maritime a/ (%)	Air b/	
1970	—	—	—	—	—	—
1971	223,409	66.0	22.8	11.2	n.s.	100
1972	231,441	66.2	21.6	12.2	n.s.	100
1973	242,237	66.0	22.1	11.9	n.s.	100
1974	267,505	62.4	23.1	14.5	n.s.	100
1975	282,130	61.7	22.4	15.9	n.s.	100
1976	287,791	62.5	21.8	15.7	n.s.	100
1977	291,487	64.7	23.5	11.8	n.s.	100
1978	305,954	65.7	22.7	11.6	n.s.	100
1979	337,614	66.5	20.1	13.4	n.s.	100
1980	381,893	66.3	18.3	15.4	n.s.	100
1981	409,579	67.4	18.0	14.6	n.s.	100

Source: Based on data from the Dirección General de Planeación, Secretaría de Comunicaciones y Transportes.

a/ Refers exclusively to domestic shipping.
b/ Domestic service.
n.s. - Not significant.

TABLE 6.4
Structure of Passenger Transportation by Main Transportation Means

Year	Passengers Transported (thousands)	Highway	Railroad	Maritime	Air [a]
1970	471,824	91.6	7.9	n.s.	0.5
1971	510,392	92.9	6.6	n.s.	0.5
1972	536,202	93.1	6.3	n.s.	0.6
1973	542,020	93.9	5.3	0.1	0.7
1974	555,684	94.5	4.5	0.1	0.9
1975	620,351	94.9	4.0	0.1	1.0
1976	732,244	95.6	3.3	0.1	1.0
1977	820,448	95.4	3.5	0.1	1.0
1978	875,075	95.5	3.3	0.1	1.1
1979	1,041,318	96.4	2.5	0.1	1.0
1980	1,188,282	96.9	2.0	0.1	1.0
1981	1,277,626	97.0	1.8	0.1	1.1

Source: Based on data from the Dirección General de Planeación, Secretaría de Comunicaciones y Transportes.

a/ Domestic service.
n.s. - Not significant.

TABLE 6.5
Energy End Use in the Transportation Sector (Kcal x 10^{12})

Year	Petroleum	Derivative	Electricity
1970	100.1	---	1.0
1973	132.1	---	1.0
1975	146.2	---	1.0
1976	165.5	---	1.0
1977	177.0	---	1.0
1978	184.2	---	2.0
1979	219.2	---[a]	2.0
1980	241.6	266.7[a]	2.0
1981	269.1[a]	308.7[a]	2.0
1982	271.3[a]	296.1[a]	2.0

Source: Secretaría de Patrimonio y Fomento Industrial, Dirección General de Energía.

[a] Estimates. The essential difference stems from the methodologies employed to calculate the energy balance. SEPAFIN makes estimates related to the destination of the fuel because it does not have detailed statistics that give the precise final destination.

TABLE 6.6
Structure of Energy End Use in Mexico by Sector Destination (in percentages)

Sector	Year					
	1970	1975	1980	1981	1982
Industrial	37.6	35.6	32.6	31.2	31.8
Transportation	38.2	39.2	40.6	41.0	41.3
Other Sectors	17.3	17.6	17.4	16.9	16.8
Non-Energy	6.9	7.6	9.4	10.9	10.1
Total	100.0	100.0	100.0	100.0	100.0

Source: Secretaría de Patrimonio y Fomento Industrial, Dirección General de Energía

Note: The energy sector's consumption is not included.

TABLE 6.7
Fuel Destination by Transportation Means, 1982 (in percentages)

Fuel	Transportation Means				
	Highway	Railroad	Maritime	Air	Total
Gasoline[a/]	99.5	—	—	0.5	100
Diesel	89.0	7.6	3.4	—	100
Liquefied Gas	100.0	—	—	—	100
Turbosine	—	—	—	100.0	100

Sources: Based on data from Petróleos Mexicanos, Anuario estadístico 1983 (Mexico, 1984), p.132; Comisión Intersecretarial del Transporte; Dirección General de Energía; and direct research.

a/ Includes automobile gasoline and aviation fuel.

TABLE 6.8
Vehicle Statistics by State and Type of Vehicle for Liquefied Gas

State	Cars	Trucks	Chassis	Buses	Tractors	Total
Aguascalientes	30	19	1	64	5	139
Baja California Nte.	875	213	4	825	34	1,951
Baja California Sur	168	31	—	29	1	229
Campeche	50	41	8	49	—	148
Coahuila	256	100	23	352	100	831
Colima	13	26	—	55	—	94
Chiapas	84	143	4	123	1	355
Chihuahua	222	153	5	554	53	987
Federal District	756	414	30	450	41	1,691
Durango	54	58	12	133	31	288
Guanajuato	156	155	9	621	84	1,025
Guerrero	164	99	3	338	9	613
Hidalgo	107	52	8	994	10	1,171
Jalisco	260	210	14	1,189	96	1,769
State of Mexico	125	85	4	1,301	15	1,530
Michoacán	77	99	8	451	7	732
Morelos	54	60	3	338	3	348
Nayarit	12	25	1	79	2	119
Nuevo León	1,085	238	27	898	420	2,668
Oaxaca	98	61	3	301	4	467
Puebla	295	148	15	950	31	1,439
Querétaro	15	28	—	85	3	131
Quintana Roo	26	8	—	8	2	44
San Luis Potosí	78	78	1	335	15	507
Sinaloa	153	160	7	316	7	663
Sonora	149	114	7	292	44	606
Tabasco	56	42	9	268	1	376
Tamaulipas	356	57	10	377	101	901
Tlaxcala	49	16	1	122	—	188
Veracruz	189	129	24	839	32	1,213
Yucatán	67	64	8	55	6	200
Zacatecas	16	14	1	86	2	119
Total	6,095	3,160	250	12,877	1,160	23,542

Sources: Secretaría de Comunicaciones y Transportes and based on unpublished data of Petróleos Mexicanos.

FIGURE 6.1
Development of Real Prices for the Principal Hydrocarbons

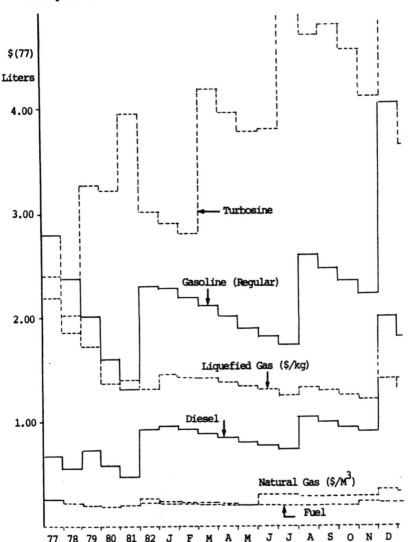

Sources: Based on unpublished data of Petróleos Mexicanos and the Banco de México, Indicadores económicos (Mexico, 1983).

TABLE 6.9
Relative Prices for Fuel Used in Transportation (in percentages)

Fuel	1973	1975	1977	1979	1980	1981	1982	1983
1.	4.38	4.20	4.30	2.80	2.80	2.40	2.00	1.58
2.	4.93	5.25	4.84	3.15	3.15	2.70	2.25	1.76
3.	0.41	0.95	0.57	0.57	0.60	0.35	0.16	0.24
4.	1.99	4.47	2.77	1.80	1.86	0.95	0.35	0.42

Source: Based on unpublished data of Petróleos Mexicanos, Anuario estadístico 1983 (Mexico, 1984), p.122.

Note: 1. Gasoline prices (regular) / diesel prices (volume).
2. Gasoline prices (regular) / diesel prices (Kcal).
3. Liquefied gas prices / gasoline prices (regular) (Kcal).
4. Liquefied gas prices / diesel prices (Kcal).

FIGURE 6.2
Fuel Consumption in Diesel Compared to Gasoline Engine

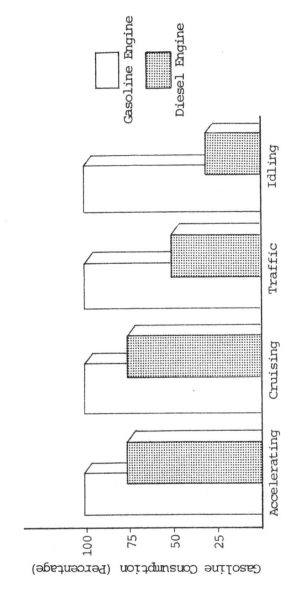

Source: Diesel Nacional.

TABLE 6.10
Estimates of Energy Savings by 1990 and by 2000

Potential Savings (10^{12} Kcal)

Year	Base Projection[a/]	Projection with Energy-Efficient Measures	Savings
1985	296	259	37
1990	422	380	42
2000	670	610	60

Energy Consumption by Transportation Group Using Energy-Efficient Measures and Conservation (10^{12} Kcal)

| Transportation | Year | | | AAGR[b/] |
	1985	1990	2000	1985-2000
Car[c/]	86	106	170	4.5
Trucks[d/]	155	249	390	6.3
Air[e/]	18	25	50	7.0
Total	259	380	610	5.9

Source: Estimates of authors.

a/ The base projection was made taking into account the relationship between the growths in GNP (the added value of transportation), energy consumption and the product elasticity of consumption.

b/ AAGR - Average annual growth rate.

c/ Cars: The energy consumed is calculated using the following formula:

$$Energy = (Efficiency) \times (Cars\ per\ capita) \times (Population) \times (kilometers\ traveled/year)$$

A decrease in the rate of growth of the number of cars per capita is assumed, reversing the trend up until now (6% during the 1970s). An efficiency of 10 km/liter is assumed, once energy use is improved.

d/ Freight: It is assumed that the railroad will have a larger share of any future transportation system, which will decrease demand for highway freight transportation.

e/ Air: Only turbosine is included, taking into account the historical development of the product elasticity of energy consumption for this means of transportation.

TABLE 6.11
Structure of the Transportation System by the Year 2000

Distribution Trend (in percentages)

Transportation means	Year	
	1982	2000
Highway	54	57
Railroad	13	11
Maritime	4	4
Pipelines	29	28
Total	100	100

Adequate Intermodal Distribution (in percentages)

Transportation means	Year	
	1982	2000
Highway	54	44
Railroad	13	20
Maritime	4	6
Pipelines	29	30
Total	100	100

Source: Estimates of authors.

7

Industrial Sector

The importance of the industrial sector in a nation's economy is beyond doubt. One must recognize that the only way that countries such as Mexico can attain higher levels of development is by their capacity to create diversified industrial structures that satisfy the population's basic requirements. In Mexico's case, the industrial sector contributes an important part of the country's total aggregate value and has wide intersectorial relationships. This sector is characterized by the ability of its industries to transform certain input materials into intermediate and final products.

From the relationship between the gross domestic industrial product (GDIP), the GDP, as well as the sector's consumption and share of energy since 1975, we can observe that the ratio of GDIP to total GDP remained virtually unchanged during the period 1975-1982 (see Table 7.1). In contrast, industrial energy consumption decreased. The ratio of industrial energy to total energy progressively declined, from 36.4% in 1975 to 33.2% in 1982. The reason for this reduction seems to be related to the increase in the transportation sector's share of energy, caused by low gasoline and diesel prices, among other factors (see Chapter 2).

From the two indicators mentioned in the previous paragraph, we obtain the ratio between the industrial sector's share in the GDP and its share in national energy consumption. This figure, which can be taken as a way of specifying the ratio of energy to GDIP, shows a tendency to decrease. For the economy as a whole, however, this ratio has steadily increased, especially since 1975 (from 1.3 that year to 1.7 in 1980). Taking this into account, it is probable that the industrial sector has become more efficient in using energy than other sectors of the Mexican economy.

Mexican industry has traditionally depended on four secondary energy sources: coke, bunker oil, gas, and electricity. The characteristics of the trends in these energy sectors during the period 1960-1981 are as follows (see Table 7.2):

1. The consumption of coke increased 3.5 times in the twenty-one years being considered: The share was 9.6% in 1960 and 9.9% in 1981.
2. Electric power consumption grew 6.9 times during this period, increasing from 5.3% to 10.9%.
3. Total consumption of gas and bunker oil rose from 44.49 X 10^{12} Kcal to 150.64 X 10^{12} Kcal, that is 3.4 times in twenty-one years. Worthy of note are the high degree of substitutability between the two energy sources and the short time in which their use was implemented.[1]/

Within the industrial sector, several branches stand out because of their intensive energy use. These are, in order of their share in the energy used by industry (see Table 7.3):

Branch	Share in Industry's Consumption of Energy Purchased, 1981
Steel	27.1
Chemical (basic, fertilizers, resins, and synthetic fibers)	11.1
Cement	10.1
Mining-Metallurgy	8.5
Sugar[2]/	4.9
Glass	3.2
Food and Drink	1.9
Total	71.1%

With regard to the history of industrial energy consumption from 1960 on, excluding the food and drink branch, we can observe that in 1960 these industries consumed 51.0% of the energy. This figure rose to 65.0% in 1973 and 69.2% in 1981. Total energy consumption increased 3.9 times during the period from 1960 to 1981: In the steel industry it grew 4.2 times; in mining-metallurgy, 5.0 times; in cement, 3.5 times; in glass, 3.1 times; in paper and cellulose, 3.9

times; in chemicals, 12.4 times; and in sugar, 4.5 times.3/
The high growth rates in consumption in these energy-
intensive industries seem to point to a certain inefficiency. The need to achieve a more rational use of energy
in the sector, thereby conserving nonrenewable energy resources, becomes more relevant if the time perspective is
taken into account. As the process of industrialization becomes firmly established, energy requirements will be guided
by the direction of the industrial development strategy. It
will become apparent that the impact of development will be
greater in energy-intensive industries than in industries
with a low energy profile, for instance, the cement and
electronics industries.

The industrialization process is favored by the availability of sufficient and easily obtainable energy, but energy is not the driving force behind the process. At current world oil-market prices, if Mexico did not possess
sufficient hydrocarbon resources, it would be difficult for
her to guarantee her industrial growth. However, because
we are talking of a nonrenewable resource, it is extremely
important to assess industry's use of energy, as well as energy's relationship to production.

Proposals for measures directed toward energy savings
and efficiency in industry must be based on a knowledge of
the production processes in specific industrial sectors.
Energy consumption not only varies in proportion to the relative size of the economy but also according to the structure and composition of the industrial sector, hence the importance of analyzing the needs of the major branches. To
do this, we look at some of the elements characterizing the
use of energy in industry, and then we discuss the results
from specific studies of the most important branches.

The first analysis is based on the results of a 1982
study by the Secretaría de Patrimonio y Fomento Industrial
(SEPAFIN) that evaluates the consumption of energy in industry in 1981.4/ This overview allows us to identify specific areas where a deeper analysis of efficient or wasteful
energy is needed as well as the possible corrective measures to be devised and the general policies to be planned
and implemented.

The study covered 289 industries. These industries
consumed 146.5 X 10^{12} Kcal, while total industrial consumption was 205.0 X 10^{12} Kcal. The study thus includes 71.5%
of total sectorial consumption (see Tables 7.4 and 7.6).5/
The ten major industrial branches account for almost 93% of
energy requirements in the industries analyzed. Among these,

the steel and cement industries are responsible for more than 50% of the consumption.6/

If one considers energy bought in relation to sales as an indicator of intensive energy use, one might conclude that the major industrial branches are, in order of importance, steel, manures and fertilizers, mineral extraction and processing, cement, and basic chemicals. The results of the study show that in 1981 industrial energy requirements were less than 10% of the amount of sales.7/ With the exception of these major industrial branches, these requirements were less than five percent in many cases. Thus, one can infer, at a first glance, that energy costs are not a significant part of industrial production costs.8/

This information allows us to identify certain characteristics, by branch and overall, about energy use from a sample of the major energy-intensive industries. Energy use can be divided into four basic categories:

1. Fuels used directly: Fuel is used directly in a wide variety of furnaces, particularly blast, clinkerization and regeneration, and open-hearth furnaces. Temperatures in such processes generally exceed 500°C.
2. Fuels used to generate steam: Specific details of use depend on whether the steam is used in productive units or for generating electricity. Under steam for productive units, we can include direct-feed steam, that is, steam used exclusively as a heat conductor (at temperatures between 100°C and 300°C), and steam used for traction, principally in steam turbines. In this case, exhaust steam from the turbines is used in processes (at temperatures below 100°C). In the generation of electricity, the amount of steam passing through the turbines that drive the electric generators is measured. The fact that exhaust steam is used in processes at temperatures below 100°C is also taken into consideration.
3. Fuels used to generate electricity by internal combustion: These fuels are used basically in motor-generator groups and in small diesel plants.
4. Fuels used in steel furnaces and to drive electric motors: More than 95% of the electricity bought from the network, together with that generated by industry itself, is used in these processes.

Using the information in this study, we can classify the main industrial energy sources in terms of the industries using the greatest percentage of them (see Table 7.7).

Of the total energy used in industry in 1981, 63% was used directly as fuel, 27.3% was used to generate steam, 8.3% was electricity bought from the network, and only 1.3% was used to generate electricity through internal combustion.

The glass and cement industries used fuel directly as their primary energy source. It accounted for more than 90% of the total 1981 consumption. Somewhat lower, but no less significant, were the percentages for the mining-metal-lurgy and the steel industries: 58% and 79%, respectively.

Steam production from fuel is a distinctive character-istic of the production processes of the paper and basic chemical industries. Eighty-six percent and 65.5%, respec-tively, of the total energy required was used by these in-dustries in 1981 for steam production. Overall, these branches used close to 60% of the total energy consumed in industry for steam production, while the rest was used prin-cipally in the steel and mining-metallurgy industries. Steam was mainly directed to productive units for use as a heat conductor and, to a lesser extent, as a generator for electricity in turbines: 29% and 9%, respectively, in the production of cellulose and paper and of basic chemicals. These uses virtually balanced each other out in the case of the steel industry.

Electricity bought from the network represented a high percentage of the total energy used in industry in 1981. The remainder was supplied mainly by self-generation by steam and, to a lesser extent, by internal combustion sys-tems. These findings show the importance of self-gener-ation by steam in industry and, in particular, in the steel, paper, and basic chemical sectors.9/

ENERGY USE IN DIFFERENT BRANCHES OF MEXICAN INDUSTRY

In the remainder of the chapter, we present results on energy use in the major consumer branches, which are also the greatest energy consumers: the steel, cement, and sugar industries. Then, we make some general comments based on information in the 1982 SEPAFIN Energy Study, on the other energy-intensive branches: In increasing order of consump-tion, these branches are mineral extraction and processing, the chemical industry, and the production of synthetic fibers and raw materials, cellulose and paper, glass, and food and drink.

Through an in-depth study of the major industries, we were able to specify types of energy consumed and specific

TABLE 7.1
Some Indicators for the Industrial Sector (in thousands of millions of 1970 pesos)

Indicators	1975	1976	1977	1978	1979	1980	1981	1982
GDP a/	610.0	635.8	657.7	711.2	777.2	841.9	908.8	903.8
GDP for Industry b/	180.9	189.8	193.5	213.1	236.9	256.1	276.2	267.2
Energy End Use (Kcal x 10^{12})	392.8	429.4	444.0	495.9	544.6	598.4	656.9	657.9
Energy Consumption in Industrial Sector (Kcal X 10^{12})	143.0	153.2	154.2	186.4	195.4	198.0	205.0	218.3
Industry's share (%)								
Industry's GDP/Total GDP	29.7	29.9	29.4	30.0	30.5	30.4	30.4	29.6
Energy in Industry/Energy End Use	36.4	35.7	34.7	37.6	35.9	33.1	31.2	33.2
Energy/GDP for Industry	1.23	1.19	1.18	1.25	1.18	1.09	1.03	1.12

Sources: Energy balances for 1975-1981 and 1982; Secretaría de Programación y Presupuesto, Sistema de Cuentas Nacionales (México, 1982), p.78.

a/ GDP - Gross domestic product.
b/ Applies to manufacturing and construction.

TABLE 7.2

Energy Consumption in Mexican Industry, 1960, 1970, 1973, 1975, 1980, and 1981 (Kcal x 10^{12})

Energy Source	1960	1970	1973	Year 1975	1980	1981
Coke	5.790	11.495	14.033	14.630	20.619	20.28
Liquefied Gas	1.524	0.883	3.678	1.275	2.727	2.374
Gasoline	.468	—	0.548	—	—	—
Kerosene	2.581	—	3.589	—	—	—
Diesel	2.428	4.025	4.291	8.822	n.s.	9.393
Bunker Oil	30.236	22.768	33.639	48.081	46.801	60.016
Gas	14.259	50.472	64.867	56.992	88.490	90.625
Electricity	3.234	8.087	15.444	13.992	20.466	22.402
Total	60.520	97.730	140.089	143.720	179.103	205.090

Sources: Instituto Mexicano del Petróleo, 1960 and 1981; Secretaría de Patrimonio y Fomento Industrial, 1981. Cf. this chapter, "Consumption of Energy and Materials in Steel Production."

n.s. - Not specified.

TABLE 7.3
Energy Consumption in Major Industries, 1981 (Kcal $\times 10^9$ and in percentages)

Industry	Natural Gas	Liquefied Gas	Bunker Oil	Diesel	Coal	Coke	Electricity	Other	Energy Purchased	Self-Generated Fuel	Total
Steel	30,926.0	8.1	3,136.9	805.1	0.0	17,619.4	2,985.5	0.0	55,481.0	3,087.8	58,568.8
	52.80	0.01	5.36	1.38	0.0	30.08	5.10	0.0	94.73	5.27	100.0%
Mining-Metallurgy	8,838.1	4.1	3,165.1	877.1	6.7	1,291.4	3,097.4	72.7	17,352.6	201.6	17,554.2
	50.35	0.02	18.03	5.00	0.04	7.36	17.64	0.41	98.85	1.15	100.0%
Cement	9,203.7	0.0	9,538.3	108.9	0.0	0.0	1,760.6	5.9	20,617.4	0.0	20,617.4
	44.64	0.00	46.26	0.53	0.0	0.00	8.54	0.03	100.00	0.0	100.0%
Glass	6,119.6	3.2	0.0	82.5	0.0	0.0	426.5	11.3	6,643.1	0.0	6,643.1
	92.12	0.05	0.00	1.24	0.0	0.0	6.42	0.17	100.00	0.0	100.0%
Paper	3,686.2	16.7	4,080.6	19.0	0.0	0.0	934.3	2.5	8,738.7	2,122.6	10,861.3
	33.94	0.15	37.57	0.18	0.00	0.00	8.60	0.02	80.46	19.54	100.0
Chemical	13,591.0	6.1	6,601.5	466.8	0.0	200.6	1,858.5	77.2	22,801.7	1,200.1	24,001.8
	56.63	0.03	27.50	1.94	0.00	0.84	7.74	0.32	95.00	5.00	100.0%
Food and Drink	2,604.9	77.1	638.7	28.7	0.0	0.0	295.0	0.2	3,644.6	0.0	3,644.6
	71.47	2.12	17.52	0.79	0.00	0.00	8.09	0.01	100.00	0.0	100.0%
Sugar	0.0	0.0	9,951.0	0.0	0.0	0.0	56.0	0.0	10,007.0	17,193.0	27,200.0
	0.00	0.00	36.58	0.0	0.0	0.0	0.21	0.00	36.79	63.21	100.0%
Other	15,655.5	2,258.7	22,904.5	7,004.9	0.0	1,168.6	10,988.2	0.0	59,980.4	200.0a/	60,180.4
	90,625.0	2,374.0	60,016.0	9,393.0	6.7	20,280.0	22,402.0	169.8	205,266.5	24,005.1	229,271.6

Source: Secretaría de Patrimonio y Fomento Industrial.

a/ Estimated value.

168

TABLE 7.4
Energy Consumption in Major Industries, 1960, 1973, and 1981

Industries	1960	Year 1973	1981
Steel	13,066	31,287	55,481
Mining-Metallurgy	3,460	7,710	17,352
Cement	5,855	15,365	20,617
Glass	2,169	5,073	6,643
Cellulose and Paper	2,266	7,041	8,738
Chemical	1,839	11,560	22,801
Sugar	2,226	12,969	10,007
Other	29,639	49,084	63,625
Total	60,520	140,089	205,000

Source: Table 7.2.

TABLE 7.5
Energy Consumption in the Mexican Sugar Industry, 1960, 1973, 1981 (Kcal x 10^{12})

Year	Bunker Oil	Bagasse[a]	Total
1960	2,226	10,364	12,590
1973	12,969	18,978	31,947
1981	10,007	17,193	27,200

Source: Table 7.4.

Note: Cf. note 3, this chapter.

a/ The calculation is based on the caloric power of dry bagasse.

TABLE 7.6
Indicators of Energy Consumption in the Industrial Sector, 1981

Economic Sector	Value of Bought Energy; Value of Sales Production; Pesos of Energy / 1000 Pesos of Sales	(index[a])	Total Energy Consumption (E)b/ Kcal x 10^{12}	Share (%)	Jobs		Sales millions of pesos	Millions of Pesos per Worker	Pesos (Kcal x 10^9)
					Manual Worker	Non-Manual Worker			
Steel	100.6	1.000	50.604	36.61	55382	17172	95.494	1.316	1.887
Cement	64.6	0.636	20.935	14.30	9254	3121	27.101	2.190	1.294
Nonferrous Mineral Extraction and Processing	60.0	0.596	13.127	9.09	22969	5605	41.955	1.468	3.174
Basic Chemicals	55.8	0.555	12.468	8.52	9234	4378	25.681	1.867	2.060
Paper and Cardboard	35.9	0.357	9.847	6.73	15012	5183	36.763	1.820	3.733
Synthetic Resins and Fibers	24.4	0.243	7.594	5.19	12593	5131	33.703	1.902	4.438
Glass and Glass Products	37.0	0.368	6.456	4.41	14016	4840	18.581	0.985	2.878
Extraction and Processing of Other Minerals	87.2	0.867	5.203	3.55	4319	742	4.800	0.948	0.923
Basic Nonferrous Metal Industry	31.8	0.316	3.197	2.18	5540	3303	25.123	2.841	7.858
Manures and Fertilizers	93.2	0.926	2.935	2.00	5816	1809	9.033	1.185	3.078
Automobiles	4.9	0.049	2.203	1.50	36599	11336	120.190	2.507	54.557
Beer and Malt	9.0	0.089	1.963	1.34	8949	2409	24.539	2.161	12.500
Ferrous Mineral Extraction and Processing	86.6	0.875	0.749	0.51	806	305	1.466	1.320	1.957
Total			137.374	95.93	200489	65334	463.429	1.743	3.373
Other c/			9.046	4.07	33639	11885	93.462	2.053	10.382
Grand Total			146.420	100.00	234128	77219	556.891	2.789	3.803

Sources: Secretaría de Patrimonio y Fomento Industrial, Encuesta sobre el consumo de energía en la industria 1981 (Mexico, 1981); estimates of authors.

a/ The steel industry, which requires 100.6 pesos of energy for each 1000 pesos of sales, is the base.
b/ The calculation is based on the requirements of the companies in each branch that was studied.
c/ These include food, textiles, nonmetallic mineral products, auto parts, transport materials and equipment, rubber products, soap, detergents, cosmetics, and so on.

TABLE 7.7
Energy Use by Branch of Industry, 1981 (Kcal x 10^9)

Energy Source	Steel	Mining-Metallurgy	Cement	Glass	Cellulose and Paper	Chemical	Other	Total
Direct use of fuel	46,389.9	10,162.4	18,788.0	6,146.6	575.5	7,239.2	3,235.5	92,537.1
Fuel used to generate steam	7,621.1	4,126.0	68.8	69.5	9,351.4	14,765.8	3,988.3	39,990.9
Steam for productive units	4,169.3	2,939.8	68.8	69.5	6,673.2	13,522.0	3,622.7	31,065.3
Direct-feed steam	3,905.3	2,917.3	68.8	69.5	4,256.9	11,431.4	3,402.2	26,051.4
Traction Steam	264.0	22.4	0.0	0.0	2,416.3	2,090.6	219.7	5,013.0
Electric power generation	3,451.8	1,186.2	0.0	0.0	2,678.3	1,258.7	290.3	8,845.3
Fuel used to generate electric power by internal	1,572.3	168.4	0.1	0.4	0.0	138.3	34.7	1,914.2
Electricity purchased	2,985.5	3,097.4	1,760.6	426.5	934.3	1,858.5	1,031.5	12,094.3
Total	58,568.8	17,554.2	20,617.5	6,643.0	10,861.2	24,001.8	8,290.0	146,536.5

Source: Secretaría de Patrimonio y Fomento Industrial.

consumption, calculate possible savings and efficiency, and propose concrete measures for energy conservation. For the other industrial branches, we obtained information on the forms of energy consumed and, in some cases, on specific consumptions and the possibilities for efficient energy use.

Studies on the conservation and efficient use of energy in the steel, cement, and sugar industries were conducted with a common methodology, which could be used to study other industrial branches or even companies. This methodology entails an analysis of the following aspects relating to an industrial branch or factory:

1. Description of production
2. Present situation: Capacity and types of products
3. Historical trends of energy use and production
4. Consumption patterns in the different stages of production
5. Immediate and mediate conservation measures and cost-benefit estimates
6. New techniques and processes favoring the efficient use of energy and savings
7. Production and market outlooks for the product
8. The impact of energy saving measures on future consumption

THE STEEL INDUSTRY

The steel industry uses a variety of raw materials and processes in the production of steel, from which a wide range of products are derived. At present, the Mexican steel industry uses four processes (see Figure 7.1):

. Blast furnace   - Open-hearth furnace
. Blast furnace   - Oxygen converter
. Direct-reduction   - Electric furnace
. Scrap iron   - Electric furnace

In the first two processes, the main materials used are iron ore, which undergoes agglomeration through sintering or pelleting; coal, from which coke is produced; and limestone. The three products obtained--the agglomerated ore, coke, and limestone--are fed into the blast furnace, and pig iron or first-fusion iron is obtained. This is then transferred to the open-hearth furnace or oxygen con-

verter to produce steel. In the third process, the iron
ore is reduced directly, using natural gas, after which
the sponge iron that is produced is fed into the electric
furnace to make the steel. In the fourth process, scrap
iron is used as raw material and fed into the electric furnace to produce steel.

After the steel is made, there are two alternative
casting methods: The continuous casting and the ingot methods are used to obtain slabs, bloom, and billet. These are
fed through reheating furnaces and then rolling mills to be
transformed into new products.

Structural forms, railing, or seamless tubing are obtained from bloom. From billet come nonflat products such
as wire, corrugated bars, solid bars, and light and heavy
structural shapes. Slabs are used directly to produce
steel sheet or are treated for the subsequent production
of plates and welded pipe. Cold or hot rolling completes
the process of transforming steel, as well as other alloys,
to produce different types of plates (see Figure 7.2).

The blast furnace is the most energy-intensive stage
of consumption, followed, in order, by coke generation, direct reduction, steel production, and the soaking pits.

Mexico's steel industry presently has five integrated
plants, which are capable of transforming iron ore into
finished products; twenty-six semi-integrated plants, which
use scrap and can produce everything from steel to finished
products; and about thirty-five rolling mills, which produce finished products from rails and other raw-steel materials ready to be rolled (see Table 7.8).10/ In 1980 Altos
Hornos de México and Fundidora de Monterrey and Siderúrgica Lázaro Cárdenas-Las Truchas, S.A. (SICARTSA), produced
57.4% of domestic raw steel and 51.8% of rolled products.
Furthermore, Hojalata y Lámina, S.A. (HYLSA) and Tubos de
Acero de México, S.A. (TAMSA) contributed 27.6% of the
steel and 28.7% of rolled products. The remaining 15% of
the steel was produced by semi-integrated plants, while
19.5% of the rolled steel came from the nonintegrated
plants, that is, semi-integrated plants and rolling mills
(see Tables 7.9 and 7.10).11/

Consumption of Energy and Materials in Steel Production

A 1979 analysis of the specific consumption of energy
and materials in the different stages of Mexican steel production is important to the integrating of consumption fig-

ures for different processes and thus the calculating of specific energy consumption for each steel process. A knowledge is required of the specific consumption for the following stages:

1. Coke used in the production of sinter and pig iron (see Figure 7.3)
2. Hydrocarbons (bunker oil and natural gas) used in processes requiring the blast furnace (see Table 7.11)
3. Materials (pig iron, scrap, and steel)
4. Energy (natural gas and electricity) used in the direct-reduction process
5. Materials (sponge iron and scrap) used in electric furnaces.

Some additional clarification is needed for the specific consumption for pig iron production (see Figure 7.3 and Table 7.11). Although the Altos Hornos de México plant uses a combination of gas and bunker oil, with specific sonsumption rates of 120,000 Kcal/ton and 310,000 Kcal/ton, respectively, the Fundidora Monterrey plant consumes 250,000 Kcal/ton. This difference is not due to inefficiency. Rather, it is an attempt to reduce coke consumption. Given this measure's regulatory character, hydrocarbon consumption in blast furnaces is not included in the specific consumptions of all stages of the steel process. We should point out, moreover, that specific consumptions indicated for the open-hearth furnace are additive. This is the type of operation used at Fundidora Monterrey, which produces a total of 1,250,000 Kcal/ton of steel. For the specific consumption of materials, see Table 7.12.

Finally, specific consumption of energy and materials for the processes of direct-reduction electric furnaces and scrap electric furnaces is listed in Tables 7.13 and 7.14. Table 7.13 shows specific gas consumption in direct-reduction plants and electric consumption in electric furnaces, and Table 7.14 gives electric furnace consumptions by process.

With the information from this 1979 analysis and Figure 7.8, we can calculate the specific energy consumption by stage, by process, and by type of final product. Figures 7.4 to 7.8 illustrate this for flat products. Equivalent figures can similarly be constructed for nonflat products, using the information presented in Table 7.12 and remembering that the production of nonflat products does not require an annealing furnace stage.

Consumption Patterns and Efficient Energy Use

The major forms of energy consumed by Mexico's steel industry are, in order of importance, hydrocarbons (bunker oil and gas), coke, and electricity. The relative import- ance of hydrocarbons declined from 1970 to 1983, but they nevertheless still account for more than 50% of total ener- gy consumed in the industry. Coke use rose from 35.6% in 1970 to 40.6% in 1983, and electricity stayed at about 7% from 1975 on (see Table 7.15).

In a study of the development of specific consumption patterns by energy source, coke and hydrocarbons merit spe- cial attention, given their importance in the industry. The processes in which they are used constitute the areas of greatest potential for energy savings by the steel in- dustry. Because the patterns of hydrocarbon and coke con- sumption differ for each of the four steel-making pro- cesses, we start with an analysis of the different produc- tion stages. We can then add the consumption patterns and integrate them into a study of patterns at the present level.12/

Electric Power Consumption. The development of pro- cesses requiring greater amounts of electricity, as well as expanded production, triggered a rapid growth in the steel industry's electric power consumption during the 1960s and 1970s. In integrated and semi-integrated plants, the growth rate of electric power consumption decreased in the 1970s relative to the previous decade. Furthermore, consumption has remained relatively stable since 1979: a- round 3.1 X 10^{12} Kcal (see Table 7.16). The relative share in total consumption of purchased and self-generated elec- tric power has remained virtually constant since 1963: About 90% of electric power is purchased, and the remaining 10% is self-generated.

The specific consumption of electricity in steel pro- duction grew along with the expansion of this fluid. Although this specific consumption increased during the 1960s, at the rate of 3.5% per year, it decreased consider- ably during the 1970s, by 1.7% during the first half of the decade and 2.4% during the second half. The steel indus- try's share of total consumption became stable after 1979 (see Table 7.17).

These specific consumption figures apply to steel making as a whole. However, there are marked differences in specific consumption between the various stages of the process: Electric furnaces and cold rolling are the largest specific consumers of electricity (see Table 7.18).13/

Coke Consumption. The sum total of the input and processes related to blast furnace production of pig iron is associated with specific flows of materials, energy, and so on. From our analysis of the specific consumptions of these materials, some relevant points concerning energy can be inferred (see Figure 7.3):

a. The stage in which energy is consumed most intensively is the blast furnace, where pig iron or first-fusion iron is obtained.
b. The main energy source is coke, obtained from coke plants, which is derived from unprocessed coal.
c. In addition to coke, iron ore is fed to the blast furnace as sinter and pellets. Sinter has a significant energy content (110 Kg of coke/ton of sinter).
d. In regard to energy, the most important relationship in the blast furnace process is that between the consumption of coke and the production of pig iron.

Changes occurred in pig iron production during the period 1970-1983 (see Table 7.19). The AAGR was 6.1% for the entire period. From 1970 to 1975, it was 4.5%, rising to 7.1% from 1976 to 1983. The specific consumption of coke in blast furnaces decreased after 1975. In fact, the efficiency of pig iron production dropped slightly during the first half of the 1970s (0.1% annually) and rose considerably from 1975 to 1978 (6.9% annually). A significant change in efficiency occurred in 1978 because SICARTSA initiated operations. From 1978 to 1983, efficiency declined slightly (0.5% annually). However, the specific consumption of coke in pig iron production decreased during the second half of the 1970s. Thus, in 1983, the steel industry required 4.5×10^6 Kcal of coke to produce one ton of pig iron.

Hydrocarbon Consumption. Blast furnaces also consume gas and bunker oil. Natural gas is the principal source of energy for the rest of the processes, be they open-hearth or oxygen-converter, and for whichever form of rolling is being done, be it cold or hot. Furthermore, gas is again the main energy source in the direct-reduction electric furnace and scrap iron electric furnace processes.

There has been a marked decrease in the hydrocarbons consumed in steel making since the mid-1970s. Indeed, con-

sumption decreased at an average annual rate of 2.1% between 1965 and 1973 (see Table 7.20).14/
     In the course of the Mexican steel industry's develop-
ment, important modifications were made in processes during the 1970s, particularly in the second half. The open-
hearth method became less important than the oxygen-converter and electric furnace methods, which were more energy-efficient. The three processes contributed 58.5%, 0.0%,
and 41.5%, respectively, in 1971, but in 1983 the percentages had changed to 11.8%, 42.7%, and 45.5% (see Table 7.21
and Figure 7.9).
     This new tendency in the industry was not accompanied
by an overall reduction in the relationship between hydrocarbon consumption and steel production because hydrocarbon production grew more rapidly than steel production between 1973 and 1981 (see Table 7.20). Consequently, the specific consumption of hydrocarbons rose by 23% during this
period, reaching 4.47 X 10^6 Kcal/ton. This result contra-
dicts the hypothesis that a change in production processes
goes hand in hand with lower overall and specific consumption of these fuels.

     Consumption Patterns in Different Steel-Making
Processes. Based on the 1979 study of the consumption of
energy and materials in the different stages of Mexican
steel making, one can calculate the specific energy consumptions for the different processes currently used (see
Tables 7.22 and 7.23).
     Nonflat products are less energy-intensive, whatever
the process used. This is because there is less specific
consumption of materials with nonflat products than with
flat products. One of the most economical processes in integrated plants, both in flat and nonflat rolling, is the
direct-reduction electric furnace using the continuous-
casting method. However, if we start from the consumption
of primary energy, electric furnace consumption should be
multiplied by 2.2, according to the efficiency of the national electric power system for 1982 (46%). This means a
0.8 Kcal X 10^6/ton increase in specific consumption for
both flat and nonflat products. These figures represent an
increase of 11% and 12.3% in the respective specific consumption. Therefore, consumptions rise to 8.06 Kcal X 10^6/
ton for flat products and to 7.3 Kcal X 10^6/ton for nonflat
products.15/
     These results show that the most efficient process is
that using the converter and continuous casting, because
its specific consumptions are 6.99 Kcal X 10^6/ton for flat

products and 5.71 Kcal X 10^6/ton for nonflat products.
These levels are approximately 13% and 22% lower than those
attained by electric furnaces.

By using continuous casting, there can be significant
savings for both flat and nonflat products. Savings for
flat products are on the order of 0.97 Kcal X 10^6/ton with
the oxygen converter and 0.73 Kcal X 10^6/ton with direct
reduction. For nonflat products, savings are 1.77 and 1.03
Kcal X 10^6, respectively, for the oxygen-converter and direct-reduction processes.

The use of scrap means sharp reductions in the specific consumption of energy for both types of products. However, this has meant a notable increase in demand, which,
given the scarcity of this material, has made it more ex-
pensive.16/

Savings Potential

Potential energy savings in Mexico's steel industry
can be evaluated by comparing the specific consumptions obtained in the SEPAFIN study with those obtained internationally. These comparisons are based on the specific energy consumptions of the main stages of steel production (see
Table 7.24 and, for an overall perspective, Table 7.25).

The figures show that energy consumption in Mexico's
steel industry is considerably higher than the international norm and the norm that prevailed more than six years ago
in the market-economy industrialized countries as a whole.
Specific consumption in the sintering stage is, in fact, 40%
higher in Mexico than internationally; the blast furnace
stage, 35% higher; soaking pits, 40% higher; reheating furnaces, 17% higher; annealing furnaces, 20% higher; the direct-reduction method, 30% higher and electric furnaces,
15% higher.

The contrast between the national and international
situations allows us to make the following points:

1. The differences in relative efficiency serve as indicators of the large potential savings that exist in Mexico's steel industry.
2. Mexico's ratio of coke to pig iron is too high compared
   to the international norm. Attempts to reduce this ratio in different countries are shown in Figure 7.10.
   Any progress made by Mexico in this respect will have
   significant repercussions on the savings in every steel-
   making process that uses blast furnaces.

3. Mexico's consumption in sintering and soaking pits can be considered relatively high. These two stages are disappearing from the process: sintering in favor of pelleting and soaking pits in favor of continuous casting.

Results can be evaluated on a macro level if we compare the efficiency of Mexico's steel industry with that attained in industrialized countries (see Table 7.25). If we take into account the difference between Mexico's industry efficiency and that of Japan, Italy, West Germany, England, and the United States, there are potential savings on the order of 35%. This is the equivalent of 41.4 tbdce at 1981 consumptions levels, which corresponds to nearly 40 million dollars a year.

Measures for Savings and Efficient Use

The results outlined in the preceding paragraphs, as well as additional considerations, make it possible to propose a set of measures that if adopted could considerably reduce the energy consumed in Mexico's steel industry. Measures are presented according to the order of the production processes and include new technology adopted.

. Preparation of Materials
--Reduce coke consumption in sinter plants through better administration, the elimination of radiation and convection losses, and the use of residual gases.
. Blast Furnaces
--Improve the preparation and distribution of the charge in blast furnaces.
--Hydrocarbon injection: This measures is already being applied in Mexican furnaces. Interest in it lies more in substituting energy sources than in saving energy.
--Increase the use of continuous casting. This measure, together with those to improve the coke/pig iron ratio, shows the greatest potential savings within the steel industry. This is particularly so with the process that uses the blast furnace.
. Soaking pits, reheating and annealing furnaces.
--Improve the insulation in reheating furnaces.
--Coordinate reheating furnaces with rolling mills.
--Install heat recuperators in reheating and annealing furnaces that do not have them.
--Change radiating pipes to direct flame for annealing

furnaces that operate in batch form.
--Increase the use of refractory insulation.
--Reduce leaks in furnaces and soaking pits.
--Improve maintenance and burner design.
. General Measures
--Insulation: Radiation and convection losses are 10%,
hence the importance of reducing them.
--Instrumentation and control: A wide variety of possible
applications are available to the steel industry in these
areas.
--Combined generation of electricity and process steam in
steel plants (cogeneration): It is estimated that one-
third of the electric power requirements in steel plants
could be supplied through cogeneration. This measure
would permit significant savings when integrated with
other industries and would have a favorable impact on the
electric power industry by reducing demand.
--Improvements in electric furnaces: Improvements in the
thermal efficiencies of these furnaces are needed. Oxygen
can be injected, and the furnaces can be operated coordi-
nating high levels of power.

The technological innovations that could be implemented include the following:

. Preparation of Materials
--Technological innovations in processing minerals: This
is an important measure because energy consumption is
tied to the quality of materials, especially in blast furnaces.
. Coke Production
--Dry quenching of coke: This is a costly process and requires long-term implementation.
--Preheating of coking coal: This measure produces only
slight savings but is inexpensive and easy to implement.
. Blast Furnace Operation
--External desulphurization: This measure eliminates
sulphur from coke before it enters the blast furnace. By
doing this, bunker oil with a high sulphur content can be
used afterward, thus extending the range of energy
sources that can be used.
--High blow temperatures in the blast furnace: It has
been found that for every 100°C the temperature is increased, there is a reduction of 36 Kilos of coke for
each ton of pig iron.

--High pressure in the charging cone: One of the advantages here is the increase in the retention time of gases, improving the efficiency of the flues and reducing coke consumption.

. Oxygen-Converter Operation

--Using the gases generated by the oxygen converter: When oxygen is injected into the converter, large amounts of a gas are formed, containing 90% carbon monoxide. We recommend making use of the gas's latent heat, as well as its caloric energy.

. Operation by Direct Reduction

It is calculated that the technique employed by HYLSA leaves room for improvements in energy efficiency.17/

Consumption Patterns and Potential Savings by 1990 and 2000

According to international trends, by 1990 and 2000 the steel industry's specific consumption is expected to decrease to 4.1 Kcal X 10^6 per ton of laminated steel and to 3.4 Kcal X 10^6, respectively. Based on these trends and on consumption in the industrialized countries around the mid-1970s compared to the consumption existing in Mexico (see Table 7.25), we are able to estimate the potential savings for Mexico's steel industry in 1990 and 2000.

The projections are based on two possible scenarios, assuming that the production of flat and nonflat products will follow the established pattern of 3.5% and 6.1% AAGR, respectively (see Table 7.26).

Scenario A (reference scenario) assumes the efficiency of flat and nonflat sheet production will stay at the 1983 levels. That is, specific consumption will be 7.3 Kcal X 10^6 per ton for flat products and 6.5 Kcal X 10^6 per ton for nonflat products for the entire period under consideration.18/ Scenario B assumes that by 1990 there will be 20% savings beyond the specific consumption recorded for flat and nonflat products in 1983 and that savings will be 40% by the year 2000.

A comparison of total energy consumption for both scenarios reveals that in terms of volume the cumulative savings during the period from 1984 to 1990 would be 38.7 Kcal X 10^{12}, that is 30.2 mbce (82.7 tbdce). The corresponding amount for the period 1991-2000 would be 216.1 Kcal X 10^{12}, that is, 168.6 mbce (461.8 tbdce). Total cumulative savings would be 254.8 Kcal X 10^{12}, that is, 198.8 mbce (544.5 tbdce).

FIGURE 7.1
Production Processes for Steel Products

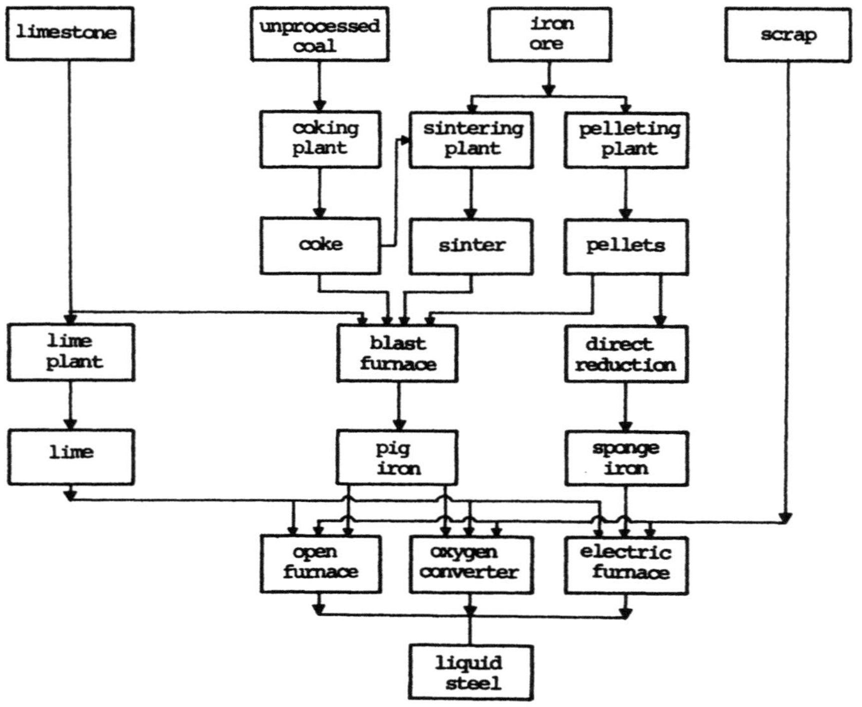

FIGURE 7.2
Production Processes for Steel Products

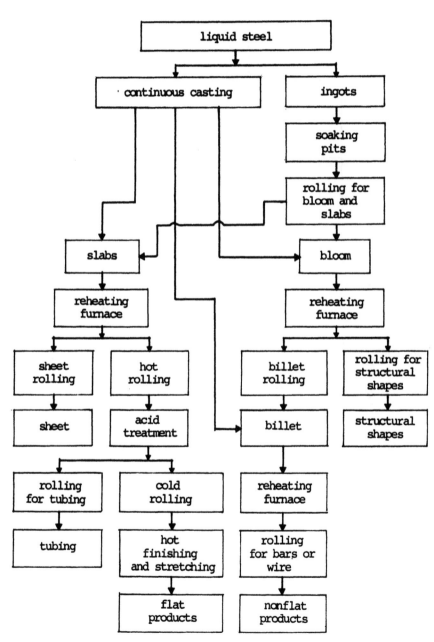

FIGURE 7.3
Specific Consumption of Materials in the Blast Furnace Process for Each Ton of Pig Iron Produced, 1979

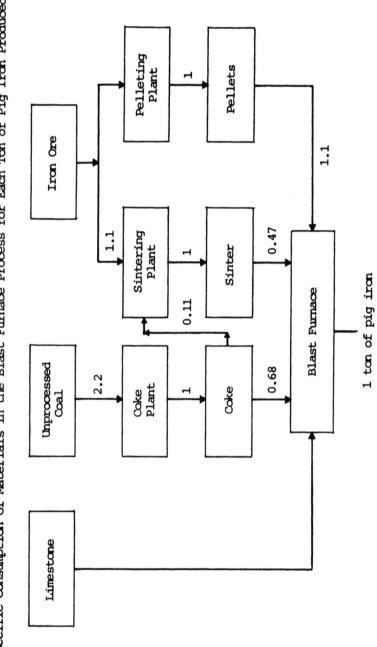

Source: Data produced by authors.

FIGURE 7.4
Energy Consumption During the Open-Hearth Process Without Continuous Casting
to Produce Flat Products

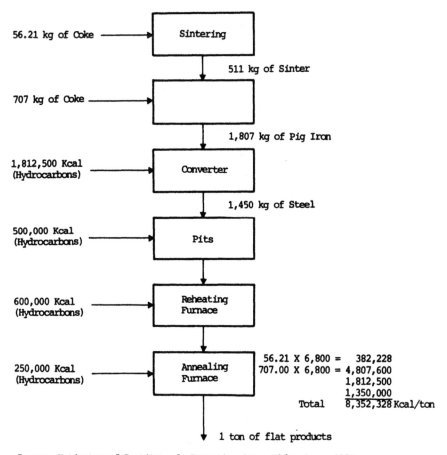

Source: Estimates of Instituto de Investigaciones Eléctricas, 1979.

186

FIGURE 7.5
Energy Consumption During the Oxygen-Converter Process Without Continuous
Casting to Produce Flat Products

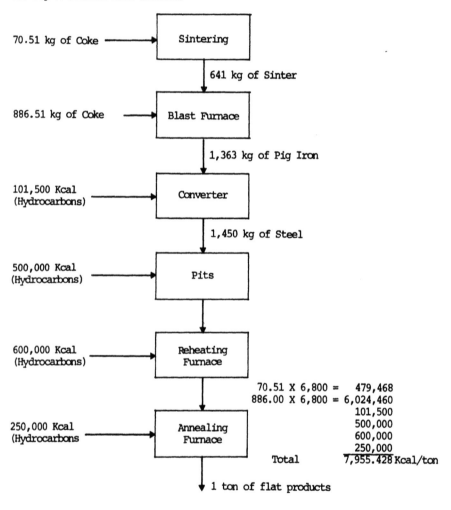

70.51 kg of Coke ⟶ **Sintering**

641 kg of Sinter

886.51 kg of Coke ⟶ **Blast Furnace**

1,363 kg of Pig Iron

101,500 Kcal
(Hydrocarbons) ⟶ **Converter**

1,450 kg of Steel

500,000 Kcal
(Hydrocarbons) ⟶ **Pits**

600,000 Kcal
(Hydrocarbons) ⟶ **Reheating Furnace**

250,000 Kcal
(Hydrocarbons ⟶ **Annealing Furnace**

```
70.51 X 6,800 =    479,468
886.00 X 6,800 = 6,024,460
                   101,500
                   500,000
                   600,000
                   250,000
Total            7,955.428 Kcal/ton
```

1 ton of flat products

Source: Estimates of Instituto de Investigaciones Eléctricas, 1979.

FIGURE 7.6
Energy Consumption During the Oxygen-Converter Process with Continuous
Casting to Produce Flat Products

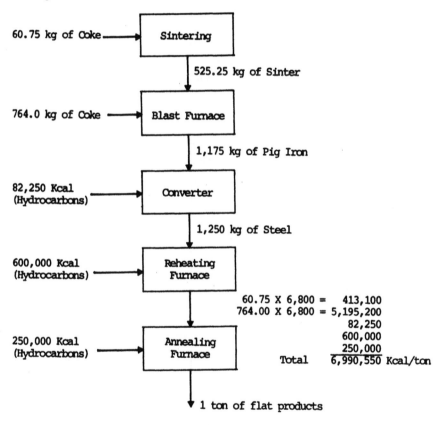

60.75 kg of Coke ⟶ Sintering

525.25 kg of Sinter

764.0 kg of Coke ⟶ Blast Furnace

1,175 kg of Pig Iron

82,250 Kcal
(Hydrocarbons) ⟶ Converter

1,250 kg of Steel

600,000 Kcal
(Hydrocarbons) ⟶ Reheating Furnace

60.75 X 6,800 =   413,100
764.00 X 6,800 = 5,195,200
                    82,250
                   600,000
250,000 Kcal   250,000
(Hydrocarbons) ⟶ Annealing Furnace   Total   6,990,550 Kcal/ton

1 ton of flat products

Source: Estimates of Instituto de Investigaciones Eléctricas, 1979.

188

FIGURE 7.7
Energy Consumption During the Direct-Reduction Electric Furnace Process
Without Continuous Casting to Produce Flat Products

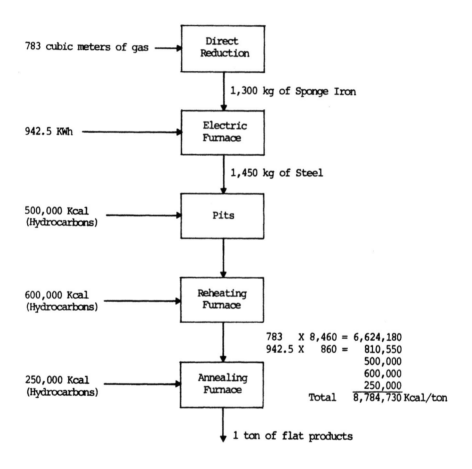

783 cubic meters of gas ⟶ Direct Reduction

1,300 kg of Sponge Iron

942.5 KWh ⟶ Electric Furnace

1,450 kg of Steel

500,000 Kcal (Hydrocarbons) ⟶ Pits

600,000 Kcal (Hydrocarbons) ⟶ Reheating Furnace

783   X 8,460 = 6,624,180
942.5 X   860 =   810,550
                  500,000
                  600,000
                  250,000
Total   8,784,730 Kcal/ton

250,000 Kcal (Hydrocarbons) ⟶ Annealing Furnace

1 ton of flat products

Source: Estimates of Instituto de Investigaciones Eléctricas, 1979.

FIGURE 7.8
Energy Consumption During the Direct-Reduction Electric Furnace Process
with Continuous Casting to Produce Flat Products

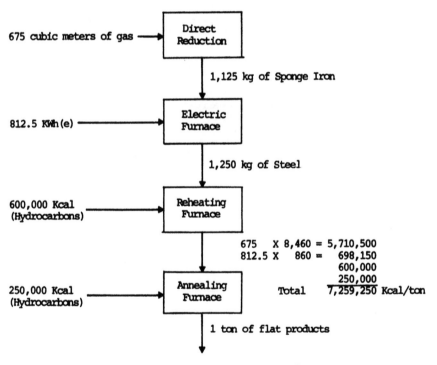

675 cubic meters of gas → **Direct Reduction**

1,125 kg of Sponge Iron

812.5 KWh(e) → **Electric Furnace**

1,250 kg of Steel

600,000 Kcal (Hydrocarbons) → **Reheating Furnace**

```
675    X 8,460 = 5,710,500
812.5 X   860 =   698,150
                  600,000
                  250,000
Total          7,259,250 Kcal/ton
```

250,000 Kcal (Hydrocarbons) → **Annealing Furnace**

1 ton of flat products

Source: Estimates of Instituto de Investigaciones Eléctricas, 1979.

TABLE 7.8
Development of Steel Production Capacity, 1976-1980

Process	Company	Nominal Capacity (millions)		Level of Use (%)	
		1976	1980	1976	1980
Blast	AHMSA[a/]	3,250	3,200	67.1	71.0
Furnace	SICARTSA[b/]	--	1,300	--	61.0
	FMSA[c/]	1,000	1,500	78.5	65.0
Direct-Reduction	HYLSA[d/]	1,445	1,600	88.0	97.4
Electric Furnace	TAMSA[e/]	360	745	97.1	51.0
Scrap Electric Furnace	SEMI-INTEGRATED	1,047	1,500	78.8	78.6
Total		7,102	9,945	74.6	72.0

Source: Cámara Nacional de la Industria del Hierro y Acero.

Note: The capacity did not change radically in 1983.

a/ AHMSA - Altos Hornos de México, S.A.
b/ SICARTSA - Siderúrgica Lázaro Cárdenas-Las Truchas, S.A.
c/ FMSA - Fundidora de Monterrey, S.A.
d/ HYLSA - Hojalata y Lámina, S.A.
e/ TAMSA - Tubos de Acero de México, S.A.

TABLE 7.9
Percentage Production Distribution of Steel and Rolled Products in Steel Industry, 1980

Company	Steel Production	Rolled Products
AHMSA[a/]	32.3	28.6
SICARTSA[b/]	11.2	10.1
FMSA[c/]	13.9	13.1
HYLSA[d/]	22.2	24.1
TAMSA[e/]	5.4	4.6
Nonintegrated	15.0	19.5

Source: Comisión Coordinadora de la Industria Siderúrgica.

Note: Figures for a base of 7.2 million tons of steel and 5.9 million tons of rolled products.

a/ AHMSA - Altos Hornos de México, S.A.
b/ SICARTSA - Siderúrgica Lázaro Cárdenas-Las Truchas, S.A.
c/ FMSA - Fundidora de Monterrey, S.A.
d/ HYLSA - Hojalata y Lámina, S.A.
e/ TAMSA - Tubos de Acero de México, S.A.

TABLE 7.10
Production of Major Products in the Steel Industry, 1970-1983 (in thousands of tons)

Product	Year														AAGR a/
	1970	1971	1972	1973	1974	1975	1976	1977	1978	1979	1980	1981	1982	1983	
Primary															
Pig Iron	1,645	1,683	1,890	2,021	2,304	2,048	2,413	3,009	3,509	3,520	3,515	3,690	3,598	3,536	6.1
Sponge Iron	617	674	784	754	903	914	1,115	1,320	1,628	1,507	1,510	1,590	1,505	1,497	7.1
Steel	3,881	3,821	4,431	4,760	5,138	5,272	5,298	5,601	6,775	7,117	7,156	7,605	7,051	6,917	4.5
Flat and Tubular															
Slab	462	472	589	586	656	670	544	556	688	744	757	783	652	487	0.4
Sheet	971	1,023	1,153	1,345	1,470	1,412	1,375	1,501	1,922	2,181	2,050	2,154	1,834	1,808	4.9
Seamless tubing	185	180	195	186	196	215	225	220	252	255	239	251	263	234	1.8
Nonflat															
Wire Rod	317	301	338	376	412	418	423	432	538	593	586	580	712	845	7.8
Corrugated Bars	570	553	628	752	784	906	849	966	1,134	1,276	1,489	1,590	1,441	1,337	6.8
Solid Bars	114	107	136	151	209	197	198	181	177	250	175	175	163	194	4.2
Light Structural	189	179	165	189	219	254	271	239	256	288	296	274	251	229	1.5
Heavy Structural Shapes	111	132	151	171	228	173	186	155	222	265	272	306	231	188	4.1

Source: Cámara Nacional de la Industria del Hierro y Acero.

a/ AAGR - Average annual growth rate.

TABLE 7.11
Specific Consumption of Gas and Bunker Oil in Blast Furnace Processes
(Kcal X 106 per ton)

Stage	Natural Gas	Bunker Oil	Total
Blast furnace	0.12-0.50	0.31	0.43-0.50
Converter	—	—	0.07
Open Hearth	0.61	0.64	1.25
Soaking pits	0.50	—	0.50
Reheating furnaces	0.60	—	0.60
Annealing furnaces	0.25	—	0.25
Total	—	—	3.10-3.17

Source: Cámara Nacional de Acero (CANACERO).

Note: These figures are in kilocalories to avoid problems about the caloric
content of the fuels. Some plants use 6.900 Kcal/liter of bunker oil,
instead of the 10,000 Kcal used here.

TABLE 7.12
Specific Consumption of Materials in Blast Furnace Processes

Stage	Input
Open-Hearth Furnace	750 kg pig iron/ton steel
	400 kg scrap/ton steel
Oxygen Converter	940 kg pig iron/ton steel
	235 kg scrap/ton steel
Sheet Bars with Continuous Casting	1,250 kg steel/ton plating
Sheet Bars without Continuous Casting	1,450 kg steel/ton plating
Skelp With Continuous Casting	1,150 kg steel/ton plating
Skelp Without Continuous Casting	1,410 kg steel/ton plating
Seamless Tubing	1,550 kg steel/ton tubing

Source: Cámara Nacional de Acero (CANACERO).

TABLE 7.13

Specific Energy Consumption by Stage and Energy Type in Direct-Reduction and Electric Processes

Stage	Natural gas cubic meters/ton (Kcal/ton)	Electricity KWh/ton (Kcal/ton)
Direct-Reduction[a]	600	—
Electric Furnaces	—	650 (560,000)

Source: Cámara Nacional de Acero (CANACERO).

a/ The HYL III method expects to consume 290 cubic meters/ton.

TABLE 7.14
Specific Consumption of Materials in Electric Furnaces

Process	Specific Input
Direct-Reduction Electric Furnace	900 kg sponge iron/ton steel 220 kg scrap/ton steel
Scrap Electric Furnace	1,200 kg scrap/ton steel

Source: Cámara Nacional de Acero (CANACERO).

TABLE 7.15
Energy Consumption in the Steel Industry in 1970, 1975, 1980, and 1983

Total	Electricity Kcal X 10^{12}	%	Coke Kcal X 10^{12}	%	Hydrocarbons Kcal X 10^{12}	%	Total Kcal X 10^{12}	%
1970	1.43	5.5	9.14	35.6	15.12	58.9	25.69	100.0
1975	2.11	6.6	11.72	37.2	17.71	56.2	31.54	100.0
1980	3.23	7.7	16.76	39.7	32.3a/	52.6	52.29	100.0
1983	3.13	7.5	17.05	40.6	34.0a/	51.9	54.18	100.0

Sources: Tables 7.16, 7.19, and 7.20.

a/ Estimated value.

TABLE 7.16
Development of Energy Consumption in the Integrated and Semi-Integrated
Steel Industry

Year	Electric Power Consumption (Kcal X 10^{12})			AAGR %[a] per Five-Year Period
	Purchased	Self-Generated	Consumed	
1963	0.5232	0.0634	.5866	—
1968	1.0047	0.1081	1.1128	13.6
1969	1.2018	0.0918	1.2936	—
1970	1.3289	0.0983	1.4272	—
1971	1.3423	0.1085	1.4508	—
1972	1.4584	0.1929	: 6513	—
1973	1.5922	0.2016	1.7938	10.0
1974	1.8013	0.2144	2.0157	—
1975	1.9435	0.1666	2.1101	—
1976	1.9857	0.1865	2.1722	—
1977	2.1437	0.2089	2.3526	—
1978	2.6812	0.2340	2.9152	10.1
1979	2.8750	0.2621	3.1371	—
1980	2.9377	0.2936	3.2313	—
1981	3.1880	0.3300	3.5180	—
1982	2.802	0.3000	3.1020	—
1983	2.843	0.2900	3.1330	1.5

Sources: Comisión Federal de Electricidad,
Secretaría de Patrimonio y Fomento Industrial.

Note: Amounts for 1976-1980 are estimated from Comisión Federal de
Electricidad figures and those from 1981 study by Secretaría de Patrimonio
y Fomento Industrial.

a/ AAGR - Average annual growth rate.

TABLE 7.17
Historical Development of the Specific Consumption of Electric Power in
Steel Production

Year	Steel Production in (tons X 10³)	Electric Power Consumption (Kcal X 10¹²)	Specific Consumption (Kcal/ton)	AAGR[a] Yearly Percentage
1963	2,026	.5866	289,536	—
1968	3,256	1.1128	341,769	—
1969	3,466	1.2936	373,225	—
1970	3,881	1.4272	367,740	3.5
1971	3,821	1.4508	379,691	—
1972	4,431	1.6513	372,669	—
1973	4,760	1.7938	376,848	—
1974	5,138	2.0157	392,312	—
1975	5,272	2.1101	400,246	1.7
1976	5,298	2.1722	410,022	—
1977	5,601	2.3526	420,034	—
1978	6,775	2.9152	430,291	—
1979	7,117	3.1371	440,799	—
1980	7,156	3.2313	451,564	2.4
1981	7,605	3.5180	462,591	—
1982	7,051	3.1020	440,000	—
1983	6,917	3.1330	453,000	0.1

Sources: Cámara Nacional de la Industria del Hierro y Acero;
Table 7.16.

a/ AAGR values are listed against the year at the end of the period for which
they are calculated.

TABLE 7.18
Specific Consumption of Electric Power in the Major Stages of
the Steel-Making Process

Process Stage	Consumption (Kcal/ton)	
Sintering	38,700	(45 KWh)
Blast Furnace	30,100	(35 KWh)
Oxygen Converter	25,800	(30 KWh)
Open hearth	60,200	(70 KWh)
Electric Furnace	559,000	(650 KWh)
Hot Rolling	73,100	(85 KWh)
Cold Rolling	129,000	(150 KWh)

Source: Cámara Nacional de la Industria del Hierro y Acero.

TABLE 7.19
Development of Specific Consumption of Coke/Pig Iron, 1970-1983

Year	Pig Iron (thousands of tons)	Coke [a] (thousands of tons)		Coke/Pig Iron Ratio for Blast Furnace	Specific Consumption [b] (Kcal X 10^6)
		Blast Furnaces	Sintering		
1970	1,645	1,262	82	.767	5.22
1971	1,683	1,290	84	.766	5.21
1972	1,890	1,453	94	.769	5.23
1973	2,021	1,597	104	.790	5.37
1974	2,304	1,725	112	.749	5.09
1975	2,048	1,619	105	.791	5.38
1976	2,412	1,809	118	.750	5.10
1977	3,009	2,258	147	.750	5.10
1978	3,509	2,272	148	.647	4.40
1979	3,520	2,396	156	.681	4.63
1980	3,515	2,320	145	.660	4.49
1981	3,690	2,398	161	.650	4.42
1982	3,598	2,375	158	.660	4.49
1983	3,536	2,351	156	.665	4.52

Source: Cámara Nacional de la Industria del Hierro y Acero.

a/ Includes imports.
b/ Coke/pig iron ratio for blast furnaces X 6,800 Kcal/kg of coke.

TABLE 7.20
Specific Consumption of Hydrocarbons for Steel Production, 1965–1983

Year	Steel Production (thousand of tons)	Hydrocarbon Consumption (Kcal X 10^{12}) Gas	Hydrocarbon Consumption (Kcal X 10^{12}) Bunker Oil	Total Specific Consumption (Kcal X 10^{6}/ton)
1965	2,454	8.13	2.12	4.17
1966	2,787	8.80	2.36	3.99
1967	3,039	10.00	2.62	4.15
1968	3,256	11.64	2.43	4.32
1969	3,466	12.86	2.29	4.37
1970	3,881	13.42	1.70	3.89
1971	3,821	14.00	1.48	4.04
1972	4,431	13.96	1.81	3.55
1973	4,760	14.80	1.96	3.51
1981	7,605	30.90	3.10	4.47

Source: Cámara Nacional de la Industria del Hierro y Acero, Secretaría de Patrimonio y Fomento Industrial.

Note: After 1973 the information available comes from the 1982 survey of industry.

TABLE 7.21
Steel Production by Process, 1971–1983 (in thousands of tons)

Year	Open Hearth	Oxygen Converter	Electric Furnace	Total
1971	2,243	—	1,578	3,821
1972	2,281	353	1,796	4,430
1973	2,336	420	2,004	4,760
1974	2,331	634	2,172	5,137
1975	2,185	687	2,400	5,272
1976	2,154	703	2,441	5,298
1977	1,628	1,504	2,470	5,602
1978	1,506	2,476	2,793	6,775
1979	1,467	2,608	3,042	7,117
1980	1,350	2,688	3,118	7,156
1981	1,309	2,981	3,315	7,605
1982	1,083	2,905	3,064	7,051
1983	811	2,956	3,148	6,917

Source: Cámara Nacional de la Industria del Hierro y Acero.

FIGURE 7.9
Steel Production by Type of Process, 1971-1983

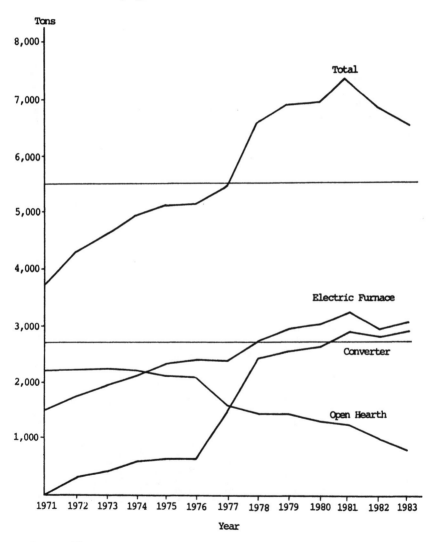

Source: Cámara Nacional de la Industria del Hierro y Acero.

TABLE 7.22
Specific Energy Consumption for Flat Products by Process, 1983

Process	Kcal x 10^6/Ton of Flat Products
Blast Furnace, Open Hearth Without Continuous Casting	8.35
Blast Furnace Converter Without Continuous Casting	7.96
Blast Furnace Converter With Continuous Casting	6.99
Direct-Reduction Electric Furnace Without Continuous Casting	8.79
Direct-Reduction Electric Furnace With Continuous Casting	7.26 (8.06[a/])
Scrap Electric Furnace Without Continuous Casting	2.14
Scrap Electric Furnace With Continuous Casting	1.55

Source: "Consumption of Energy and Materials in Steel Production," this chapter.

a/ If the efficiency of the electricity system is taken into account.

TABLE 7.23

Specific Energy Consumption for Nonflat Products by Process, 1983

Process	Kcal x 10^6/Ton of Nonflat Products
Blast Furnace Open Hearth Without Continuous Casting	7.87
Blast Furnace Converter Without Continuous Casting	7.48
Blast Furnace Converter With Continuous Casting	5.71
Direct-Reduction Electric Furnace Without Continuous Casting	8.33
Direct-Reduction Electric Furnace With Continuous Casting	6.50 (7.3[a])
Scrap Electric Furnace Without Continuous Casting	1.89
Scrap Electric Furnace With Continuous Casting	1.24

Source: "Consumption of Energy and Materials in Steel Production," this chapter.

[a] If the efficiency of the electricity system is taken into account.

TABLE 7.24
Potential Savings in the Main Stages of the Steel-Making Process

Process Stage[a]	Specific Consumption (Kcal x 10⁶/Ton)		Potential Savings[b] (%)
	Mexico	International	
Pelleting[c]	—	0.17	—
Sintering	0.75	0.45	40
Blast Furnace	4.52	3.00	35
Soaking Pits	0.50	0.30	40
Reheating Furnace	0.60	0.50	17
Annealing Furnace	0.25	0.20	20
Direct Reduction	5.00	3.50	30
Electric Furnace	0.56	0.48	15

Sources: Table 7.19 and "Consumption of Energy and Materials in Steel Production," this chapter.

a/ The open-hearth furnace is not included because internationally it is being replaced by the electric furnace and converter.

b/ $\left(\dfrac{\text{Specific Consumption in Mexico} - \text{International Specific Consumption}}{\text{Specific Consumption in Mexico}}\right) 100$

c/ Pelleting is included because it is a substitute for sintering and in order to show the reduction in energy consumption pelleting implies with respect to sintering.

TABLE 7.25

Specific Consumption in the Steel-Making Process in Different Countries, 1976

Country	Specific Consumption (Kcal x 10⁶/ton of rolled steel)	Potential Savings (%)
Japan	4.25	41.37
Italy	4.60	33.79
West Germany	5.00	31.10
England	5.90	18.62
United States	6.62	8.68
Mexico	7.25	—

Source: Gordian Associates, An Energy Conservation Target for Industry (New York, 1976), p.116.

FIGURE 7.10
Development of Specific Consumption of Coke in Different Countries

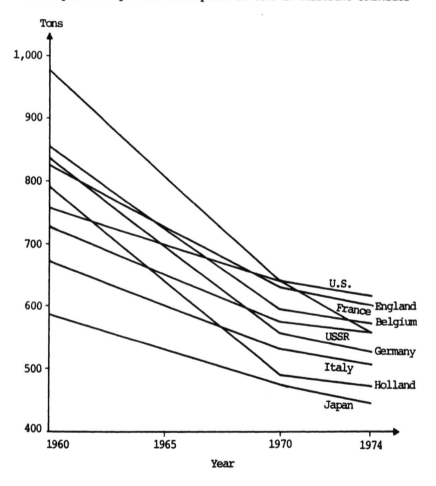

Source: Gordian Associates, An Energy Conservation Target for Industry (New York, 1976).

TABLE 7.26
Potential Savings Estimates for the Steel Industry

Year	Production (thousand of tons) Flat	Nonflat	Scenario A Total Consumption (Kcal X 10^12) Flat[b]	Nonflat[c]	Scenario B[a] Total Consumption (Kcal X 10^12) Flat	Nonflat	Total Potential Savings (Kcal X 10^12)
1983	2,529	2,793	18.5	18.2	18.5	18.2	--
1984	--	--	19.1	19.3	18.5	18.7	1.2
1985	--	--	19.8	20.5	18.6	19.2	2.5
1986	--	--	20.5	21.7	18.6	19.7	3.9
1987	--	--	21.2	23.1	18.6	20.2	5.5
1988	--	--	22.0	24.5	18.7	20.8	6.8
1989	--	--	22.7	26.0	18.7	21.4	8.6
1990	3,218	4,227	23.5	27.5	18.8	22.0	10.2
1991	--	--	24.3	29.2	18.9	22.7	11.9
1992	--	--	25.2	31.0	19.0	23.4	13.8
1993	--	--	26.1	32.8	19.1	24.1	15.7
1994	--	--	27.0	34.8	19.3	24.9	17.6
1995	--	--	27.9	37.0	19.4	25.6	19.9
1996	--	--	28.9	39.2	19.5	26.4	22.0
1997	--	--	29.9	41.6	19.6	27.2	24.7
1998	--	--	30.9	44.2	19.7	28.1	27.3
1999	--	--	32.0	46.9	19.8	29.0	30.1
2000	4,539	7,642	33.1	49.7	19.9	29.8	33.1
AAGR[d]	3.5%	6.1%	3.5%	6.1%	0.4%	2.9%	
Subtotal 1984–1990							
Subtotal 1991–2000							216.1
Total							254.8

Source: Estimates of authors.

a/ Supposes 20% savings for 1990 and 40% for 2000.
b/ Calculated on the basis of 1983 specific consumption: 7.3 Kcal X 10^6 ton (see Table 7.22).
c/ Calculated on the basis of 1983 specific consumption: 6.5 Kcal X 10^6 ton (see Table 7.23).
d/ AAGR - Average annual growth rate.

THE CEMENT INDUSTRY

In this section, we examine different aspects of cement production and the conservation and efficient use of
energy in this industry, within a context of change. We
describe the process involved in manufacturing cement, the
development of this process since the 1960s, and the present situation in the industry. Next, we examine its energy consumption patterns, discuss measures to increase efficiency, and assess the potential savings for 1990 and 2000.

Mexico's cement industry has been characteristically
dynamic since World War II. The average growth in production was 8.8% per year from 1947 to 1980. During the same
period, the number of plants increased from eighteen to
twenty-eight and the number of kilns from thirty-nine to
seventy-five. Production capacity increased at an AAGR of
7.7% (see Table 7.27).

The cement industry is concentrated in a handful of
plants, the largest having a capacity of 6,500 tons a day,
or 11.8% of the industry's total capacity. The six largest
plants account for 53% of total production and the
thirteen smallest for only 16%.19/

The following steps constitute the process of manufacturing cement:

1. Obtaining the raw materials
2. Preparing the raw materials
3. Producing clinker
4. Grinding clinker with gypsum and, occasionally, puzzolanic extenders, to obtain cement

Given the characteristics of the raw materials, there
originally were two methods of processing these materials
to create cement: "wet" and "dry." The main difference between the two methods was in the handling of the raw materials. In the wet method, the materials are used in slurry
form, and in the dry method they are used in powder form.
Around 1950, the dry method was perfected by including a
preheating stage, and, today, a further modification has
been incorporated into the method: precalcination.

There has been a strong tendency to replace the wet
method with the dry. The share of cement produced by the
wet method dropped from 22.8% in 1965 to 7.3% in 1980.
This means that by 1980 the dry method was already used in
92.7% of domestic production (see Table 7.28). There are
presently twenty-four plants using this method, while only
four use the wet method.

Compared with other industries, the cement industry can be considered to be homogeneous insofar as the characteristics of the product are concerned. The main product is known as grey or portland cement, obtained by adding 7% gypsum to the clinker.

Recently, production of puzzolanic cement has begun, where 7% gypsum and approximately 13% puzzolanic extenders are added to the clinker. The puzzolanic extender is a silica or siliceous-argillaceous material that, of itself, has few, if any, cement-like properties. However, when finely ground in a humid environment, the extender reacts chemically with calcium hydroxide at room temperature to form compounds with cement-like properties. Among major extenders are the puzzolanes, blast furnace slag, and volcanic ash. In 1981 it was calculated that 65% of domestic production was grey cement and 35% puzzolanic cement.

Consumption Patterns and Efficient Energy Use

The cement industry uses bunker oil and gas, as well as electricity, as its principal forms of energy. Data pertaining to gas and bunker oil are generally placed in the same category because both energy sources can be used interchangeably in the cement industry, unlike other industries.

The history of cement production shows that the consumption of bunker oil, gas, and electricity continuously increased from 1968 to 1981. The AAGR for production was 8.8% during this period, 9.6% for electricity consumption, and 7.04% for fuel consumption. These rates translate into a 0.9% average annual increase in the specific consumption of electricity for the whole period and a 1.6% decrease in the specific consumption of fuel (see Table 7.29).

The reduction in specific consumption of hydrocarbons means a 19% savings relative to 1968 consumption. This improvement can be attributed to a rapid increase in the use of modern production techniques, such as four-stage suspension preheaters, and the relative increase in puzzolanic production. The slight increase in specific consumption of electricity should not be interpreted as a drop in efficiency. This slight upswing in consumption is due to the increased use of electricity in the process to support the new suspension preheaters.

Based on the industry's specific consumption according to process type, we can observe that the dry method with preheaters is the least energy-intensive (see Table 7.30 and

Figure 7.11). Next is the dry method without preheating, with 45% greater specific consumption. Finally, the wet method consumes almost twice as much energy as the dry method with preheating. However, the share of the main energy forms (bunker oil and electricity) in specific consumption is similar for all three processes (7%-9% and 90%-93%, respectively).

Calcination consumes energy intensely compared to the other production stages, notwithstanding the process used. It accounts for between 86% (dry method with preheater) and 94% (wet method) of total specific consumption.

In spite of the advances that have been made in saving energy, there is still room for improvement in Mexico's cement industry, based on a comparison between Mexican rates of specific consumption and international rates. Recognizing the technology presently available on the international market and prorating the average values for pure portland cement and portland cement with extenders (used in proportions of 65% and 35%, respectively, in Mexico), we found that the average specific consumption that could be attained is 821 Kcal/kg of cement (see Table 7.31).

If we compare this figure with Mexico's specific consumption for 1981 (1103 Kcal/kg), we obtain a potential savings of 26%. If we take the technical minimum for specific consumption (223 Kcal/kg) as a reference point, based on the thermodynamic concept of work needed to produce cement, potential savings would be 80%.

Measures for Conservation and Efficient Energy Use

The following steps could be taken to save energy during cement production. Some of these measures are currently being introduced, and others are subject to new research developments.

1. Transform long, dry furnaces into systems with preheaters.
2. Increase the number of preheating stages to the maximum of four.
3. Use more hydraulic cement with extenders, recommending:
   a. Orienting users about the quality of cement required for each type of construction
   b. Studying the norms governing the ratio of clinker to cement in order to develop extenders that permit reducing this ratio without detriment to the product or increased risks to the user

4. Institute measures related to insulation. Radiation and
   convection losses from kilns are calculated at 80 Kcal/
   kg, representing as much as 10% of the energy consumed.
   To reduce this loss, we recommend selecting new, long-
   life refractors with low thermal conductivity as well as
   providing adequate maintenance.
5. Institute measures to increase energy efficiency in the
   combustion system:
   a. Using the appropriate type of burner for the fuel
   b. Maintaining and replacing burners
   c. Providing an optimum proportion of air for combustion
   d. Controlling the length, intensity, and so on, of the
      flame
6. Eliminate false air intakes

These measures vary as to the advantages they offer
and the investments needed to implement them. Generally
speaking, the first two measures, using preheaters and increasing preheating stages, can produce significant savings,
but they require investments with amortization periods of
ten to fifteen years. Measure 3, using more hydraulic cement with extenders, requires only a small investment and
would produce large energy savings. This practice is now
being rapidly implemented throughout the industry. Ongoing
care of the insulation, one part of measure 4, produces only small savings but does not require large investments.
The second part, dealing with research and improving insulation in general, is complex and requires more specialized help. Measure 5, providing energy efficiency in the
combustion system, can be controlled partly by adequate administration and partly by specialized organizations that
should be regulated by proper energy administration.

Apart from the savings obtained through these measures, the cement industry has new technology at its disposal that would permit more efficient energy use. The following items deserve special mention:

. Systems with Precalcination
. Oxygen Enrichment
. Insulation
. Instrumentation and Control

Precalcination, which was developed in Europe and Japan, is just now being practiced in Mexico. The two-stage
combustion or precalcinator process is similar to the process with a suspension preheater. The difference is that

inside the preheating tower there is an additional chamber
that acts as a preheating kiln. Although a conventional
kiln with a preheater produces 40% to 50% calcination, the
precalcinating system achieves levels of 95% calcination.

Several major advantages are offered by the new system. Because the incoming material is virtually calcinated.
the productive capacity of the rotary kiln increases from
65 kg of clinker per cubic meter per hour to 145 kg of
clinker per cubic meter per hour. Thus, one can conclude
that for a conventional system the rotary kiln can be considerably smaller, reducing radiation losses and replacement costs for refractors. Also, because the precalcinator can be operated a relatively low temperatures,
fuel with low caloric energy (even garbage) can be used at
this stage in cement manufacturing.

Oxygen enrichment is based on the principle that by
enriching the oxygen content of the air used for combustion, the productive capacity of the rotary kiln can be increased. If heat losses from the outer surfaces of the
kiln are assumed to remain constant and coke is formed more
rapidly (increasing production), then the fuel consumption
per ton of clinker produced decreases.

As mentioned previously, the problems of insulation,
common to all industrial processes, require further research.

As in other industries, increased and more precise instrumentation allows continuous control of the different
parameters regulating product quality and fuel and electricity consumption, making it possible to optimize troubled
conditions and to record information for new improvements.
These concepts apply to the process as a whole and not just
to the kiln. Significant improvements in software and control aspects can be made to provide better energy consumption and electric power.

Savings Potential

Estimates of potential energy savings in cement production for the years 1990 and 2000 are made on the basis
of a series of considerations arising from the foregoing
analysis (see Table 7.32). It is assumed that cement production will continue developing at the traditional rate (an
average of 8.8% annually). To estimate the possible savings,
three alternative future consumptions are proposed.

Scenario A assumes that there will be no changes in
the specific consumption level recorded for 1981. This im-

plies total energy consumption will grow at the same average growth rate as cement production (8.8%). Scenario B assumes that the dynamics of specific consumption will pro-
ceed as they have till now; that is, consumption level will
decrease at an average annual rate of 1.6% (see Table 7.29).
Scenario C assumes that energy consumption efficiency in
Mexican industry will reach international levels in the
long run. Efficiency will, in turn, increase at the rate
expected internationally (an average of 1.4% annually).

Scenario A is taken as the point of reference when
calculating the potential savings for the other two scenarios because it assumes a constant level of efficiency.
From a comparison of the scenarios (see Table 7.32), we can
infer that scenario B would produce energy savings of 8.5%
by 1990 and 21.7% by 2000, that is, a 17.9% savings for the
entire period. The amount of cumulative savings from 1982
to 1990 would be on the order of 23.67 Kcal X 10^{12}. From
1990 to 2000, the savings would be 150.45 Kcal X 10^{12} and,
for the overall period, 174.0 Kcal X 10^{12}. The cumulative
savings translate into 18.46 mbce (50.58 tbdce) for 1982 to
1990, 117.35 mbce (321.52 tbdce) for 1990 to 2000, and 135.81
mbce (372.10 tbdce) for rhe entire eighteen-year period.20/

Scenario C would produce savings of 34.57% by 1990
and 42.58% by 2000, which means savings of 40.29% over the
eighteen years. In cumulative terms, these percentages
would amount to 96.27 X 10^{12} by 1990, 295.22 X 10^{12} by 2000,
and 391.54 X 10^{12} Kcal overall. In terms of crude oil, these
savings are equivalent to 75.09 mbce (205.73 tbdce) by 1990
and 230.28 mbce (630.90 tbdce) by 2000. The total saved
over the entire period would be 305.37 mbce (836.64 tbdce).

The cumulative energy savings for the period, according to scenarios B and C, would be equivalent to approximately 3,700 and 8,400 million dollars, calculated at 27.5
dollars per barrel of equivalent crude.

THE SUGAR INDUSTRY

There has been little study of conservation and efficient energy use in Mexico's sugar industry. Only recently
has there been any official concern in this respect. As
yet, there has been no definition of objectives or policies affecting consumption.21/

Sugar production requires a great deal of energy. Its
bunker oil consumption is among the highest within the different branches of Mexican industry. It was 17% of overall
industrial consumption in 1983 and 5.5% of domestic con-

TABLE 7.27
Cement Industry Production Plants in Mexico

Year	Plants	Kilns	Capacity (thousands of tons per year)	Average capacity (tons/ plant/year)	Production (thousands of tons per year)
1947	18	39	1,475	81,945	999
1950	18	44	1,953	108,500	1,419
1955	18	50	2,757	153,167	2,086
1960	20	60	3,876	193,800	3,086
1965	22	61	5,236	238,000	4,199
1970	27	74	8,034	297,000	7,180
1975	28	85	13,654	487,643	11,612
1976	28	79	13,844	494,429	12,584
1977	28	79	13,844	494,429	13,227
1978	28	73	14,844	530,143	14,057
1979	28	75	16,400	585,714	15,178
1980	28	75	17,021	607,893	16,243

Source: Cámara Nacional del Cemento.

TABLE 7.28
Percent Production of Cement by Wet and Dry Processes

Year	Wet Process	Dry Process
1965	22.8	77.2
1970	15.0	85.0
1975	10.9	89.1
1978	8.3	91.7
1980	7.3	92.7

Source: Cámara Nacional del Cemento.

TABLE 7.29
Total and Specific Consumption of Fuel and Electricity in Cement Production, 1968-1981

Year	Production (thousands of tons) (1)	Total Consumption of Energy (10^{12} Kcal/year)		Specific Consumption of Energy (Kcal/kg)	
		Electricity (2)	Fuel (3)	Electricity (2)/(1)	Fuel (3)/(1)
1968	6.008	0.605	8.18	100.70	1,364.0
1969	6.674	0.663	8.95	99.34	1,342.0
1970	7.180	0.782	9.47	108.90	1,321.0
1971	7.362	0.790	9.57	107.30	1,300.0
1972	8.602	0.896	11.00	104.20	1,280.0
1973	9.789	1.027	12.32	104.90	1,259.0
1974	10.595	1.063	13.12	100.33	1,240.0
1975	11.612	1.170	14.16	100.76	1,220.0
1976	12.584	1.310	15.10	104.10	1,201.0
1977	13.227	1.470	15.03	111.40	1,182.0
1978	14.056	1.550	16.35	110.30	1,165.0
1979	15.178	1.690	17.36	111.35	1,144.0
1980	16.243	1.787	18.27	110.00	1,125.0
1981	17.971	2.000	19.82	111.30	1,103.0
AAGR[a]	8.79%	9.63%	7.04%	0.77%	1.62%

Sources: Instituto de Investigaciones Eléctricas,
Cámara Nacional del Cemento; and author's information.

a/ AAGR - Average annual growth rate.

TABLE 7.30
Specific Consumption of Energy by Process Type, Energy Source, and Stage (Kcal/ton of cement)

Process Type	Initial Stages	Drying, Milling, Homogenization	Calcination	Final Milling	Total
Wet					
Electricity	2,040	71,422	23,812	38,108	135,382
Gas and Bunker Oil	—	—	1,874,683	—	1,874,683
Other	13,310	—	—	—	13,310
Total	15,350	71,422	1,898,495	38,108	2,023,375
Dry					
Electricity	3,774	31,171	24,021	40,027	98,992
Gas and Bunker Oil	—	66,020	1,219,443	—	1,285,963
Other	4,586	—	—	—	4,586
Total	6,560	97,191	1,243,964	40,027	1,389,541
Preheater					
Electricity	3,774	31,171	23,482	40,027	98,404
Gas and Bunker Oil	—	66,020	901,178	—	967,198
Other	4,586	—	—	—	4,586
Total	6,560	97,191	924,660	40,027	1,070,238

Sources: Instituto de Investigaciones Eléctricas; author's information.

FIGURE 7.11
Energy Consumption in the Cement Industry by Process, 1977

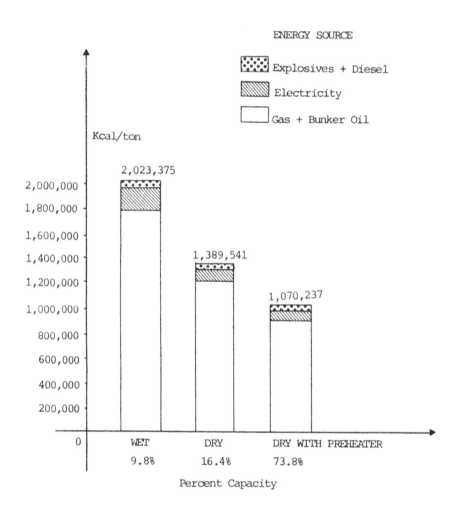

Sources: Instituto de Investigaciones Eléctricas,
authors' information.

TABLE 7.31

Specific Consumption for Pure Portland Cement and for Portland Cement with Extenders (international standards)

Cement Type	Minimum Value (Kcal/kg)	Average Value (Kcal/kg)	Maximum Value (Kcal/kg)
Clinker	890.0	950.0	2,200.0
Pure Portland Cement	800.0	870.0	1,500.0
Portland Cement with Extenders	650.0	750.0	1,200.0

Source: Gordian Associates, An Energy Conservation Target for Industry (New York, 1976), p.62.

TABLE 7.32
Total Consumption for Policy A and Lines of Reference

Year	Production (thousands of tons) (1)	Scenario A Total Consumption[a] (Kcal x 10^12) (2)	Scenario B Specific Consumption (Kcal/kg) (3)	Total Consumption (Kcal x 10^12) (4) (1) X (3)	Scenario C Specific Consumption (Kcal/kg) (5)	Total Consumption (Kcal x 10^12) (6) (1) X (5)
1982	19,552	21.56	1,085.4	21.22	767.50	15.00
1983	21,273	23.46	1,068.0	22.72	757.14	16.11
1984	23,145	25.53	1,050.0	24.30	746.91	17.29
1985	25,182	27.78	1,034.0	26.04	736.83	18.55
1986	27,398	30.22	1,017.0	27.86	726.88	19.91
1987	29,809	32.88	1,001.0	29.84	717.07	21.37
1988	32,432	35.77	985.3	31.95	707.39	22.94
1989	35,286	38.92	969.5	34.20	697.84	24.62
1990	38,391	42.35	954.0	36.62	688.42	26.43
1991	41,770	46.07	938.7	39.21	679.13	28.37
1992	45,445	50.13	923.7	41.98	669.95	30.44
1993	49,445	54.54	909.0	44.95	660.91	32.68
1994	53,795	59.34	894.4	48.11	651.99	35.07
1995	58,529	64.56	880.1	51.50	643.19	37.64
1996	63,680	70.24	866.0	55.15	634.50	40.40
1997	69,284	76.42	852.0	59.03	625.94	43.37
1998	75,381	83.15	838.0	63.17	617.49	46.54
1999	82,015	90.46	825.0	67.66	609.15	49.94
2000	89,232	98.42	812.0	72.46	600.93	53.62
Subtotal 1982-1990		278.47		254.75		182.21
Subtotal 1991-2000		693.33		543.22		398.09
Total 1982-2000		971.80		797.97		580.30
AAGR[b]	8.8%	8.8%	1.6%	7.1%	1.4%	7.3%

Source: Estimate of authors.

a/ Based on specific consumption for 1981: 1,103 Kcal/kg (see Table 7.29).
b/ AAGR - Average annual growth rate.

sumption.22/ In this section, we outline the major aspects
of the sugar industry's patterns of growth and energy consumption. The most general points cover the period from
1970 to 1983. It is during this period that the structural problems of energy consumption in the industry became acute. The period is characterized by increases in
consumption, heterogeneous energy use in sugarcane factories, and stagnant sugar production.

We describe the main stages of the production process,
and we deal with the patterns of consuming the major
sources of energy (bagasse and bunker oil), along with the
factors affecting these patterns. In a study of energy consumption during the various stages of the production process, we consider sugarcane factories producing regular
sugar, which account for 64% of the industry's total production. Finally, we arrive at a number of conclusions that
give us a general view of the sugar industry.

The sugar industry is the country's major agribusiness.
It comprises 69 factories distributed through 15 states, of
which Veracruz and Jalisco have 33% and 14%, respectively,
of the total.

There are fifty-one state-owned factories, sixteen are
privately owned, and two are cooperatives. There is an installed capacity for harvesting sugar of 4.5 X 10^6 tons,
with a daily milling capacity of 0.31 X 10^6 tons. For the
1981-1982 harvest, the agribusiness employed 284,725 persons directly in the field and factory, with consequent multiplying effects. In the same period, 469,175 hectares
were planted, of which 40.8% were irrigated and the rest
rain fed. The average production unit is 6 hectares in
area.23/

One of the industry's most important characteristics
is its seasonal nature: It operates an average of six
months a year. It is subject to agricultural production
conditions as well as to sugarcane supply, quality, and a-
vailability.

The industry has shown only slight improvements during
the last thirteen years in terms of yields and the amounts
produced. Production first grew at an average of only 2.1%
a year and has remained stationary since 1977 (see Table 7.33).

In contrast to the above, domestic sugar demand has
risen continuously, at an AAGR of 4.9% annually during these
thirteen years. This is due to increases in industrial, not
domestic, consumption. Industrial consumption grew at an
average rate of 8.3% a year, while the domestic consumption

remained stationary. The most marked increases in demand relative to internal supply have made it necessary to import increasing amounts of sugar. (see Figure 7.12).

The sugar industry is, furthermore, one of the oldest industries in the country, and the development of its installed capacity, structure, growth, and replacement of machinery and equipment has been heterogeneous. This is apparent in many sugarcane factories, where the machinery and equipment are old and obsolete. In other factories, however, they are relatively new and modern. Thus, it is not surprising to find a wide variety of energy consumption rates among the factories, a fact that complicates our analysis of these factories. Another important aspect of the industry is that the installed capacity for sugar production underwent a marked growth from 1978 to 1982 (an average of 8% annually). There were, however, no corresponding increases in either sugar or sugarcane production (see Table 7.33).

The major stages in the production of sugar are sugarcane preparation, juice extraction, clarification, evaporation, crystallization, centrifugation, and drying and packing.

In the factory grounds where raw materials enter, sugarcane is handled by cranes and, in some cases, by mechanical dumpers that unload the sugarcane onto conveyor belts to transport it into the plant for the preparation stage. The sugarcane is prepared by shredding it with a set of knives and crushing it with a set of hammers. In some sugarcane factories, washing the sugarcane has recently been introduced. The increasing mechanization of sugarcane gathering in the fields has meant that it reaches the factory with a high percentage of dirt, stones, and other elements that later impede milling.

The juice is extracted by squeezing the sugarcane stalks in a series of mills. During this stage, the mills are sprayed with water (imbilition) to improve juice extraction. During the process, bagasse (cane fiber) is produced as a by-product and is transported by conductor directly to the boilers to be used as fuel.

During the clarification process, as much as possible of the nonsugar compounds contained in the extracted juice is removed. To do this, the juice is limed and subjected to heat to produce the desired reaction. The clarified juice is then separated from the precipitate, or mud, and is sent on to the evaporation stage.

The clarified juice contains approximately 85% water.

The evaporation process eliminates two-thirds of this water with a system of multiple-effect evaporation in a vacuum, where a concentrated juice or syrup is obtained.

During crystallization, the syrup undergoes a process of concentration and saturation in order to form sugar crystals. This is done by mixing the syrup with sowing crystals in single-effect vacuum pans.

The centrifugation process consists of separating the crystallized sugar from the noncrystallized molasses by means of high-speed revolving cylinders equipped with metal mesh.

To produce the standard type of sugar, the depuration process is intensified, which increases the sugar's purity and decoloration. In the clarification stage, the extracted juice is treated with sulphites to produce greater decoloration. Later, at the centrifugation stage, the process is complemented by rinsing the product with condensation water to remove the molasses covering the crystallized sugar. Finally, the sugar is dried.

Refining is a process that improves the quality of the product: its purity, texture, color, and moisture content. The prime material is raw sugar, which undergoes further clarification. This stage includes a number of phases, the most important of which are melting, dissolving the raw sugar in condensation water, and chemically treating the raw sugar. In this last phase, the syrup is treated with sulphites and lime before being aerated, heated, and clarified. The syrup is then filtered and again decolored with industrial absorbents (activated charcoal) and filters. Finally, the syrup undergoes crystallization and centrifugation.

Drying the sugar is the final process. The sugar should have a certain moisture content to comply with commercial norms for packing.

Consumption Patterns and Efficient Energy Use

Energy input has had an AAGR of 3.8% from 1970-1983. In contrast, sugar milling and production rose at an average rate of 2.2% and 2.1%, respectively (see Tables 7.33 and 7.34).

Bagasse consumption, excluding sales to the paper industry, grew on the order of 1.9% annually, while bunker oil consumption rose at a rate of 9.6%. Consequently, the share of total energy consumption held by bagasse decreased from 83.1% in 1970 to 67.8% in 1983 (see Table 7.35).24/

Bunker oil has shown a significant increase as an energy source. The practice of exchanging bagasse for bunker oil by the paper industry has intensified and has kept bunker oil's share of total hydrocarbon consumption high, at 24% annually.

Specific consumption in sugar production has risen continuously at an annual rate of 1.6% for the past thirteen years, which can be explained by the increase in bunker oil use. The specific consumption of this energy source rose from 1,313 Kcal/kg of sugar in 1970 to 3,284 Kcal/kg of sugar in 1983. This means that inefficiency rose at an average annual rate of 7.7%. The specific consumption of bagasse has not varied significantly: It went from 6,476 Kcal/kg of sugar to 6,326 Kcal/kg (see Tables 7.33 and 7.34 and Figure 7.13). This proves that the same quantity of bagasse was available for energy consumption in 1983 and in 1970. Meanwhile, the bunker oil used increased significantly.

To find an explanation for the increase in bunker oil production, we analyzed factors that have an effect on energy consumption and, most definitely, on specific consumption. These are production capacity and how it is utilized; lost working hours and their fluctuations; and the amounts of sugar produced during the thirteen-year period. These factors, however, do not suffice to explain the dynamics of the bunker oil consumption observed.

A study of the characteristics of the sixty-six sugarcane factories did not disclose any relationship between specific consumption levels and their variations and installed production capacity, plant size, and plant utilization. In 1983 different levels of energy were required for each unit produced for plants of similar size, production volume, and degree of utilization (see Tables 7.36 and 7.37).

Changes in specific consumption by plant during the thirteen years examined bear no relation to the changes that took place in 1970, the first year of the study. For example, of twenty-six factories with relatively low specific consumptions in 1970, six continued to reduce consumption over the next thirteen years, four showed slight increases, and the rest showed marked increases. By way of contrast, of fourteen factories with high specific consumptions in 1970, three reduced their levels, two increased them slightly, and nine increased them considerably by 1983.

(see Table 7.38).

The inquiry into possible explanations of the increases in the specific consumption of bunker oil was extended to include the number of working days and lost working days and the use of bunker oil during the thirteen-year period. However, this examination bore no fruit because variations in the effective milling and lost working days do not correspond, either in time or number, with bunker oil consumption. It was observed, for example, that the notable increase in consumption between 1979 and 1981 coincided with a marked drop in the number of milling days and a constant number of lost working days (see Figure 7.14).

There is, then, no doubt that the reasons for the increase in the sugar industry's specific consumption of bunker oil lie beyond the scope of the technical considerations set forth here. What is evident from this discussion is the heterogeneity of the energy use in the industry's plants and the tendency to use a nonrenewable energy source less and less rationally.

Specific consumption levels recorded for sugar production in Mexico (around 10,000 Kcal/kg of sugar) are much higher than international levels (6,000 Kcal/kg. The difference stands out all the more if we consider that the technology and production processes are similar. The increasing inefficiency in using energy is confirmed by these figures: During the 1970 harvest, the Mexican sugar industry consumed 11.8 liters of bunker oil per metric ton of sugarcane (MTSC). For the 1983 harvest, the levels were 29.2 1/MTSC and 0.33 1/MTSC for Mexico and Cuba, respectively.25/

The consumption of steam in sugar production is governed by two basic factors: the productive efficiency of each stage of the process, in overall terms, and the efficiency in generating and using steam. It has been observed that the industry is presently operating with low yields in the different stages of the process, regardless of the quality or quantity of sugarcane processed. Overall yield is, consequently, also low. The ratio of sugar/ton of ground cane is 9.0%, with 75% utilization. These percentages contrast with those of the industry in Cuba, where overall yields are 12.5%, with 85% utilization. The low yields and utilization directly condition the energy balance because large amounts of energy are required for each unit produced.

As far as steam generation is concerned, boilers also show low levels of utilization, with an efficiency of close to 55% when burning bagasse. In other words, Mexico obtains 1.56 kg of steam per kg of bagasse, while the industry norm in other countries is 65%, with 2 kg of steam produced per kg of bagasse. To these low generating figures, we can add the additional consumption of bunker oil. It was 23.6 1/MTSC for the effective grinding during the 1982-1983 harvest.26/

Finally, the specific process consumption is 5,846 Kcal/kg of sugar.27/ As a point of comparison, the Cuban specific process consumption is between 3,500 and 4,500 Kcal/kg of sugar. Moreover, it can be reduced further to 2,050 Kcal/kg of sugar by evaporation with extraction for heating and boiling, which significantly lowers the demand for process steam.

In summary, energy consumption in Mexico's sugar industry can be characterized as follows:

1. Factors Influencing Consumption Patterns
   a. The low efficiency of the various stages of the production process causes considerable increases in the demand for energy.
   b. The disproportions in installed production capacity in different areas, caused by successive factory expansions, have created imbalances in both production and energy consumption levels.
   c. The industry is generally characterized by a high percentage of old or obsolete machinery and equipment, mainly in the area of mills, boilers, and power plants.
   d. The number of lost working days in the industry is high: one day of stoppage for every three days of operation. The amount of time lost is even worse if we consider the frequency of the stoppages.
   e. The industry considers bagasse as "free input." This fact, together with subsidized bunker oil prices, distorts the understanding of energy costs and means that little attention is given to waste.
2. Imbalances in Steam Generation and Demand
   a. Low boiler efficiency, which affects both the quantity and quality of steam, requires consuming bunker oil to improve the quality of combustion and to cover steam requirements.
   b. The limited use of exhaust steam from turbines means that live steam must be used to do low-pressure thermal work, with a resulting loss in energy.28/
   c. The frequency and level of overloading is considerable. This exerts pressure on the feeder lines and,

particularly, on the boilers, to the detriment of the
equipment and the preparation of sugar itself.
d. Maintenance and instrumentation of machinery and
equipment are poor because of the inadequate training
of personnel.

The practice of consuming as much bunker oil as necessary to assume a steady supply of steam, without regard for
cost, shows that bunker oil hides the inefficiency of the
process and allows enough slack for irrationality to be the
dominating factor.

Measures for Efficient Energy Use

The heterogeneous way in which the industry's plants
function impedes proposing concrete measures applicable to
all the factories. Energy waste is not merely a technical
question; it is the result of many problems, all characteristic of the industry and the state's interest in it. A
large number of workers, from sugarcane producers to factory workers, earn their livelihood from sugar production.
The internal supply of the product and good relations between workers and the state are matters of constant concern to the Mexican government.

To initiate a program of rational energy use in industry thus requires a rigorous process of planning and political cooperation among the various groups involved. It is
clear, moreover, that some initiatives will require considerable investment. The investment, however, would be
easy to recover, given the degree of waste and, therefore,
the potential savings. Finally, using sugarcane (a renewable resource) as a source of energy has been successful,
to varying degrees, in Brazil, Cuba, and Hawaii. There is
no reason why Mexico should not make efforts in this direction.

The possibility also exists of creating industries
parallel to, or integrated with, the sugar industry. These
would be based on sugarcane by-products, such as cellulose,
fuel alcohol, agglomerates, cogeneration, and so on. Such
an effort is closely related to solving the industry's energy problems. The state has the obligation to go about
paving the way for an integral exploitation of sugarcane,
particularly as a renewable energy source.

Potential Savings

The results we have presented clearly demonstrate the ample possibilities for industry to use energy more efficiently, either by producing more sugar with the same energy or by reducing energy consumption itself. The sucrose losses are evidence that more sugar could be produced with the same energy. Average losses are 25%, although there are some factories with losses fluctuating between 10% and 15%. It is thus possible to reduce specific consumption by the same proportion.

The possibility of savings through a reduction in energy consumption is more significant, however. Taking studies done by the Instituto Cubano de la Industria Azucarera (Cuban Sugar Industry Institute) as a point of reference, we can obtain savings varying between 20% and 50% in the use of process and low-pressure steam. On the supply side (boilers), studies done for the Mexican sugar industry itself show that 65% efficiency can be obtained, which is ten points higher than the present level. If we assume 46% moisture in bagasse, the increase in efficiency would mean a savings of 4.9 million barrels of bunker oil for each sugar harvest.

These two possibilities for using energy more efficiently would yield savings of 50.8% over present energy consumption. This means energy savings of 14.12×10^{12} Kcal, or 11.01 mboe (30.175 tbdoe). The amount of savings would be higher if lost working days, presently 30%, were reduced.

Based on these estimates of potential savings and on the historical rate of sugar production, we can present calculations of possible savings to be made by the years 1990 and 2000 (see Table 7.39). Two projections are given, both based on the historical dynamics of sugar production. Scenario A assumes that energy consumption will continue growing at the traditional rate of 3.8% annually.

Scenario B assumes that by the year 2000 the inefficiency of energy consumption will be reduced 60%, compared to the trend to date. In other words, scenario B supposes that the trend up till now will be reversed, going from a 1.7% AAGR (scenario A) to an average decrease of 3.8% annually for the remainder of the century.

If the goal in scenario B were achieved, energy savings would be on the order of 43.5×10^{12} Kcal from 1984 to 1990 and 219.0×10^{12} Kcal from 1991 to 2000. Cumulative savings would be 262.5×10^{12} Kcal for the sixteen-year period (see Table 7.39). This means a savings of 33.93 mboe

TABLE 7.33
Development of the Sugar Industry, 1970-1983

| Year | Field | | Number of Factories | Factory | | | | Overall Yield (tons of sugar/ hectare) | Consumption (thousands of tons) |
	Area Cultivated (thousands of hectares)	Yield (tons/hectare) (%)		Installed Capacity	Sugarcane Milled (thousands of tons)	Sugar Production (thousands of tons)	Yield (%)		
1970	413.6	60.9	63	3,356	24,524	2,208	8.9	5.4	1,841
1971	427.4	62.4	65	3,333	25,985	2,398	9.1	5.7	1,775
1972	426.9	63.4	65	3,303	26,254	2,359	8.9	5.7	1,910
1973	452.7	67.8	64	3,243	29,849	2,592	8.6	5.8	2,125
1974	456.4	68.2	65	3,334	30,492	2,649	8.6	5.8	2,173
1975	460.4	64.4	66	3,533	28,949	2,548	8.7	5.6	2,387
1976	446.2	62.7	64	3,432	27,237	2,547	9.3	5.8	2,473
1977	431.3	67.2	65	3,358	27,947	2,541	9.1	6.1	2,477
1978	461.1	72.7	66	3,317	32,348	2,849	8.8	6.4	2,717
1979	474.2	73.2	67	3,443	33,865	2,881	8.5	6.2	2,855
1980	488.7	65.5	68	3,655	31,343	2,603	8.3	5.4	2,921
1981	452.8	65.3	69	3,831	28,677	2,367	8.2	5.4	3,020
1982	469.2	69.9	69	4,535	31,769	2,677	8.4	5.9	3,226
1983	—	—	69	4,541	32,482	2,893	8.9	—	—
AAGR[a]	1.1%	1.2%		2.4%	2.2%	2.1%	0.0%	0.1%	4.9%

Source: Azúcar, S.A., Estadísticas azucareras (Mexico, 1983), p.28.

a/ AAGR - Average annual growth rate.

FIGURE 7.12
Installed Capacity, Production, and Consumption of Sugar, 1970–1983

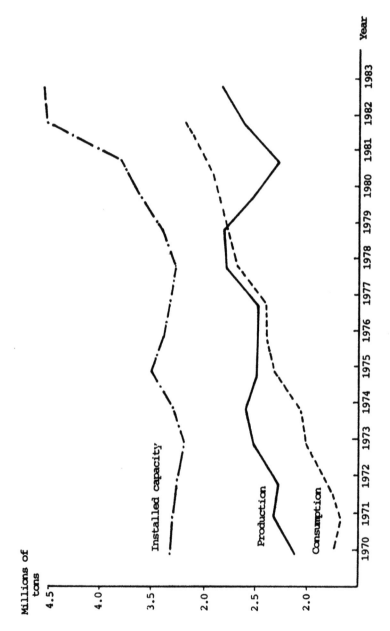

Source: Table 7.33.

TABLE 7.34
Energy Consumption (Kcal x 10^{12})

Year	Bagasse	Bunker Oil	Total	Specific Consumption (Kcal/kg sugar)
1970	14.3	2.9	17.2	7,818
1971	14.7	3.4	18.1	7,542
1972	14.3	4.0	18.3	7,625
1973	17.0	4.9	21.9	8,423
1974	17.2	4.9	22.1	8,500
1975	16.3	5.1	21.4	8,560
1976	15.5	5.4	20.4	8,160
1977	15.6	5.9	21.5	8,600
1978	18.0	7.4	25.4	9,071
1979	19.3	8.2	27.5	9,483
1980	18.3	8.7	27.0	10,385
1981	16.5	8.9	25.4	10,583
1982	17.9	9.3	27.2	10,074
1983	18.3	9.5	27.8	9,586
AAGR[a]	1.9%	9.6%	3.8%	1.6%

Source: Official reports on sugarcane factory operation for 1970–1983 and authors' information.

a/ AAGR - Average annual growth rate.

TABLE 7.35

Bagasse Production, Consumption, and Sales (thousands of tons, wet base)

Year	Production	Consumption	Sales	Equivalent in Bunker Oil (millions of liters)
1970	8,155	7,625	529	89.9
1971	8,426	7,848	578	98.3
1972	8,243	7,655	587	99.8
1973	9,797	9,105	692	117.6
1974	9,963	9,196	767	130.4
1975	9,371	8,721	650	110.5
1976	8,924	8,264	720	122.4
1977	9,194	8,326	868	147.6
1978	10,632	9,616	1,017	172.9
1979	11,507	10,319	1,188	202.0
1980	11,033	9,793	1,240	210.8
1981	10,098	8,829	1,268	215.6
1982	10,772	9,585	1,186	201.6
1983	11,167	9,777	1,390	236.3
AAGR[a]	2.4%	1.9%	7.7%	7.7%

Source: Official reports on sugarcane factory operation for 1970-1983.

a/ AAGR - Average annual growth rate.

FIGURE 7.13
Energy Consumption by kg of sugar, 1970–1983

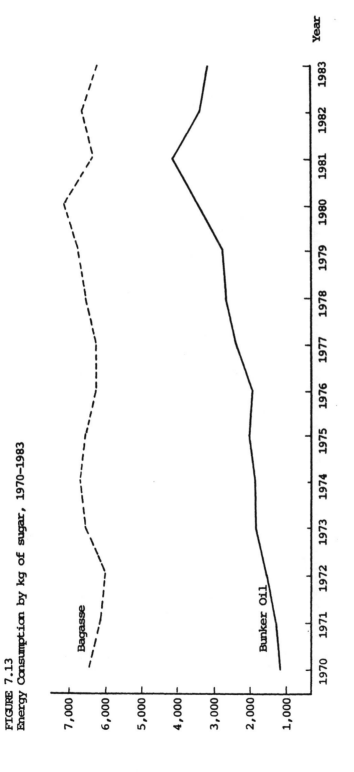

Source: Estimates of authors.

TABLE 7.36
Factory Distribution: Specific Consumption Relative to Plant Size and Production, 1983

Specific Consumption (strata)	Installed Capacity (thousands of tons, %)						Production (thousands of tons, %)					
	0	20	40	60	80	100	0	20	40	60	80	100
0 – 5.9	—	—	—	1	—	2	—	1	—	—	—	2
6.0 – 6.9	—	2	1	3	4	—	1	3	3	3	—	—
7.0 – 7.9	—	3	2	4	—	1	—	4	4	1	1	1
8.0 – 8.9	1	3	4	2	1	1	2	7	2	—	—	1
9.0 – 9.9	2	2	1	—	4	1	3	2	3	1	1	—
10.0 and Over	4	3	4	5	3	4	7	8	6	2	—	1
Number of Factories	7	13	12	15	12	9	13	25	18	7	2	4

Source: Authors' data.

TABLE 7.37

Factory Distribution: Specific Consumption Relative to Use of Installed Capacity, 1983

Specific Consumption (Strata)	Percent of use								Number of Factories
	30	40	50	60	70	80	90	100	
0 – 5.9	—	—	—	—	1	1	1	—	3
6.0 – 6.9	—	—	3	1	5	1	—	—	10
7.0 – 7.9	—	—	—	4	5	—	1	—	10
8.0 – 8.9	—	2	3	2	4	1	—	—	12
9.0 – 9.9	1	3	3	1	1	1	—	—	10
10.0 and over	3	5	2	8	4	—	1	—	23
Number of Factories	4	10	11	16	20	4	3		68

Source: Authors' data.

Note: Installed Capacity — 4,541,159 tons
Production — 2,892,716 tons
Use — 63.7%

TABLE 7.38
Rates of Growth of Specific Consumption by Factory, 1970–1983

Specific Consumption (margins)	Factories		Growth Rates					
	Number	%	Negative	0–0.99	1.0–1.99	2.0–2.99	3.0–3.99	4.0 and over
0 – 5.9	5	7.6	—	3	1	1	—	—
6.0 – 6.9	8	12.1	1	1	3	2	1	—
7.0 – 7.9	13	19.7	5	1	3	2	1	1
8.0 – 8.9	16	24.2	—	2	5	6	3	—
9.0 – 9.9	8	12.1	2	2	1	1	2	—
10.0 –10.9	2	3.0	1	—	—	—	1	—
11.0 –11.9	6	9.1	1	1	—	—	2	2
12.0 and over	8	12.1	2	1	2	1	2	—
Number of Factories	66		12	11	15	13	12	3
%		100.0	18.2	16.7	22.7	19.7	18.2	4.5

Source: Authors' data.

FIGURE 7.14
Working Days Lost and Energy Consumption Percent Variation (1970 = 100)

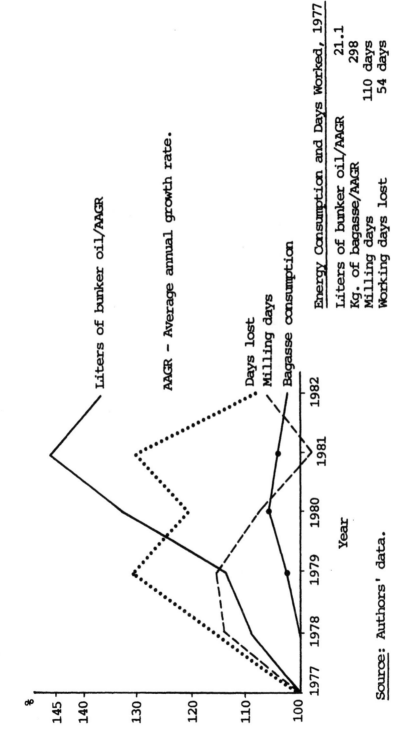

Source: Authors' data.

TABLE 7.39
Sugar Production Energy Consumption and Savings, 1983–1990–2000

Year	Production (thousands of tons)	Scenario A		Scenario B	
		Total Consumption (Kcal x 10^{12})	Specific Consumption (Kcal/kg of sugar)	Total Consumption (Kcal x 10^{12})	Specific Consumption (Kcal/kg of sugar)
1983	2,893	27.8	9,609	27.8	9,609
1990	3,346	36.1	10,789	24.7	7,382
2000	4,119	52.4	12,722	21.0	5,098
Subtotal 1990/1983		254.5		211.0	
Subtotal 2000/1991		445.7		226.7	
Total 2000/1983		700.2		437.7	
AAGR[a]	21.1%	3.8%	1.7%	-1.7%	-3.8%

Source: Authors' data.

a/ AAGR – Average annual growth rate.

(92.963 tbdce) from 1984 to 1990, 170.83 mbce (468.019 tbdce) from 1990 to 2000, and 204.76 mbce (560.981 tbdce) cumulatively. In monetary terms, cumulative savings would be approximately 5,600 million dollars, at the average price for Mexican export crude.

THE MINING-METALLURGY INDUSTRY

This industry includes the extraction and processing of ferrous (iron), nonferrous (lead, copper, coal, and zinc), and other minerals (basically sulphur compounds). Energy consumption for 1981 was 13.12, 5.2, and 0.74 Kcal X 10^{12}, respectively, for the three mineral types. In other words, the branch as a whole consumed as much energy as the cement industry: 19.08 X 10^{12} Kcal compared to 20.94 X 10^{12} Kcal (see Table 7.6). The lack of homogeneity between the companies studies by SEPAFIN precludes an analysis of specific consumptions.

Direct use of fuels was 57.9% of total consumption in the mining-metallurgy branch, and 23.5% of total consumption was used to generate steam. Self-generation of electricity by steam provided nearly 30% of the total electric power consumed (see Table 7.7). Among the fuels used in productive activities, natural gas covered half the demand and was complemented mainly by bunker oil (see Table 7.3).

In the ferrous and nonferrous mineral branches, consumption of fuels and electricity showed similar proportions. By way of contrast, consumption in sulphur extraction and processing is basically of fuel, the move being toward natural gas.

In the mining-metallurgy industry, the relationship of energy costs to sales is one of the highest of all industries, from 6% to 9% (see Table 7.6). Studies of the efficient use of energy should concentrate on the direct use of fuel and on the production of steam for use as a heat conductor. For this purpose, a breakdown of the different production processes is needed, along with a balance of the flow of energy and materials.

THE CHEMICAL INDUSTRY

The industries forming the chemical and fertilizer-producing group are relatively diverse in nature and produce a number of different products by varied processes.

This industry's energy consumption is most significant because it represents between 4% and 10% of sales and 8% of industrial consumption (see Table 7.6).

In terms of calories, 85% of the branch's consumption comes from fuel and the rest from electricity. Among the fuels used by the chemical industry, natural gas accounts for 56.6%, followed by bunker oil with 27.5% of total consumption (see Table 7.3). A large percentage of fuel is destined to produce steam for productive units and, to a lesser extent, to generate electricity. Nevertheless, self-generated electricity supplied nearly 40% of the total electricity consumed (see Table 7.7).

An examination of the specific consumptions in the chemical industry reveals a considerable degree of dispersion among them. For example, in the very same plant there were differences of 100% in the specific consumption obtained for the production of a single product. The following table illustrates this dispersion:

Product	Level (Kcal X 10^3 tons)
Sulphuric Acid	0 – 650
Hydrofluoric Acid	3,000 – 10,700
Ammonium Sulphate	75 – 420

It is necessary, therefore, to do a more detailed study that considers the types of products and processes in order to determine potential savings. However, given the dispersion of the consumptions, it is clear that a number of measures can be introduced to use energy more efficiently. In this respect, it should be noted that all types of heat recuperation, reaction, cogeneration, back-pressure turbines, and so on, can be implemented in the chemical industry. The high percentage of energy used in generating steam and in its various applications suggests that it would be worthwhile to examine, in detail, heat losses in the different processes, as well as the possibility of utilizing the residual heat from exhaust steam.

We should also mention one branch, in particular, of the chemical industry: resins and synthetic fibers. This branch consumed close to 5% of the total energy requirements, according to the SEPAFIN study, and 30% more than the glass-making sector. Energy was only 2.4% of its production (see Table 7.6). Some of the major characteristics of this branch's energy consumption were:

1. Seventy-five percent of the total fuel consumed was dedicated to generating steam.
2. Of this, 75% was supplied by bunker oil and 25% by natural gas.
3. Less than 20% of the energy consumed was electricity, and 25% of that was self-generated.

The study by types of products revealed that the branch's energy consumption is relatively homogeneous. Moreover, in certain companies, using energy efficiently has been an established practice for years. Such is the case with Celanese, which has had a program of this nature for more than twenty years. Resistol industries also have such a policy. If we compare Celanese consumption with that of Resistol, we find that the Resistol consumed 45% more energy to produce the same synthetic fiber. This is a marked difference because both plants are just as old, and Celanese has half the capacity of Resistol. Such disparities reveal the large potential savings within this branch.

THE CELLULOSE AND PAPER INDUSTRY

The cellulose and paper industry is relatively labor-intensive, and its energy bill was 3.6% of its production, low in comparison to other industries (see Table 7.6).29/ In terms of calories, energy bought consisted of 10% electricity and 90% fuels. Of the fuels, 47% was bunker oil and 42% natural gas, the two major sources of heat (see Table 7.3). Electricity, however, accounted for 30% of total consumption, given the amount supplied by self-generation. This industry generates the greatest percentage of its own electricity compared to what it consumes. However, it is still a long way from matching international levels of self-generation. Considerably higher levels of self-generated electric power could be reached in Mexico. Although there are some companies that generate all the electricity they consume, there are still others firms that buy 100% of their energy requirements.

In the manufacture of cellulose, the lowest specific consumptions, approximately 1000 Kcal/kg, are held by those plants working with used paper. At the other end of the scale is the manufacture of special types of cellulose, for which consumption is around 13,000 Kcal/kg.

The energy consumed in producing paper also varies according to type. Newsprint consumes the least energy, around 3,000 Kcal/kg. The production of Kraft paper, the most commonly produced, consumes between 2,700 and 4,700 Kcal/kg. The production of industrial grades of paper consumes in the range of 4,000 Kcal/kg to 9,000 Kcal/kg. The exception here is a two-year-old plant producing 80,000 tons a year and consuming 3,000 Kcal/kg.

It is clear, then, that there is ample room for energy savings in this industry, given the dispersion in consumptions, the potential for increasing cogeneration, and the importance of steam both for productive units and for electricity generation.

THE GLASS INDUSTRY

A large part of the market in this branch is dominated by a single company, Vitro, which is characterized by an intensive use of manpower. The energy consumption in this industry was 4.4% of total energy consumption in the SEPAFIN study. It was based mainly on the direct use of gas and only to a small extent on electricity. In this case, there was no self-generation of electricity, and the fuel burned to produce steam was marginal. The relationship of energy costs to sales was relatively low, scarcely 3.7%. This leads us to suppose that priority need not be given to improving this industry's energy use in production. (see Tables 7.3, 7.6, and 7.7).

THE FOOD AND DRINK INDUSTRY

The SEPAFIN study only covered the large companies operating in the food and drink industry. These companies were grouped according to product type: condensed and dehydrated foods, corn derivatives (starches and others), edible oils and fats, and beer and malt. Given the great variety of products among the first three groups, we restrict our analysis to the brewing industry. Its product is homogeneous and represents 60% of consumption in the establishments investigated.

Beer production is not labor-intensive, and its energy costs are less than 1% of sales. However, because of its relative size, this branch consumed considerable amounts of energy: 1.96×10^{12} Kcal. This figure is practically the same as the automobile industry's and represents more than 70% of the energy consumed by the manure and fertilizer branch of the chemical industry. It is also double the amount required to produce rubber and tires (see Tables 7.6).

The energy consumed in the brewing industry comes from electricity (25%) and fuel (75%). Eighty percent of the fuel is natural gas. Moreover, four-fifths of this fuel was used to generate steam.

Consumptions recorded in this branch were relatively homogeneous, amounting to about 800 Kcal/liter of beer. the variation ranges from 580 to 1,354 Kcal/liter. Because the companies on the extremes were isolated cases, it can be said that the industry's specific consumption varied within the range of 700 to 900 Kcal/liter.

Because energy has such a low value among the inputs in this industry, there is probably a large potential for saving energy. Moreover, because the industry is concentrated in a limited number of plants, it would be relatively easy to advise the breweries and to stimulate them toward more efficient consumption.

APPENDIX TO CHAPTER 7

SEPAFIN ENERGY STUDY

This survey was directed at the companies with the greatest energy consumption in the country and covered the following industries:

. Basic iron and steel
. Cement
. Mineral extraction and processing
. Chemicals
. Paper and cardboard
. Glass
. Manures and fertilizers
. Secondary petrochemical industry
. Beer and malt
. Other

It is estimated that the information used in the survey represented slightly less than 70% of the energy requirements for the industrial sector in 1981. Given the high concentration of energy consumption in the sector, it was only necessary to survey 289 establishments. Their energy consumption was about one-third of the country's end consumption of energy.1/

The information was gathered by means of a questionnaire, which was applied the months of August to October 1982 by trained survey personnel in 310 industrial establishments. The survey obtained a 93% response.

The questionnaire is divided into four chapters. The first identifies the establishment. In the second, overall data on sales and personnel are recorded. The third describes the plant, breaking it down into productive units. Finally, in the fourth chapter, energy consumption is analyzed by type of energy source, by productive units, by production processes and finished products. The energy consumption data is supplemented by information on the amount of primary energy used to produce steam and generate electricity, as well as the distribution of secondary energy within the plant.

Industrial cogeneration of electricity necessitated designing a questionnaire to record the amount and destination of extraction steam as well as fundamental data on turbogroup operations. The charts containing this information were integrated into the rest of the questionnaire only when the company being interviewed used cogeneration. This instructions for these questionnaires also included the relevant guidelines for filling out the charts. Both types of questionnaire and instructions were, therefore, prepared to distinguish those plants having cogeneration of electricity.

A basic problem in the design of the questionnaire was deciding on the appropriate degree of detail with which energy consumption should be recorded. The simplest solution would have been to consult the companies' energy expenditure records. In such records, companies list, in no more than twelve entries, the different items included in their purchases of energy and electricity. However, even though this procedure was quite practical, it dis not offer access to information on how the energy acquired was used, nor did it identify the products and processes to which the energy was applied. It would also have been impossible to glean relevant data from this source on whether secondary energy was generated within the company, either by producing steam or generating electricity.

A very complete and detailed survey would have included energy flows within the plant; energy consumption for each piece of machinery and equipment; thermal balances for transformation operations; and, in general, the problems and itineraries of the package of kilocalories that each industry receives, uses, transforms, and discards during its production activities. However, this course presented serious obstacles in the conception and size of the questionnaire; its completion; and, subsequently, in the processing of the information and the presentation of the results.

A middle course between the two extremes was chosen, using the concept of a productive unit. A productive unit is defined as any group of machinery or equipment used to manufacture a product or a variant of the same that can be sold directly by the plant. These same products can be consumed as raw materials by other units of the same plant to manufacture another product or products. If two or more productive units exist, making the same product and using the same process, each is considered separately. When two or more manufacturing processes are used for the same product, each of them is linked to one or more different productive units. Using the productive unit as a point of reference in the analysis of energy consumption made it possible to compromise between the two possible questionnaires.

The concept of the productive unit allows a breakdown of the plant into main groups and, based on these groups, an identification of energy use and transformation. In the questionnaire, energy flows can be followed very simply: In general terms, energy is bought or self-generated. This energy is used either directly by productive units or indirectly for generating steam and electricity. The questionnaire's structure allows one to follow up this secondary energy and evaluate how it is used within the plant. In short, the analysis of energy consumption provides a quantifiable all-inclusive sketch of the origins and destinations of energy.

NOTES TO APPENDIX

1. At the present time, the Energy Economics Board of the Subdirectorate for Planning and Coordination in PEMEX has, with support from the Instituto Mexicano del Petróleo (IMP), undertaken the job of continuing this initial effort by SEPAFIN. It did the survey on 1982 energy consumption in industry. It should be pointed out that the area consulted will now be extended to 700 establishments, and the questionnaire will be more ample.

NOTES TO CHAPTER

1. This can clearly be seen from the pertinent data in Table 7.2. Present policy again favors going back to consuming bunker oil instead of natural gas.

2. Table 7.5 shows bagasse consumption in the sugar industry, which was not included in the previous tables because it was not bought energy. If this energy source were included in the industry's consumption, the latter's share of overall industrial consumption would increase notably (Cf. Table 7.3).

3. The 1973 figure for the consumption of bought energy in the sugar industry, recorded in Table 7.4 (in which bunker oil is the major source of energy Table 7.6), differs from the figure obtained from the detailed study of the industry. According to information obtained directly, this consumption rose considerably from 1973 to 1981, at an annual rate of 7.7% (Cf. Table 7.34).

4. The survey is described in detail in the appendix to this chapter.

5. Table 7.6 contains the overall results of the survey. The different branches are subdivided, with more detail than previously. The chemical industry is divided into basic, resins and synthetic fiber, and manure and fertilizer, and the brewing and automobile branches are set apart from their primary industry.

6. These two branches account for 25% and 10%, respectively, of overall energy consumed in the industry (Cf. Tables 7.4 and 7.6).

7. The highest was recorded by the steel industry; the percentage was 10% in 1981.

8. To make a more detailed evaluation of the structure and share of energy in the industrial context, it is necessary to analyze other variables that form part of the production process. The most important variables are the work force and capital. However, such is beyond the objectives of this book. One such study, which should be updates because it only covers up to 1975, is Santiago Levy's 1982 study.

9. The relative share of self-generated electricity in total electricity consumed in the industry shows an upward bias. This is due to the fact that the sample's figure for the steel industry (3.09 to 5.0 Kcal X 10^{12}, Tables 7.3 and 7.7) is too high compared to figures obtained in the detailed branch study (0.33 Kcal X 10^{12}; Cf. "The Steel Industry" and Table 7.16).

10. Table 7.8 gives information on the importance of the industry and its recent development (1976-1980). It shows the production capacity of steel in tons per year for the five integrated plants and for the semi-integrated plants as a group.

11. In order to give a complete sketch of the main products of the steel industry, we present Table 7.10, which shows the production volumes for primary products (pig iron and steel), as well as for flat and tubular and nonflat products.

12. The study of the consumption of energy and materials in the various stages for manufacturing final steel products is presented in "Consumption of Energy and Materials in Steel Production" in this chapter.

13. The specific consumptions of electric energy in the main stages of steel making are given in Table 7.18. This information will later serve as a point of comparison with international patterns and to calculate the possibilities for using electric energy more efficiently in the industry.

14. Cf. appendix, this chapter.

15. Cf. the figures in the appendix.

16. Consumption figures for the scrap electric furnace process have been obtained directly because, unlike the other figures, these do not require a detailed study.

17. Some of this new technology is already in commercial use in other countries but has not been implemented in Mexico.

18. These figures are for consumption in the direct-reduction electric furnace process with continuous casting and assume 100% efficiency of electric power production (see Tables 7.22 and 7.23).

19. Cámara Nacional del Cemento.

20. The calculation is based on 1.282×10^6 Kcal/barrel.

21. This situation required doing a detailed study of the industry, by factory and by the flow of energy and materials. In this section, we present the main results to date. A monograph is being prepared that will include the details of this study, with 1983 data collected directly from the major factories.

22. Petróleos Mexicanos, Anuario Estadístico 1983 (Mexico, 1983) and internal data.

23. Azúcar S.A., Estadísticas azucareras (Mexico, 1983).

24. The fiber content in bagasse has not changed (it varies between 43% and 44%), nor has the moisture content

(between 50% and 52%). In other words, the available caloric power has not varied significantly.

25. Data were presented in the Second Latin American Meeting on the Regional Use of Energy in the Sugar Industry, Veracruz, Mexico, 1984.

26. Secretaría de Energía, Minas e Industria Paraestatal, "Encuesta sobre el consumo de energía en la industria azucarera: zafra 1982-1983," internal document (Mexico, 1983).

27. Specific consumption of energy input is 9,586 Kcal/kg of sugar (see Table 7.34).

28. Steam is generated at an average pressure of 17.5 kg/square centimeter, and, by expansion, it is used at 1.0 kg/square centimeter.

29. It should be pointed out that neither cogenerated electricity nor black liquor are included here. The latter represents 20% of consumption in the branch and is self-generated when producing cellulose.

8

Residential, Commercial, and Public Sector

Although the residential, commercial, and public sector (RCP) is not a major national consumer of energy in quantitative terms, it is, in fact, an important consumer of energy in qualitative terms because its basic requirements are electric power and liquefied gas. Since 1970 this sector's share of secondary energy end use has fluctuated between 13% and 16%, with a tendency toward the lower figure (see Table 8.1).

PATTERNS OF CONSUMPTION AND ENERGY USE

During the twelve-year period from 1970 to 1982, total energy consumption in the sector grew at an AAGR of 8.2% (see Table 8.1). There was notable growth in liquefied gas consumption. This is reflected in the 12.4% AAGR between 1970 and 1982 (the percentage of total national consumption went from 31.4% in 1970 to 49.3% in 1982) and a fourfold increase in consumption during the same period. Practically all liquefied gas consumed in the country is for domestic purposes.

The demand for electric power also grew notably, at an AAGR of 8.7%. It increased its share of total RCP consumption from 24.6% to 26.1% between 1970 and 1982. The electricity consumed in this sector accounted for, on the average, close to half of the domestic sales of this energy source. Kerosene and natural gas lost their position of importance in the consumption hierarchy. Annual demand grew at a rate of 1.7% for kerosene and 0.5% for natural gas, much lower than the consumption growth of the RCP as a whole.

Information on this sector's consumption is not sufficient to classify it according to type of energy and user. This limitation is especially apparent in the case of fuel derived from hydrocarbons. As for electricity, indirect estimates can be made of consumption rates for each and of the development of these rates.

ELECTRICITY

The best way to approach patterns of electric power consumption and their development, according to types of users, is through the tariffs fixed by CFE. The following summarizes the tariffs, relating energy consumers to the types of service given:

Tariff Number	Type of Service
1	Domestic
1A	Domestic in hot climates
2	General, up to 25W contracted
3	General, more than 25W contracted
4	Cornmeal mills
5	Public lighting
6	Pumping potable water and sewage
7	Rain-fed agricultural areas
8	General, high voltage
9	Irrigated agricultural areas
10	High voltage for resale
11	High voltage for mines
12	General, more than 5,000W contracted

CFE tariffs 1 and 1A are basically for domestic uses; so is, however, the tariff small merchants pay, given their low levels of consumption. Tarif 1A is for warm climates. Sales associated with these tariffs represent about 20% of the total sales of electricity for 1982 (see Tables 8.2 and 8.3).

Between 1962 and 1972, total sales grew at a slightly higher annual rate than between 1974 and 1982, 12.1% versus 10.8%, while specific consumption (KWh/consumer) grew twice as rapidly, 12% versus 4%.1/ This phenomenon indicates that in the 1960s demand expanded because of new users and later increased in intensity because of greater specific consumption.

Domestic consumption in warm climates was decisive in

extending the total demand for these tariffs during the second half of the 1960s. Hence, domestic consumption grew from being less than one-fourth of total demand in 1974 to close to one-half in 1982, although it included only slightly more than one-third of the users. The foregoing reflects not only the rapid expansion of the number of new clients in the network but also the sharp increase in specific consumptions (see Table 8.3). In fact, electric power consumption in warm climates (tariff 1A) was 72% higher than that of the rest of the country (tariff 1): 1,775 KWh/consumer as opposed to 1,034 KWh/consumer in 1982.

Tariffs 2 and 3 correspond to small businesses and some public services. The already difficult task of separating businesses from public services is complicated even more by the fact that the areas incorporated by tariffs 2 and 3 also include some small- and medium-sized industries. Tariff 8 (general, high-voltage service) includes large commercial firms as well as many large industries (see Tables 8.4 and 8.5).

With respect to tariff 2, the growth in demand over consumption was due as much to new users as to increased specific consumption between 1974 and 1982. The number of users rose at 4.3% annually, and sales grew an average of 7.4%. Demand for this tariff was 8% of total sales in 1982.

With respect to tariffs 3 and 8, the new users were the determining factor in the increase in demand. This is shown by the decrease in electric needs for each consumer from 1962 to 1982. The consumption levels associated with these tariffs accounted for 33% of electric power sales in 1982.

Part of the electric power demands of the public sector correspond to tariffs 5 and 6, which are for specific services. Their development is shown in Tables 8.6 and 8.7.

After decreasing during the 1960s, specific consumption levels tended to stabilize. This indicates that the demand grew because of the expansion of the activity, as shown by the increase in the number of users. Consumption at these tariffs was 6.9% of electric power sales in 1982.

It is important to point out that the average real price of a kilowatt hour sold by the CFE has shown a marked decline during the period studied: In 1962 it was 25.08 centavos, in 1970 it dropped to 19.39 centavos, and in 1980 it dropped to 12.45 centavos. These calculations take 1962 prices as a base.2/

This decline could be one of the factors that partially explain the increases in the specific consumption of the

domestic subsector. In fact, the real price of tariff 1
was twice as high in 1962 as in 1980.3/

The same cannot be said of the other two subsectors.
The decrease in their specific consumptions has occurred at
the same rate as the decline in the real prices of the tariffs. One should remember, however, that the way in which
a tariff is grouped, as well as the implicit overlaps, impede the separation of industrial from commercial and public consumption.

RESIDENTIAL SUBSECTOR

The few detailed studies existing on this subsector
and the limited information available make it necessary to
specify some methodological aspects in order to probe
deeper into the analysis of residential energy uses. It is
important to obtain specific information about housing and
energy-consuming appliances.

From an energy standpoint, it would be useful to have
information on the number of square meters of housing space
and the number of inhabitants in these areas, as well as
the characteristics of the building materials. The data
should be classified by state and by income strata, so as
to be a study of the country as a whole. Appliance data
should include information on income strata. Precise records should be obtained of the type of appliance, the
amount of energy available for each user, specific energy
consumption, how much energy is used as well as pertinent
technical characteristics.

CONSUMPTION PATTERNS AND EFFICIENT ENERGY USE

There are practically no studies on housing, and up-to-
date information on housing in Mexico is not available.
Analysis of consumer appliances is limited for these same
reasons. Nevertheless, we can make certain observations.

The main energy-consuming appliances found in Mexican
households include the following:

. Gas stove
. Gas water heater
. Electric refrigerator
. Black-and-white television set
. Color television set

. Iron
. Washing machine
. Electric water pump
. Electric heater
. Air conditioner
. Fan
. Other (blender, vacuum cleaner, dryer, and so on)

The limited information available on the energy consumed by domestic appliances is an impediment when trying to study the two main commercial energy sources used: liquefied gas and electricity. However, domestic sales of the main appliances can be used as an indirect reference point from which to judge appliance use. Sales grew at an annual rate of 9.9% between 1970 and 1980, totaling 5.5 million units by 1980. Major appliances (stoves, refrigerators, washing machines) accounted for 40% of sales in 1980, while the remaining 60% (3.3 million units) covered minor appliances (irons, small washing machines, fans, and vacuum cleaners). During the 1970s, both appliance groups grew at a similar rate: 10.2% annually for major appliances and 9.8% for minor appliances (see Table 8.8).

The increase in sales meant more appliances were available for each household in 1980. Refrigerators went from 2.4 units for each 100 families in 1970 to 4.6 in 1980, washing machines from 2.0 to 3.8, and stoves from 4.9 to 6.0. In 1982 an estimated 6 million refrigerators were operating in the country, with a specific consumption of 700 KWh per unit. From this data, one can infer that refrigerators consumed 4,200 GWh that year, that is, 33.5% of tariffs 1 and 1A.

Completing the category of domestic appliances, consumer electronics included black-and white and color television sets and audio equipment (consoles, radios, record players, modular sets, table radios as well as portable and car radios). Consumer electronics production had an AAGR of 3.6% between 1970 and 1977. However, from 1978 to 1980, the rate was 19.8% annually, with 2.9 million units manufactured (see Table 8.9).

The percentage of television sets has risen from 27.7% in 1970 to 34.9% in 1980. As a consequence, the number of sets to a family rose rapidly, from more than 0.16 in 1965 to 0.40 in 1975 to 0.58 in 1980. The figures were above average for Latin America but only a little more than half that of Western Europe in 1980 (see Table 8.10).

We can make a series of assumptions about the number of units in service and their specific consumption.4/ It is

estimated that television sets used 1,090 GWh of electricity in 1980, that is, close to 10% of the sales for
tariffs 1 and 1A that year.

Lighting is another aspect that plays an important
role in residential electric power demand. The prevailing
system uses incandescent lamps, which are not very efficient compared to other types of lamps. Their efficiency
is estimated to be almost four times less than fluorescent
lamps and as much as eight times less than low-pressure ra-
dium lamps (see Table 8.11).

MEASURES FOR EFFICIENT ENERGY USE AND POTENTIAL ENERGY SAVINGS

Because of the unavailability of data, we can only attempt an evaluation of the energy savings possible for refrigerators and television sets. In this study of potential energy savings, we take into account the way these
products are used in the country as well as future technological developments.

Refrigerators have always consumed a large amount of
electricity. However, since the 1970s, the technical innovations incorporated into their production in industrialized countries have led to a reduction in their specific
consumption of energy. This is clear in the case of Japan,
where, in spite of using increasingly larger refrigerators
(from 110 liters in 1970 to 233 liters in 1982), electric
power consumption decreased from 42 KWh per month to 24 KWh
per month (see Table 8.12). The same tendency can be observed in Europe and the United States. The more efficient
models have design changes and better components, such as:

. Fiberglass insulation rather than polyurethane foam
. Thicker insulation
. Better door seals
. More efficient compressors and motors
. Longer heat-exchange coils
. Evaporator fan motors placed away from the cold area

Modifications leading to a more efficient use of energy in refrigerators would have a significant impact on residential energy consumption. In fact, as mentioned
earlier, electric power consumption for refrigerators could
be close to 33% of the sales (tariffs 1 and 1A) in the sector by 1984.

If one considers that there will be another fifteen million units by the year 2000 (totaling twenty-one million units in operation) with no change in their specific consumption, some 14,700 GWh will be required just for refrigerators, that is, 10,500 GWh per year more than in 1982. If refrigerator power demands were met by electricity generated from hydrocarbons until the year 2000 and if we assume an efficiency of 33% in thermoelectric plants, 85 tbdce would be consumed.

However, if the average specific consumption of refrigerators could be reduced, there would be important energy savings. If an average specific consumption of 400 KWh per year were achieved by the year 2000 (a feasible level), savings would be considerable. Instead of 14,700 GWh per year, only 8,400 GWh per year would be required, a savings of 6,300 GWh per year. This would mean 35 tbdce would no longer be burned, approximately one million dollars a day by the year 2000 just for fuel alone.

Although information is fragmentary, we can make similar calculations of energy savings for television sets. Assuming that by the year 2000 the number of television sets to a family will be the same as the number in Western Europe in 1980 (1.04 sets per family) and that the population will be 100 million, with 5.5 individuals to a family, we can calculate that there will be close to 19 million units in service. If, moreover, one assumes that the percentage of black-and-white sets to color sets will be 60% to 40%, one can estimate how much energy can be saved by using energy-efficient units, as is currently the trend in industrialized countries. Using the percentages of 60% to 40% and assuming the new, more efficient sets will be present in all homes, we can calculate a savings on the order of 2,743 GWh per year, that is, 15.3 tbdce.5/ This would be the equivalent of close to 153 million dollars a year by 2000. If our hypothesis is less optimistic and we calculate that only one-half of the sets would include such improvements, potential savings would also be reduced by half.

Our observations on refrigerators and television sets depend on modifications in the units. One could also add, if necessary, the average viewing time for the television sets, which would depend on the length of the broadcasting day.

The gradual substitution of incandescent lighting with more energy-efficient systems can be analyzed in detail and implemented as part of a policy on energy savings and conservation. This modification of the lighting system should be complemented by campaigns to change user habits. Users put unnecessary pressure on electric power demand and thus on the installed capacity, as well as on the CFE's finances and, in the final analysis, on the country's balance of payments.

Future energy consumption in the residential sector cannot be calculated with any degree of accuracy using current information on consumption. The same is true for the commercial and public sectors. Extrapolating trends of the last ten or twenty years to determine future numbers of users and specific consumption gives unsatisfactory results for an energy consumption analysis (see Table 8.13). If this trend were to continue, however, there would be 3 million new consumers by the year 2000, compared to the present 600,000. The effective physical impact of this number seems difficult to grasp. At the same time, specific consumption throughout the country will exceed 2,000 GWh per user. A consumption of this magnitude exceeds the present-day requirements of the regions with a warm climate. It also goes against efforts to decrease the specific consumptions of appliances and achieve more efficient use of energy.

Vast sectors of the population in Mexico currently have no access to electricity. Their gradual inclusion as consumers will lead to increased future consumption. This trend will be difficult to reverse because it means opposing the need to improve the living conditions of the socially and economically marginated sectors. However, this does not mean the idea that well-being is inextricably linked to the wasting of resources, in particular, energy sources, should not be modified. The timely provision of electricity for the entire population is possible and desirable. The efficient use of energy should be promoted. This will regulate the growth of demand and, therefore, reduce pressure on the country's energy and financial resources, liberating them for other uses.

COMMERCIAL AND PUBLIC SUBSECTORS

The commercial and public subsectors are less important than the residential subsector. These subsectors merit a treatment similar to the one suggested for the residential subsector, but again there is the problem of insufficient information.

In regard to the energy consumption in the commercial

and public subsectors, an initial listing of their component parts indicates that it is worth classifying the different types of buildings and, later, considering the nature of the energy-consuming equipment.

The most important types of buildings are:

. Shopping centers (supermarkets)
. Offices
. Warehouses and storerooms
. Schools
. Hospitals
. Public buildings
. Hotels
. Churches
. Theaters and cinemas
. Other

The energy consumed in these structures is primarily for
air conditioning, hot water heating, and lighting. An overall study of both areas would require finding out which
electric power tariffs correspond to which building types.
This is a research project in and of itself and, therefore,
is beyond the scope of the present study.

NOTES

1. The separation of the two periods is due to the
creation of tariff 1A in 1973.
2. Comisión Federal de Electricidad, "Evolución de las
tarifas de energía eléctrica en México 1962-1980," (Mexico,
June 1981), pp. 9-10.
3. Ibid., pp. 19-20.
4. Seven million units were assumed to be operating in
1980, 60% black and white and 40% color. They were attributed a specific consumption of 66.1 KWh/year and 300 KWh/
year, respectively.
5. In the case of color and black-and-white television
sets, a specific consumption of 311.7 KWh/year and 66.1
KWh/year per unit, respectively, was assumed for the first
generation and 80.1 KWh/year and 52.5 KWh/year per unit,
respectively, for the second generation. Cf. Institute of
Energy Economics, National Living Standards and Energy Demand (Tokyo, 1980).

TABLE 8.1
Residential, Commercial, and Public Sector Share of Secondary Energy, 1970-1982 (Kcal x 10^{12})

Year	Liquefied Gas	Gasoline	Kerosene	Diesel	Combustóleo	Natural Gas	Electricity	Total	Participation in the final consumption
1970	11.709	—	13.076	—	—	3.35	9.193	37.328	15.2
	31.4		35.0			9.0	24.6	100	
1975	20.615	—	14.604	—	0.049	4.027	14.274	53.569	17.5
1976	22.229	—	16.121	—	0.068	4.461	15.249	58.128	16.4
1977	22.166	—	14.998	—	0.046	4.734	15.748	57.692	15.9
1978	27.341	—	15.390	0.368	0.128	5.271	18.000	66.498	13.4
1979	31.294	—	15.893	—	0.049	4.161	19.519	70.916	12.4
1980	36.469	—	16.532	0.463	0.056	4.938	20.967	79.425	15.1
1981	40.840	—	16.664	4.029	0.056	4.669	22.958	89.216	13.7
	49.3		16.6	4.0	0.1	3.7	26.1		
1982	47.426	—	15.975	3.919	0.141	3.579	25.120	96.160	13.5
TMCA[a]	12.4%	—	1.7%	—	—	0.5%	8.7%	8.2%	—

Source: Secretaría de Energía, Minas e Industria Paraestatal, Balances de energía 1975-1981 (México,1982), p.118.

a/ TMCA - Average Annual Increase Rate.

TABLE 8.2
Number of Users and Sales (GWh) for the Residential Subsector, 1962-1982

Year	Tariff 1		Tariff 1A		Total	
	Thousands of Users	Sales	Thousands of Users	Sales	Thousands of Users	Sales
1962	1,978	1,419	--	--	1,978	1,419
1963	2,218	1,579	--	--	2,218	1,579
1964	2,458	1,816	--	--	2,458	1,816
1965	2,666	1,971	--	--	2,666	1,971
1966	2,886	2,256	--	--	2,886	2,256
1967	3,120	2,548	--	--	3,120	2,548
1968	3,412	2,804	--	--	3,412	2,804
1969	3,892	3,152	--	--	3,892	3,152
1970	4,409	3,582	--	--	4,409	3,582
1971	4,769	3,980	--	--	4,769	3,980
1972	5,110	4,442	--	--	5,110	4,442
1973	5,453	4,943	--	--	5,453	4,943
1974	4,845	4,202	999	1,307	5,844	5,509
1975	5,031	4,272	1,224	1,784	6,255	6,056
1976	4,704	4,177	1,914	2,529	6,618	6,706
1977	4,562	4,174	2,416	3,188	6,978	7,362
1978	4,796	4,531	2,595	3,738	7,391	8,269
1979	5,068	4,896	2,779	4,314	7,847	9,210
1980	5,409	5,214	2,992	4,824	8,401	10,038
1981	5,760	5,744	3,243	5,467	9,003	11,211
1982	6,139	6,348	3,472	6,163	9,611	12,511
AAGR[a]						
1962-1972	10.0%	12.1%	--	--	10.0%	12.1%
1974-1982	3.0%	5.3%	16.8%	21.4%	6.4%	10.8%

Source: Comisión Federal de Electricidad, Sector eléctrico nacional: Estadísticas 1962-1982 (Mexico, 1982).

a/ AAGR - Average annual growth rate.

TABLE 8.3
Development of Specific Consumption per Consumer for Tariffs 1, 1A, and Total, 1962-1982 (KWh/consumer)

Year	Tariff 1	Tariff 1A	Total
1962	--	—	717.4
1963	--	—	711.9
1964	--	—	738.8
1965	--	—	739.3
1966	--	—	781.7
1967	--	—	816.7
1968	--	—	821.8
1969	--	—	809.9
1970	--	—	812.4
1971	--	—	834.6
1972	--	—	869.3
1973	--	—	906.5
1974	867.3	1,308.3	942.7
1975	849.1	1,457.5	968.2
1976	888.0	1,321.3	1,013.3
1977	915.6	1,319.5	1,055.0
1978	944.7	1,440.5	1,118.8
1979	966.1	1,552.4	1,173.7
1980	963.9	1,612.3	1,194.9
1981	997.3	1,685.8	1,245.3
1982	1,034.0	1,775.1	1,301.7
AAGR[a]			
1962-1972	--	--	1.9%
1974-1982	2.2%	3.9%	4.1%

Source: Comisión Federal de Electricidad, Sector eléctrico nacional: Estadísticas 1962-1982 (Mexico, 1982), p. 34.

a/ AAGR - Average annual growth rate.

TABLE 8.4
Number of Users and Sales of Electricity (GWh) to Commerce and Industry

Year	Tariff 2 Thousands of Users	Tariff 2 Sales	Tariff 3 Thousands of Users	Tariff 3 Sales	Tariff 8 Users	Tariff 8 Sales
1962	---	---	---	---	5,975	3,315
1963	---	---	---	---	6,636	3,643
1964	---	---	---	---	7,088	4,142
1965	---	---	---	---	7,802	4,630
1966	---	---	---	---	8,506	5,202
1967	---	---	---	---	9,346	5,875
1968	---	---	---	---	10,424	6,679
1969	---	---	---	---	11,183	7,834
1970	---	---	---	---	12,362	8,212
1971	---	---	---	---	13,785	8,676
1972	---	---	---	---	14,574	9,428
1973	---	---	---	---	16,189	10,423
1974	906	2,754	10	1.147	17,941	11,957
1975	938	2,876	11	1.167	19,589	12,635
1976	964	3,047	11	1.187	21,629	13,012
1977	1,002	3,273	11	1.189	23,100	13,231
1978	1,952	3,584	11	1.235	25,004	14,540
1979	1,107	3,877	12	1.325	27,666	15,692
1980	1,159	4,201	13	1.429	31,082	16,489
1981	1,215	4,550	14	1.512	34,000	18,094
1982	1,264	4,861		1.581	37,000	18,692
AAGR[a] 1962-1972	---	---	---	---	9.3%	11.0%
1974-1982	4.3%	7.4%	4.3%	4.1%	9.5%	5.7%

Source: Comisión Federal de Electricidad, Sector eléctrico nacional: Estadísticas 1962-1982 (Mexico, 1982), p. 57.

[a] AAGR = Average annual growth rate.

TABLE 8.5
Development of Specific Consumption for Tariffs 2, 3, and 8

Year	Tariff 2	Tariff 3	Tariff 8
1962	--	--	554,811.7
1963	--	--	548,975.3
1964	--	--	584,367.9
1965	--	--	593,437.6
1966	--	--	611,568.3
1967	--	--	628,611.2
1968	--	--	640,732.9
1969	--	--	700,527.6
1970	--	--	664,293.8
1971	--	--	629,379.8
1972	--	--	646,905.4
1973	--	--	643,832.2
1974	3,039.7	114,700.0	666,462.3
1975	3,066.1	106,090.9	645,004.8
1976	3,160.8	107,909.1	601,599.7
1977	3,266.5	108,090.9	572,770.6
1978	3,406.8	112,272.7	581,506.9
1979	3,502.3	120,454.5	567,194.4
1980	3,624.7	119,083.3	530,499.9
1981	3,744.9	116,307.7	532,176.5
1982	3,845.7	112,928.6	505,189.2
AAGR[a]			
1962-1972	--	--	1.5%
1974-1982	3.0%	-0.2%	-3.4%

Source: Comisión Federal de Electricidad, Sector eléctrico nacional: Estadísticas 1962-1982 (Mexico, 1982), p.37.

a/ AAGR - Average annual growth rate.

TABLE 8.6
Development of Users and Their Consumption for Tariffs 5 and 6,
1962-1982 (in thousands)

Year	Tariff 5		Tariff 6	
	Users	Sales (GWh)	Users	Sales (GWh)
1962	3,236	274	1,265	391
1963	4,070	303	1,549	405
1964	4,909	360	1,854	495
1965	5,614	436	2,052	514
1966	6,199	509	2,324	543
1967	7,064	558	2,786	590
1968	8,606	624	3,284	651
1969	9,795	685	3,811	738
1970	11,102	746	4,416	826
1971	12,768	822	5,052	938
1972	14,262	911	5,667	1,012
1973	15,381	1,047	6,478	1,085
1974	17,038	1,236	7,428	1,198
1975	18,110	1,240	8,259	1,349
1976	19,342	1,302	9,206	1,561
1977	19,017	1,460	9,839	1,667
1978	20,439	1,527	10,331	1,737
1979	21,723	1,537	11,069	1,808
1980	23,570	1,666	11,719	1,939
1981	25,573	1,854	12,399	2,049
1982	27,747	1,947	13,118	2,243
AAGR[a]				
1962-1972	16.0%	12.8%	16.2%	10.0%
1974-1982	6.3%	5.8%	7.4%	3.2%

Source: Comisión Federal de Electricidad, Sector eléctrico nacional:
Estadísticas 1962-1982 (Mexico, 1982), p.119.

a/ AAGR - Average annual growth rate.

TABLE 8.7
Development of Specific Consumption for Tariffs 5 and 6 (KWh/consumer)

Year	Tariff 5	Tariff 6
1962	84,935	309,091
1963	74,447	261,459
1964	73,335	266,990
1965	77,663	250,487
1966	88,110	233,649
1967	78,992	211,773
1968	72,507	198,234
1969	69,934	193,650
1970	67,195	187,047
1971	64,380	185,669
1972	63,867	178,578
1973	68,071	167,490
1974	72,544	161,282
1975	68,470	163,337
1976	67,315	169,563
1977	76,773	169,428
1978	74,710	168,135
1979	70,754	163,339
1980	70,683	165,458
1981	72,498	165,255
1982	70,170	170,986
AAGR		
1962-1972	-2.9%	-5.2%
1974-1982	-0.4%	0.7%
1962-1982	-0.1%	-3.0%

Source: Comisión Federal de Electricidad, Sector eléctrico nacional: Estadísticas 1962-1982 (Mexico, 1982), p.117.

TABLE 8.8
Consumption of Main Household Appliances (in thousands of units)

Product	Year			AAGR (%) [a]
	1970	1975	1980	1970-1980
Refrigerators	210	418	594	11.0
Stoves	429	570	852	7.1
Washing Machines	195	322	510	10.1
Blenders	300	516	1,026	13.0
Irons	700	1,260	1,536	7.6
Fans	145	285	487	12.9
Vacuum Cleaners	50	63	120	9.1

Source: Secretaría de Programación y Presupuesto.

a/ AAGR - Average annual growth rate.

TABLE 8.9

Development of Consumer Electronic Industry: Audio and Television (in thousands of units)

Product	Year		
	1970	1975	1980
Audio Equipment			
Consoles and Radios	158	225	229
Record Players	64	54	26
Juke Boxes	3	3	5
Modular Sets	—	64	259
Table and Portable Radios	675	616	1,016
Car Radios	142	234	334
Subtotal	1,042	1,196	1,869
Television Sets			
Black and White	349	504	826
Color	50	65	175
Subtotal	399	569	1,001
Total	1,441	1,765	2,870

Source: Cámara Nacional de la Industria Electrónica y Comunicaciones Selectivas.

TABLE 8.10
International Development of Number of Television Sets per Family

Area	Year		
	1965	1975	1980
World	0.23	0.41	0.51
United States	1.13	1.48	1.82
Western Europe	0.50	0.83	1.04
Japan	0.74	1.40	1.71
Latin America a/	0.15	0.35	0.52
Mexico	0.16	0.41	0.58

Source: Cámara Nacional de la Industria Electrónica y
Comunicaciones Selectivas.

a/ Mexico included.

TABLE 8.11
Efficiency of Different Electric Lamps

Type	Efficiency[a]
Low-Pressure Sodium	180
High-Pressure Sodium	130
Metal Halide	100
Fluorescent	80
Mercury Vapor	56
Incandescent	23

Source: Comisión Federal de Electricidad.

a/ Metal halide lamps were taken as a base.

TABLE 8.12
Development of Refrigerator Efficiency, 1970-1982

Year	Volume (liter)	KWh/ Month	KWh/ Month-Liter
1970	110	42	0.382
1971	131	54	0.412
1972	152	57	0.375
1973	170	57	0.375
1974	170	56	0.329
1975	170	53	0.312
1976	170	53	0.312
1977	200	46	0.230
1978	200	44	0.220
1979	233	44	0.189
1980	233	36	0.155
1981	233	28	0.120
1982	233	24	0.102

Source: Institute of Energy Economics, National Living Standards and Energy Demand (Tokyo, 1980), p.116.

TABLE 8.13
Development of Users and Their Consumption for Tariffs 1 and 1A
by 1990 and 2000

Year	Users (thousands)	Consumption (GWh)	Specific Consumption (GWh/users)
1983	10,401	13,949	1,341
1984	11,255	15,553	1,381
1985	12,181	17,342	1,423
1990	18,081	29,887	1,652
1995	26,838	51,506	1,919
2000	39,837	88,764	2,228

Source: Estimates of authors.

9

Rural Sector

Analysis of potential conservation and energy savings in the rural sector must begin with an identification of this sector's current national energy consumption pattern. This pattern, based on agricultural, livestock, and domestic activities and their evolution, is closely linked to Mexico's economic development model for rural areas. This energy consumption pattern can be understood only through a study of the relationship between these activities and the economic model.

Some of the most relevant characteristics of the country's overall rural development that directly or indirectly determine and direct energy consumption in the sector had their origins in the socioeconomic development that the country has undergone since the 1940s. This socioeconomic development favors industrialization. This has meant that agriculture and the rural sector, in general, have maintained a share in the GDP and the economically active population (EAP) similar to that observed in industrialized countries. However, the specific internal characteristics of the rural sector, as well the sector's relationship with the economy as a whole, show grave structural deficiencies, which are further complicated by the current economic crisis.

Although Mexico has managed to come very close to the international average for irrigated and rain-fed land under cultivation in the last few decades (15.5% irrigated and 80.2% rain fed), there are marked productive and social differences between the two land types that grow larger as time goes by. Over the last fifteen years, a pattern of gradual change in crop composition has set in: There is a tendency to substitute export crops and cattle feed for basic grain crops. Thus, since the 1970s, the drop in the production of basic grains, together with the growth in population, has meant the country is no longer self-sufficient in foodstuffs and has become a net importer of food.

Some 70% to 80% of rural producers are located in rain-fed areas, concentrated mainly in southern and central Mexico. These producers have little or no capital and use inefficient techniques for approximately 80% of their productive activities. However, they support a high percentage of the country's population. At the other end of the spectrum, a small fraction of the productive units that we classified as businesses have agricultural, livestock, and capital input; are situated predominantly in irrigated areas; and control commercial farm export products as well as the most profitable products on the domestic market.

Poverty, although it exists in irrigated areas, is more apparent in most rain-fed areas, as far as levels of nutrition, health, clothing, and education are concerned. These problems are aggravated by the fact that the population is highly dispersed in small rural communities.

The heterogeneity of the country's agricultural and agrarian structure explains some of the characteristics and basic problems in the sector's energy consumption. Until now, this situation has, to a good measure, determined trends in development. Intensive use of commercial (nonrenewable) energy sources in irrigated areas,1/ the increasing use of rain-fed and irrigated areas for pastureland, to the detriment of the forests, and, finally, the gradual change in crop composition, oriented toward animal feed, have led the country to use solar energy less than efficiently in the production of foodstuffs.

Two negative synergisms can be used, therefore, in a general diagnosis. First, rural resources (land and forests) have been voraciously decimated, in spite of their renewable nature. Second, the drop in the production of basic foodstuffs has been resolved by importing what is lacking and by exporting hydrocarbons, which implies additional pressures on the remaining reserves. In 1983 close to 1,500 million dollars in agricultural products were imported. This is equivalent to exporting approximately 150 million barrels of oil daily, or 80% of the 1980 domestic energy consumption in the rural areas. Achieving self-sufficiency in food and renewing and using rural resources efficiently are undoubtedly of utmost priority, not only for an overall development policy but also for a specific policy leading to the conservation and rational use of the country's nonrenewable resources.

One of the conditions for implementing these proposals is a familiarity with the patterns of energy use in the rural sector. If some of these measures are adopted, a diagnosis of the energy situation will allow us to analyze how future consumption will evolve and, thus, to evaluate possible future energy savings. These measures should be part of a set of transitional proposals that would tend to form a balanced, long-term energy system in rural areas. This would necessitate diversifying sources, with a marked tendency toward renewable sources, and a more efficient use of energy, favoring the conservation of natural resources.

The efficient use of energy must be set within a context of rational and efficient use of other national resources. Efficient energy use that does not break the biotic cycle can have a favorable influence on how other resources (forests, for example) are treated, because energy is a common substratum for all of them. Moreover, improving the ways energy is used in different productive and domestic tasks would permit substantial improvements in material living standards with no increase, and perhaps even a decrease, in the total amount of primary energy required. Thus, with proper land use, only 4.4 million hectares would be needed to provide a basic diet for a population of 120 million inhabitants by the year 2020. At the same time, essential domestic energy needs could be satisfied with only 27% of the 1980 consumption.

CONSUMPTION PATTERNS AND EFFICIENT ENERGY USE

The rural sector's importance within domestic energy consumption cannot be determined correctly form the information given in the different versions of the country's energy balance. The data corresponding to some energy sources show such variation, over time and between versions, that one is led to doubt the validity of these energy balances. This is particularly true for the hydrocarbon-derived fuels destined for production but not for electricity. The discrepancies are critical in the case of domestic uses. A major drawback in the conception and structure of energy balances is the exclusion of all types of noncommercial energy forms, particularly, firewood. As a consequence, the importance of one form of primary energy (biomass, in general) tends to be underestimated. This

distorts the observation of national energy use characteristics and impedes the understanding of an important aspect of everyday life in rural areas.2/

The agricultural sector, as defined in the country's
energy balances, refers solely to the productive activities of the rural areas and excludes domestic energy consumption. Commercial forms of domestic consumption are incorporated into the RCP sector, where they cannot be separated from urban consumption. A distinction between domestic and urban consumption is indispensable if we are to
correctly interpret the rural sector's importance in the
country's energy consumption. When considering the agricultural sector, one can see that, historically, its share
of national end use is not very significant: This share
ranged from 0.8%-2.6% in 1970 and from 0.7%-3.1% in 1980,
depending on which information source is consulted. From
such results, one concludes that the country's rural areas
are not very important within a national energy context.

Moreover, we can draw contradictory conclusions from
this diverse set of statistics. In one case, energy consumption seems to have grown at a lower rate, and, in another case, the rate was considerably higher than national
end use, which was 8.7% annually during this same period.
What is at issue here is not the degree of precision of
simple growth rates but the understanding of the under-
lying phenomena: intensive or extensive use of energy, the
technicalization or mechanization of different rural productive areas, the transition from one energy source to another, efficient use or waste of energy, and so on.

Incorporating estimates of the rural sector's domestic consumption into the energy accounting system implies
a considerable increase in the sector's share of overall
domestic consumption. In fact, rather than an average level of approximately 1% to 3% end use, its share of total
domestic consumption rose perhaps several times. This,
it seems, would modify the prevailing erroneous view
(see Table 9.1). The level of consumption was roughly
equal to the 1970 industrial consumption and to some
80% of that same consumption in 1980.

In view of these results, we can conclude the following:

1. During the 1970s, the rural sector lost some of its impact on total national consumption. Its overall demand
   grew at less than 1% annually.

2. The domestic subsector is the most influential factor, requiring ten times more energy than the productive subsector in 1970 and almost five times more in 1980.
3. The domestic subsector's consumption level stayed more or less stable during that period, around 103 X 10^{12} Kcal, while productive consumption requirements almost doubled, to 17.0 X 10^{12} Kcal in 1980.

The fertilizers used in productive areas have a high energy content. This should be taken into account when a-nalyzing the needs of rural areas. If we add the consumption of the productive subsector to that of the domestic subsector, the rural sector's share of national consumption rises to 26.2% for 1970 and 18.3% for 1980.3/ Given the different characteristics and uses of fuels and fertilizers, we believe it wise to separate them in this study.

The different goals that the productive and domestic circles have in using energy oblige one to specify their characteristics carefully. This will help us to detect those categories where a more efficient use of the energy can be developed and where conservation of natural resources can be instituted.

RURAL PRODUCTIVE SUBSECTOR

The different productive activities involved in agriculture required increasing amounts of energy during the 1970s. Also, there was a progressive change in the overall distribution of consumption in the rural sector as a whole. The apparent level of energy used for productive ends was 10.0% of the total rural energy use in 1970 and 15.7% in 1982. These percentages would go up if the useful end-use energy was considered, using the transformation yields (see Table 9.1).

The commercial energy consumed (fossil fuels and electricity), as well as the fertilizers used by the sector, is concentrated in rural production. However, human and animal energy is also required for rural activities, especially farming. Given the limitations of the existing information, we can only make a partial, indirect, and approximate estimate of the levels of use for each of these energy forms and of their relative importance. Any study of the consumption patterns in this subsector that aims to detect inefficiencies and propose guidelines for correcting them needs a good data base. With this data base, energy demands can be assigned to specific rural activities, taking into consideration transformation devices as well as their yields. We are, at present, far from this optimal situation. This does not prevent us, however, from identifying the basic characteristics of the subsector's consumption, taking into account the different forms of energy we have mentioned: commercial energy, human and animal work, and fertilizers.

Commercial Energy

Commercial energy includes petroleum derivatives and electricity, which have different specific applications. Petroleum derivatives are used mainly in agricultural machinery, and electricity is primarily for pumping water to irrigate crops.

The petroleum products most used in the subsector are diesel and kerosene. Both are used in tractors and in other agricultural machinery as well as in stationary engines that are used for different purposes.4/ The data available for analyzing the consumption of these fuels, as well as of bunker oil and liquefied gas, are partly contradictory (see Tables 9.2 and 9.3). We can, nevertheless, state that the use of diesel expanded rapidly during the 1970s, while kerosene use was practically stationary during this period. In 1982 the fuel situation was such that diesel predominated (close to 83% of the total), followed by kerosene (15.6%), and, to a lesser degree, liquefied gas (1.4%). The increase in the consumption of these fuels was due to the growing mechanization of agriculture, principally through the introduction of tractors.

The number of tractors available in rural areas in Mexico went from 91,534 units in 1970 to 164,000 in 1980, and the power per unit went up as well. It is estimated that 90% of the fuel was used for tractors, while the remaining 10% was used for other machines, such as threshers, reapers, seeders, and so on. We do not yet know the impact that tractors used in agriculture have had on the relationship between the size of the land plowed and the energy used in plowing it.

Electricity plays a role in irrigation similar to that played by fuel in the mechanization of agriculture. Electric power consumption grew at a rate of 10.8% between 1970 and 1980, going from 1,349 GWh to 3,746 GWh (see Table 9.2). This increase in consumption is associated with the increase in the total installed power of the country's pumping plants as well as with the country's annual level of usage. The 281 MW of installed electric power in 1970 represented 24% of the sector's total power, including stationary engines. Although the installed power corresponding to both engine types probably increased during the 1970s, no data is available for 1980.

Human and Animal Labor

The characteristics of Mexican rural areas, where there are still notable differences between producers and the way in which they exploit the land with available technical and economic resources, have an impact on both the use of energy and the prevailing methods of achieving production goals. The use of commercial energy sources typifies the consumption pattern in the most technical irrigation-agriculture zones. The sources are not entirely limited to these areas, but they are not available in the major part of the peasant ("campesino") economies, which predominate in the rain-fed areas. A wooden plow that is pulled by animals or pushed by the peasant on poor rainfed land, often under unfavorable orographic conditions, is a salient description of peasant labor. Human energy and animal energy, although prevailing in the peasant economy, complement the commercial energy used in exploitative activities that are technically modern.5/

The energy provided by human labor in 1970, based on the number of working days, was close to 13% of the total amount of fossil fuel used in agricultural tasks, not including electricity or fertilizers. Of this total, approximately 12% corresponded to irrigated areas and 88% to rainfed areas. Despite the large number of days worked, relatively little is contributed in energy terms, because of the low efficiency in transforming energy consumed into useful energy (2.5%).6/ The undernourishment affecting 80% of the economically active peasant population diminishes the effectiveness of their labor and also their hope for a lifestyle similar to the "ejido" owners, day workers, and small landowners.7/

The work done by animal traction is almost totally concentrated in the rain-fed areas (98%). It represents about 8.0% of the energy used in agricultural production in 1970, with an efficiency varying between 9% and 11%. The importance of the animal labor is reflected in the statistics for that year. Estimates of the animal work capacity differ widely, from 2.3 million horsepower to 7.7 million horsepower.8/ The second figure, however, could be considered an exaggeratedly high upper limit.

During the 1970s, as the mechanization of farm work expanded, human labor and animal labor were progressively displaced by commercial energy. Despite this tendency, one can suppose that both human labor and animal labor still prevail in farming of the basic crops that make up the popular diet. This situation is reflected in the energy profile for the main crops produced by peasants. In 1975 human and animal energy probably represented close to 51.0% of the energy required to produce maize and 52.0% and 76% of the energy to produce beans and sesame seed. These percentages are higher than those for the same energy sources in the energy profile of agricultural production in Mexico as a whole.9/

Fertilizers

Along with mechanization, the use of fertilizers in agriculture has increased. Domestic production doubled from 1970 to 1980, reaching 4.9 million tons in 1980. On the average, approximately 25% is destined for irrigated crops and an undetermined fraction for rain-fed crops.

If the energy employed in producing fertilizers is added to the total energy consumed, including human and animal energy, it is estimated that human energy probably represented about 38.0% of the 1975 energy profile for the rural productive subsector.10/ Organic fertilizers do not constitute an important means of improving productivity in rain-fed and irrigated areas. Chemical fertilizers have been progressively favored because of advertising and low cost.

RURAL DOMESTIC SUBSECTOR

The energy used in rural areas, in terms of the apparent energy required, is strongly centered around domestic activities. Even though the subsector's consumption has been stationary for the last fifteen years, with a slight downward tendency, it was close to 86.0% of the total energy used in rural areas in 1980.

The importance of rural domestic activities to the

country's overall energy perspective transcends its present impact on total consumption (9.0% in 1980) and can be included among the problems of national socioeconomic development for the population's largest sectors. In rural areas, even minimal living standards leave much to be desired, and energy is no exception to this.

The energy consumption patterns associated with the characteristics of rural production and lifestyle differ from urban patterns in the make-up of energy sources; in the way these sources are used; and, moreover, in the low level of use per capita. A detailed knowledge of the subsector's energy situation is indispensable when trying to understand and solve the problems affecting the 23 million people living in Mexico's rural areas, close to one-third of the country's population. In making future plans to satisfy the energy needs of this population, attention should be paid to the concrete possibilities for success, the pressure that would be placed on renewable and finite resources, the solutions or combination of solutions thought to be viable, and the policies that should be implemented to substantially modify the present situation. Such transformations should be introduced rapidly if the political and social stability of the nation is to be preserved.

The set of energy sources used in the subsector includes firewood and organic residues, light oil, and liquefied gas among fuels, with electricity as a complement.11/ Firewood is, without a doubt, the most widely used fuel for cooking food and heating water. Light oil and liquefied gas are used increasingly and in combination. Electricity, if it is available, is consumed specifically for lighting dwellings. If it is not available, kerosene is used, and, occasionally, if subsistence conditions are difficult, wood is used. (Human and animal labor account for an important part of the daily subsistence activities, and women and children play a central part in this. However, a precise analysis is almost impossible from the information currently available.)

At present, the study of the efficient use of energy refers, within a generalized context of relative subconsumption, to highly inefficient ways of using firewood. This fuel dominates the possible energy sources in rural areas. Its low yield leads to a strong increase in demand, thereby putting pressure on a resource that is, in principle, renewable. In terms of useful energy, firewood's share has gone down a considerable degree. At best, it now represents some 10% of what it was at the beginning of the 1980s. This fact clearly reveals how much firewood is wasted, which is a problem because of the accelerated depletion of forests and because of the critical subsistence conditions of the majority of the peasants.

What follows is an analysis of the energy consumption patterns in rural areas. The sources are classified according to their main use or uses: (1) cooking and heating water, (2) lighting, (3) heating, and (4) fetching water and products. Patterns are examined with respect to specific energy sources.

Cooking and Heating Water

From 1970 to 1980, firewood was the main fuel used in cooking and heating water. This was due to the number of consumers, 84% of the 1980 rural population, and to the amount of energy consumed, 96 X 10^{12} Kcal for 1980, or 94% of the subsector's total consumption (see Tables 9.4, 9.5, 9.6, 9.7, and 9.8). (The lack of information, its questionable worth, and its level of generality impede a separate analysis of energy consumption for cooking and heating.[12]/

Generally speaking, it can be stated that firewood was replaced to some extent by light oil and liquefied gas during the 1970s. The share of both fuels in energy consumption went from 0.3% in 1970 to 6.6% in 1980 (see Tables 9.5 and 9.6). This general tendency did not apply uniformly to all regions of the country; for example, in the most socioeconomically deprived states, the rural population cooking with firewood even increased.

Mixed firewood-gas cooking is practiced throughout some states (Mexico and Morelos, for example), especially in areas where liquefied gas is distributed. The number of people using this method has not yet been determined, nor has its impact on energy consumed. It is estimated that the firewood consumed per capita by those using mixed cooking is equivalent to 60% of the level of those cooking only with wood. This puts strong pressure on forest resources.

Firewood and Other Vegetable Fuels. Official statistics on firewood are particularly representative of the poor quality of the information at hand (see Table 9.9). The official information corresponds to wood cut and used directly as fuel or in the production of vegetable coal but only as market products. This wood is consumed mainly by small industries, such as brick makers, potters, bakers, and so on, and a part of the urban sector. It does not represent the domestic consumption of firewood in the rural sector.

In the rural sector, the firewood consumed for domestic purposes does not necessarily pass through the market. Firewood is generally gathered by the people directly. In certain regions, where there is a shortage of resources, it can even be commercialized among the inhabitants.

Some studies have tried to rectify the lack of information on true firewood consumption by making estimates (see Table 9.10). Even in these cases, there are large differences between results. The figures proposed vary from 1.1 X 10^{12} Kcal, in López Portillo's fourth state of the nation address, to 91.9 X 10^{12} Kcal, according to OLADE. Because of the criteria used, the second estimate is closest to the figures used in our study.

We base our estimate on census material and on the few studies about energy consumption done on the rural communities in Mexico. The amount of firewood consumed per capita is not homogeneous throughout the country. It varies according to the type of stove used, the caloric content of the wood and the percent of humidity, the scarcity of fuel, the climatic conditions of the region, types of food, and family size. Determining these variables implies an in-depth knowledge of how firewood is used as a fuel. Such knowledge is not presently available.

Taking an average of 3.5 kg/per capita, we can calculate that 33 X 10^6 cm of firewood were consumed in 1970 and 32 X 10^6 cm in 1980 (see Table 9.11).13/ These amounts represent 6 and 3 times, respectively, the total wood produced during these years. The importance of domestic firewood consumption compared to commercial wood production is reflected in the fact that the domestic consumption was close to 85% of the total consumption of wood for energy and non-energy purposes in 1970 and 78% in 1980 (see Table 9.12).

The relatively high per capita firewood consumption is a function, among other factors, of the cooking devices used. In the majority of cases, they are hearths with three stones, with 4% to 7% efficiency.14/ In some places, such as the central highlands of Michoacán, they use semi-closed clay boxes that increase efficiency slightly.

There is marked selectivity in the type of tree used for firewood, at least in those places where there is not

yet a scarcity problem. The types selected as fuel do not
always coincide with the dominant tree type. This selectivity produces the premature depletion of certain species
in the first phases of deforestation.15/

In those places where the preferred species for fuel
have already been exhausted, inhabitants consume any type
of wood and even manure and maize stubble. In these
places, the acute scarcity of wood causes further deterioration in an already poor diet. Because of the lack of
fuel, less food is cooked. The time and work needed to
gather wood, found at distances of up to 10 km from the locality, thus increase.

Firewood is selected as an energy source for cooking
for economic reasons. Its low (or free) cost, the possibility of using it without a stove, and its availability
in the majority of towns and villages are incentives for
using it. This contrasts with the situation of other energy sources, such as light oil and liquefied gas.

Light Oil and Liquefied Gas. From 1970 to 1980, the
country as a whole showed a considerable increase in the
number of liquefied gas consumers and a corresponding decrease in consumers of light oil. In the rural sector,
however, the number of users of both fuels went up. Thus,
light oil was displaced toward the rural sector during
this period.

Light oil is used as an alternate form of energy in
areas where firewood is scarce and where there is no gas
delivery. Generally speaking, light oil is not considered
a transition fuel (from wood to gas) in rural areas. The
increase in the number of light oil consumers in 1980 is
an additional indicator of the depletion of forest resources. In the future, two factors could accelerate substitution of light oil for other energy sources: a decrease in its quality as a fuel because it is sold with increasing degrees of impurity and the variation in its relative price compared to liquefied gas, which has made it
progressively more expensive.

Liquefied gas is essentially an urban fuel. Consumption in rural areas is limited by difficulties in delivery
to small towns and by the initial investment required to
use it.

Although light oil might appear to be a transition
fuel toward gas, frequently, and where distribution permits, the inhabitants of rural communities change directly
to liquefied gas or combine the use of both fuels. The pro-

cess of substituting energy sources is conditioned by
economic and social factors that transcend the trend in
relative fuel prices. The progressive proletariarization
of the peasants, which often forces them to work outside
the community and gives them a relatively regular cash income, modifies the pattern of energy consumption. The
worker changes from using gathered firewood to using commercial fuels because, now, the worker has the minimal resources to pay for commercial fuels and no longer has time
to gather firewood. This phenomenon is accentuated by the
increased number of children going to school and changing
meal times.16/ Moreover, liquefied gas permits women to
use less effort in cooking food, making time available for
other activities. Access to liquefied gas is restricted,
in part, by the string of intermediaries involved in its
distribution. They raise its cost up to 100% above the
original price.

There are no official studies on the consumption of
these fuels in the rural domestic subsector. According to
the estimates made for this book, the amount of light oil
and liquefied gas used by the rural domestic subsector for
cooking in 1980 was 8.2% and 3%, respectively, of the total domestic consumption for these fuels.

Both light oil and liquefied gas are used in commercial stoves, with a 30% efficiency. They are suited to urban consumption but not necessarily to the way in which
food is prepared in rural areas. For this reason, mixed
cooking, with firewood-commercial fuel (mainly gas), con-
tinues in rural communities.

Lighting

Firewood, light oil, electricity, and gas make up the
energy package used for lighting in rural areas. In areas
with coniferous forests, ocote is often burned for light.
Ocote is burned directly after being cut into small sliv-
ers. It gives off poor light and produces a good deal of
smoke. Electricity and light oil are the main sources of
energy used in lighting. Light oil is widely used where
electricity is not available: 69.7% of all consumers in
1970 and 66.2% in 1980 used this liquid fuel as a source
of light.

The development of rural electrification during the
1970s contributed to the progressive displacement of light
oil as a light source. In spite of this, in 1980 some 90%

of all lighting was provided by kerosene and some 10% by electricity.

Electricity. According to 1970 census information, 30.3% of the rural population, or six million inhabitants, had electricity.17/ The 1980 census indicates that the percentage had risen to 34%. The information presented by CFE seriously disagrees with the census results for both years.18/

The company estimated that 9.9 million rural inhabitants had access to electricity in 1970, that is, 65% more than the number indicated in the 1970 census. The differences did not disappear by 1980 because in 1982 the CFE estimated that the rural population with electricity had risen to 15.2 million people, double the number indicated in the 1980 census (7.6 million people).

The criterion used to count the number of people with electricity is a possible reason for the marked discrepancy between these results. CFE considers all inhabitants of a locality to have access to electricity when the supply line reaches that locality. The census bureau, however, as well as the most recent studies done on energy in rural areas, does not follow this principle in assessing its figures.19/

Several factors limit the possibility that all persons in the rural areas with electricity have electric power. The first is the size and dispersion of the communities. Given the centralized nature of present electric power production, laying out power lines is onerous and difficult as the size of towns decreases and the dispersion of towns increases. In 1970 96% of the localities with less than 500 inhabitants were without electricity. By the end of the 1970s, the size of the localities was so important that the program of rural electrification itself left out close to 700,000 people who were living in communities with less than 30 inhabitants.

In each town, the dispersion of the houses also influences access to electricity. Although in urban sectors there are 7 to 10 users per post, in rural sectors the number decreases to 1.8. Even when the power line reaches the community, not all the population can shoulder the cost of installing the service. This situation is accentuated in economically deprived communities.20/

In rural areas, the majority of the population uses electricity almost exclusively for lighting. In regard to light quality, it is undoubtedly the best option.

Light Oil. It is estimated that in 1980 2.2×10^{12} Kcal of light oil was consumed for lighting. This corresponds to 13% of the total domestic demand for this fuel. Just as in the case of electricity, the number of consumers is distributed in different ways throughout the states, with a high concentration in more deprived areas.

According to case studies, per capita light oil consumption shows a wide range of variation, depending on the community. However, in two different localities, it was about 16 liters per year.[21]/

This energy source is used because of its low cost and because it is distributed better than electricity. The light it gives off, however, is deficient, and it fills the homes with smoke. It is usually used in rustic lamps that are not very efficient and that have no way of increasing their luminosity.

Heating. The poverty of vast sectors of the peasantry does not allow the peasants to use their income for anything but basic needs. Given the conditions in which they live, heating does not appear to be one of these basic needs. It is not common, therefore, for energy to be used for heating, not even in cold climates. The low winter temperatures recorded in the north of the country lead one to think these areas use firewood, gas, or electricity for heating, but because there is absolutely no information available, no estimate has been made of the energy requirements for heating.

Fetching Water and Products. This activity uses human and animal labor exclusively. Fetching water is a necessary chore for that part of the rural population that does not have piped-in water. When the source of water is far from the home, the activity can require several hours a day and considerable effort. The time and effort are even greater if there are no beasts of burden to do the work, which is true in the majority of cases. Any member of the family—man, woman, or child—can do this work. In case studies, it was determined that fetching water takes up to 180 days a year of animal labor.[22]/ However, there is no complete and detailde information on the human and animal labor used for this purpose.

MEASURES FOR EFFICIENT ENERGY USE AND CONSERVATION

From an examination of energy use in rural areas and the main trends of the 1970s, some facts emerge about how energy is used in Mexico's rural areas, the difficulty or ease the rural population has in gaining access to energy sources, the regional and rural-urban imbalances in consumption levels, and those energy uses with the lowest energy efficiency.

The relative underconsumption characterizing close to one-third of the country's population means we have to analyze the possibilities of more efficient energy use and of the savings and conservation associated with this more efficient use from a different standpoint for the rural sector than that for the consumer sectors. This, however, does not invalidate efforts toward better energy use. In the rural sector, this concern must be reconciled with the growth in consumption.

In Mexico, as in the rest of Latin America and in other countries where there is a significant peasant population, the need for improvements in the living conditions of that population makes it necessary to conceive and implement energy and socioeconomic development policies based on an in-depth knowledge of the sector's overall and particular characteristics and problems. These characteristics and problems should be approached from a multidimensional view. They should not be restricted by the economic laws of a nonexistent free market and should include social, cultural, and anthropological elements that define the essential features of a rural population whose ethnic diversity forms a part of the substratum on which the nation is founded.

In rural areas, there is a certain uniformity to the pattern of energy source consumption and the way in which these sources are used that goes beyond the social heterogeneity already mentioned. Any energy policy should take this as a central factor if one expects a favorable response to an energy policy from the rural population.

In the future, the incorporation of isolated communities and marginated peasant groups and the resulting higher per capita energy consumption should not be at odds with efficient and nonpredatory use of the finite or renewable energy resources. Development and energy policies have to be limited so as the harmonize different objectives, for example, bringing power to the entire rural population at levels adequate for its needs, using energy ef-

ficiently, and conserving energy and natural resources.
Improving people's living conditions can occur simultane-
ously with recuperating and supporting self-sufficiency in
foodstuffs.

Given the present energy situation in rural areas and
our knowledge of them, we need to do the following:

. Make detailed studies of the characteristics of the rural energy system throughout the country, carefully specifying the sources, uses and intervening devices, and
  the factors defining the interrelationship of the characteristics, be they economic or other.
. Do the analyses on a regional level, defining the regions according to energy, production, and socioeconomic
  criteria.
. Make precise evaluations of the renewable energy resources in the different regions.

The isolation and the dispersion of the rural communities, the characteristics of the energy consumption patterns, and the need for a balanced use of resources suggest that it would be worth promoting decentralized systems of energy production. These systems would be based on
renewable sources and technology appropriate to the environment in which they are developed.23/ This position implies the following:

. Supporting research on and technological development of
  energy sources using renewable resources.
. Openly promoting the production of these energy sources
  on an industrial scale, with an explicit policy of incentives
. Supporting the diffusion of installations and equipment
  through economic and financial measures, as well as the
  training of rural users to maintain them, eliminating
  the need for technical help outside the community.

It will probably take a long time before the preceding general guidelines can be instituted and can result
in a substantial change in the country's energy policy.
This new position should be accompanied by a set of measures leading to a more efficient short- and medium-term
use of energy overall. Specific measures can be suggested
for each of the subsectors, depending on their particular
characteristics.

DOMESTIC SUBSECTOR

To improve cooking efficiency, Lorena-type stoves, made from local materials, should be introduced. This could increase cooking efficiency two or three times over the traditional system. Also, these stoves do not require outlays.

Another effort would be to design and apply programs to reforest the tree species most affected by the preferred selection of wood for fuel. The use of commercial fuels should be promoted to decrease the pressure on forest resources. There are price advantages in using liquefied gas over light oil. However, there are distribution problems because the domestic supply must be complemented by imports. In order to substitute some of these fuels for firewood, using conditions beneficial to the rural population, pricing policies should be reviewed and specified, domestic availability should be examined, and the adaptation of stoves for fuel use, as well as their production and sale, should be promoted. Installing Lorena-type, mixed gas-firewood stoves with a device for using gas could constitute an alternative in a transition toward a stable use of renewable sources.

Finally, pressure cookers, which allow one to reduce cooking time substantially and, therefore, the energy needed for cooking, could be promoted.

The quality of lighting could be improved in the most marginated areas by the massive introduction of commercial kerosene-type lamps. These, along with the use of fluorescent discharge lighting, with an appropriate policy for advertising and prices, should be promoted. With these proposals, lighting would be improved, and electric power consumption would be reduced.

Finally, there are energy needs not yet satisfied under the present living conditions of the rural population, and it would be worth developing the following programs quickly:

. A program of animal stables that would utilize the organic waste and gas generated by the animals
. Hydraulic microplants to provide electricity for rural lighting and workshops
. Partial introduction of economical and easily made solar heaters, that is, those that can be reproduced in local workshops

PRODUCTIVE SUBSECTOR

Measures can be instituted to make farm machinery using diesel and kerosene more efficient. In the selection, maintenance, and adequate operation of tractors, the type of soil, relief, and other factors related to the surface under cultivation should be considered. The tractor's power should be geared to the type of soil and crops, and periodic tune-ups of the tractors should be conducted. Studies should be done on transportation and evaporation losses that can occur during the handling and storing of fuel, in order to develop devices that would reduce these losses to a minimum.

To these measures can be added those related to ploughing methods. New ploughing methods should be introduced that permit sowing in a minimum of time, soil movement, and work in the different crop phases. Research is presently being done in Mexico on techniques that reduce the use of the tractor and, at the same time, fuel consumption and that also avoid soil erosion.

A good number of peasant farmers use animal traction and traditional crop techniques with a low commercial energy consumption per hectare. There is, therefore, a need for a permanent program to use animal energy efficiently and to improve ploughing methods. This can be accomplished by using versatile and easy-handling farm implements for animal traction, incorporating sowing techniques that require a minimum of work, and finding a balance between the use of human and animal labor.

To make water use more efficient, which is necessary with the possible increase in the land under irrigation, the consumption of electric power and hydrocarbons can be reduced with improvements in irrigation techniques. This can be achieved through drop and aspersion irrigation, canal systems that distribute water more efficiently, and the partial introduction of air pumps and the widespread introduction of pumping systems that use renewable energy sources.

In spite of numerous studies on techniques and the need for correct fertilizer application, there is no national study of the effects of chemical fertilizers on the soil and its net utilization. Therefore, it is necessary to offer permanent consultation throughout the country on using manure, with periodic follow-ups on yields; to utilize organic fertilizer techniques; and to encourage the use of biodigesters and the utilization of the energy and fertilizer these machines produce.

POTENTIAL ENERGY SAVINGS

PROJECTIONS FOR 1990

The savings derived from using energy more efficiently are obvious when comparing the consumptions associated
with two different scenarios for a fixed-time horizon. In
the first case, the traditional consumption tendencies are
projected, and in the second case, it is assumed that a set
of measures for efficient energy use will be applied.

Given the limitations of information and the unknown
potential energy savings in the productive subsector, any
estimate is limited in its scope to the domestic subsector
and in time to the year 1990 (see Table 9.13).

By applying efficiency measures, it should be possible to reduce the sector's total energy consumption by a-
bout 40%, based on the historical trend. This percentage
means 69.5 X 10^{12} Kcal, that is, approximately 149 tbdce
in 1990, an amount greater than the potential savings in
the electric power sector for the same year.

The distribution of energy consumption among the subsectors will tend to balance out. The productive sector's
share will be 40.5% in 1990, compared to 14.0% in 1980.24/
Domestic energy consumption would be reduced 3.3 times to
a level equivalent to 29% of the consumption projected by
the historical trend.

The use of firewood for cooking food and heating water will be the origins of almost all the energy savings
that can be derived from more efficient energy use. These
savings will be achieved mainly by introducing Lorena-type
stoves and gradually replacing firewood with commercial
fuels. Liquefied gas is preferred because of the advantages it offers to users.

Potential savings for electricity are also proportion-
ally high; they would be 12% of the amount consumed if corrective measures were not taken. However, their impact
would be relatively minor, only about 140 tbdce for 1990.

THE CONSERVATION OF ENERGY RESOURCES: LONG-TERM
PROSPECTS

The transformation of energy consumption patterns and
a more efficient use of energy will not take place before
the 1990s. We can then move toward a more radical solu-

tion by the beginning of the year 2000.

The amount of renewable natural resources that can be applied to provide energy for rural areas and the country in general has not yet been sufficiently estimated. However, our first approximations (see Table 9.14) show that the energy potential contained in animal and vegetable residues from the rural sector would have been sufficient to satisfy the total demand of the rural sector in 1970 and 1980 and will also be sufficient in 2020. It is imperative, then, to think about measures and policies leading to the utilization of these sources.

Resources can be utilized close to their source. To what extent they are exploited will depend, to a good degree, on the socioeconomic characteristics of the area in which they are located. It is also necessary to develop technology for converting these resources into useful energy. Table 9.15 contains a possible series of long- and short-term measures.

A coordinated effort will be required by the 1990s for conservation measures, both on a regional and a national level, to be initiated and for the resources to be assigned and distributed to the areas most needing them. The distribution should be based on regional studies done all over the country as part of a general evaluation policy.

During this period, it will be possible to spread the use of new equipment and technology that utilize renewable resources. It is hoped that this equipment and technology will be available to users through financing programs launched by the federal government.

Moreover, several of the measures proposed for 1990 should be continued. A complete and well-distributed reforestation of at least 40 million hectares is vitally important. The return to the use of firewood instead of commercial fuels for cooking food will depend on this. Such a policy also requires developing an integral program of cattle stables that will allow using the animals more efficiently for work and using their manure to produce biogas and fertilizers (see Table 9.15).

If this radical change in the energy system of rural areas were to take hold by the year 2020 at the latest, the basic needs of the rural population could be covered entirely by renewable resources. This could mean that total energy consumption would no longer absorb a percentage of finite resources and would be only about 43% of the rural sector's total 1980 consumption (see Table 9.16).

On this basis, we can conclude that it is not the re-

strictions of a technical or natural reserve nature that
prevent satisfying the energy needs of the rural sector.
Rather, it is the development models that give advantages
to centralized, large-scale technology and that polarize
access to energy sources, to the exclusive benefit of
those who already have the most resources.25/

NOTES

1. This was done by promoting and subsidizing the development of the infrastructure needed to introduce technical advancements into the production process.

2. The Organización Latinoamericana de Energía included an estimate for firewood consumption in the RCP sector of its balance for Mexico. However, the national version of the balance, when trying to present a homogeneous
view for all of Latin America, left out all references to
firewood and vegetable fuels. Cf. Organización Latinoamericana de Energía, Balances energéticos de América Latina,
Serie Documentos OLADE, No. 13 (Quito: OLADE, 1981), Secretaría de Patrimonio y Fomento Industrial (SEPAFIN), Balance de energía (Mexico, 1975-1981).

3. In this estimate, the energy content of the fertilizers was subtracted from the industrial sector to
avoid counting it twice.

4. In 1970 there were 46,633 stationary engines fed
by hydrocarbons. Their total power was 886 MW. Cf. Secretaría de Agricultura y Recursos Hidráulicos, Censo agropecuario y forestal (Mexico, 1970).

5. Cf. Oscar M. Guzmán, "Energía y sector agrícola de
subsistencia" in Miguel S. Wionczek, comp., Energía en
México: Ensayos sobre el pasado y el presente (Mexico: El
Colegio de México, 1982); Instituto de Investigaciones Elec-
tricas, "Evaluation of Energy Supply and Demand in Four Rural Communities," mimeographed (Mexico, 1984).

6. There is no data in Mexico on the energy humans
and animals use in different activities; therefore, we
used several sources: M. Haswell, Energy for Survival
(Cambridge, 1981); Food and Agriculture Organization, Informe sobre tracción animal (Rome, 1981); and S. Vaclar,
"China's Energetics: A System Analysis" in
Energy in the Developing World (Oxford, 1980).

7. Coordinación General del Plan Nacional de Zonas
Deprimidas y Grupos Marginados, Las necesidades esenciales
de México (Mexico, 1981).

8. J. Ibarra, Los energéticos en el desarrollo revolucionario de México (Mexico, 1982). The difference comes from SARH, Censo agropecuario, which takes into account only the number indicated as work animals, because there can be horses and mules that are not used as such.

9. It was estimated that for production as a whole in 1975, human and animal energy would be close to 20.7% of the energy consumes. This includes the energy used in irrigation, drying, farm machinery and transportation to the distribution centers. Cf. Guzmán, "Energía," p.128.

10. Oscar M. Guzmán, "Energía y sector agrícola de subsistencia" in Miguel S. Wionczek, comp., Energía en México: Ensayos sobre el pasado y el presente (Mexico: El Colegio de México, 1982), p.128.

11. Light oil is a type of kerosene.

12. Only one study exists that separates both categories, but its conclusions are not valid at a national level.

13. This figure is of the same magnitude as the averages for firewood that appear in even the most precise studies on Mexico and Latin America (see Table 9.11).

14. R. Giesecke, et al., Leña y carbón vegetal: Su incorporación en la planificación y política energética (Managua: CEPAL and Instituto Nicaraguense de Energía, 1981).

15. In the community of Guacamaya, Michoacán, oak is used for cooking, even when the main species is pine. This is because oak burns slower and produces less smoke. Cf. IIE, "Evaluation of Energy Supply."

16. M. Evans, Aspectos socio-económicos de la carencia de combustibles domésticos: Un estudio empírico de México rural (Mexico, 1984).

17. National statistics do not provide any information on the level of electric power consumption in the rural domestic subsector. The evaluation here is based on the information available in the few existing studies. We generalized the patterns of electric power applied to the rural population in these studies.

18. Comision Federal de Electricidad, Plan nacional de electrificación rural 1979-1982 (Mexico, July 1978).

19. Cf. IIE, "Evaluation of Energy Supply."

20. In Los Reyes, Veracruz, only 22% of the homes have electricity. IIE, "Evaluation of Energy Supply."

21. Although in Guacamaya, Michoacán, where ocote is burned, per capita consumption was 4 liters/year, in San Jerónimo Tulija, Chiapas, and Coscatlán de Los Reyes, Vera-

cruz, it was 16 liters/year. Cf. IIE, "Evaluation of Energy Supply."

22. IIE, "Evaluation of Energy Supply,"

23. This is an environment in which social, economic, and political relationships within the community are included as well as outside ties to the community.

24. If fertilizers are included in the productive subsector, this subsector's role in consumption would be greater than that of the domestic subsector (80% and 20%, approximately).

25. There is one concrete example in Muñoztlán, Tlaxcala, where the so-called sistemas ecológicos autosostenidos (self-sustaining ecological systems) are being developed and seem promising. These systems make use of very simple synergisms on a domestic level, such as digesters, Lorena-type stoves, water regenerators, and so on, that can be interconnected with certain productive activities, thereby raising the standard of living of the population adopting them. With the cost of a single 1200-MW nuclear plant, one could finance the construction of 3 million such systems. This would benefit some 18 million people, close to the total number of marginated population members existing at the present time and also close to the population projected for the rural sector by the year 2020.

TABLE 9.1
Sector Consumption Patterns and Efficient Energy Use

Sector	1970			1980			1982		
	10^{12} Kcal	%	%	10^{12} Kcal	%	%	10^{12} Kcal	%	%
Rural									
Productive	11.34	10.0	2.0	16.67	14.0	1.5	19.08	15.7	1.6
Domestic	103.46	90.0	18.6	102.94	86.0	9.0	103.0	84.3	8.7
Subtotal	114.80	100.0	20.6	119.61	100.0	10.5	122.08	100.0	10.3
Domestic (Commercial Energy) a/	441.78	--	79.4	1,023.95	--	89.5	1,056.18	--	89.7
Total	556.58	--	100	1,143.60	--	100	1,178.26	--	100

Sources: Secretaría de Patrimonio y Fomento Industrial, Balance de energía 1970 (Mexico, 1982), p.118; Balance de energía 1975-1980 (Mexico, 1982), p.112; Balance de energía 1982 (Mexico, 1982), p.119. Petróleos Mexicanos, Mexico: Balance de energía 1982 (Mexico, 1983), p.168. Comisión Federal de Electricidad, Sector eléctrico nacional: Estadísticas 1965-1982 (Mexico, 1982), p.171.

Note: Energy use corresponds to the gross domestic supply of energy plus un-utilized energy, but it does not include fuel consumption from the agricultural sector.

TABLE 9.2

Agricultural Sector's Estimated Energy Consumption and Share of End-Use Domestic Energy

Year	Petroleum Products		Electricity			Total Commercial Energy	
	10^{12} Kcal	%	GWh	10^{12} Kcal	%	10^{12} Kcal	%
1970	5.38	2.0	1,349	1.16	6.2	6.54	2.6
1975	2.30	0.7	2,257	1.94	6.5	4.23	1.2
1978	11.69	2.8	2,932	2.52	6.5	14.21	3.1
1980	13.45	2.7	3,746	3.22	6.5	16.67	3.1
1982	15.51	2.8	4,152	3.51	7.2	19.08	3.2
AAGR							
1970–1980	9.6	—	—	10.8	7.8	9.8	—
1970–1975	-15.7	—	—	10.7	—	-8.3	—
1975–1980	42.5	—	—	10.7	—	31.6	—

Source: Secretaría de Patrimonio y Fomento Industrial, Balance de energía 1982 (Mexico, 1983), p.182; Comisión Federal de Electricidad, Sector eléctrico nacional: Estadísticas 1965-1981 (Mexico, 1982), p.116.

Note: Data corresponding to petroleum products show a tendency that leads one to doubt their precision and magnitude, especially when Table 9.3 is examined. This fact underlines the need to improve the system of gathering and processing the existing information.

TABLE 9.3
Consumption of Petroleum Products in Rural Productive Subsector (10^{12} Kcal)

Petroleum Product	1970	1975	1980	1982	%
Diesel	—	—	—	12.86	83.0
Kerosene	2.51	2.30	2.78	2.42	15.6
Liquefied Gas	—	—	—	0.23	1.4
Bunker Oil	2.87	—	10.67	—	—
Total	5.38	2.30	13.45	15.51	100

Sources: Secretaría de Patrimonio y Fomento Industrial, Balance de energía 1970 (Mexico, 1982), p.119; Secretaría de Patrimonio y Fomento Industrial, Balance de energía 1982 (Mexico, 1983), p.112.

Petroleum Product	1970	1975	1980	1982	%
Diesel	5.60	n.s.	15.30	14.86	84.2
Kerosene	2.41	n.s.	2.68	2.30	15.8
Total	8.01	n.s.	17.98	17.69	100

Source: Based on unpublished data of Petróleos Mexicanos, Concentrado de las operaciones realizadas por las compañías distribuidoras (Mexico, 1983).

n.s. - not specified

TABLE 9.4
Number and Percentage of Consumers in Rural Domestic Subsector, 1970

Use	Firewood[a] Kcal x 10^{12}	%	Liquefied[b] Gas Kcal x 10^{12}	%	Light[c,d] Oil Kcal x 10^{12}	%	Electricity[e] Kcal x 10^{12}	%	Total Kcal x 10^{12}	%
Cooking and Heating Water	19,413,230	97.5	50,430	0.3	453,060	2.2	—	—	19,916,630	100
Heating	n.s.	n.s.	n.s.	n.s.	—	—	—	—	—	—
Lighting	n.s.	n.s.	n.s.	n.s.	13,884,120	69.7	6,032,510	30.3	19,916,630	100
Fetching Water and Products	—		—		—		—		—	

Source: Census data.

Note: Localities of less than 2,500 inhabitants were considered rural population.

a/ Cooking: (Rural population consuming firewood) x (3.5 kg per capita/daily) x (365 days) x (4,000 Kcal/kg).
b/ Cooking: (Rural population cooking with gas) x (0.14 kg per capita/daily) x (365 days) x (12.248 Kcal/kg).
c/ Cooking: (Rural population consuming light oil) x (0.14 kg per capita daily).
d/ Lighting: (Population lighting with light oil) x (16 liters per capita/year) x (9,221 Kcal/liter).
e/ Lighting: (Number of rural electrified dwellings) x (120W x 4hrs. x 3,600) x (365 days) x (0.2389) x (10^3 Kcal/J).
n.s. - Not specified.

TABLE 9.5
Number and Percentage of Consumers in Rural Domestic Subsector, 1980

Use	Firewood[a]		Liquefied Gas[b]		Light Oil[c, d]		Electricity[c]		Total	
	Kcal x 10^{12}	%	Kcal x 10^{12}	%	Kcal x 10^{12}	%	Kcal x 10^{12}	%	Kcal x 10^{12}	%
Cooking and Heating Water	18,734,947	83.5	23,911,823[f]	6.6	2,220,060	9.9	—	—	22,433,415	100
Heating	n.s.	n.s.	n.s.	n.s.	—	—	n.s.	n.s.	—	—
Lighting	n.s.	n.s.	n.s.	n.s.	14,843,686	66.2	7,589,729	33.8	22,433,415	100
Fetching Water and Products	—		—		—		—		—	

Source: Census data.

a/ Cooking: (Rural population consuming firewood) x (3.5 kg per capita/daily) x (365 days) x (4,000 Kcal/kg).
b/ Cooking: (Rural population cooking with gas) x (0.14 kg per capita/daily) x (365 days) x (12.248 Kcal/kg).
c/ Cooking: (Rural population consuming light oil) x (0.14 kg per capita/daily).
d/ Lighting: (Population lighting with light oil) x (16 liters per capita/year) x (9,221 Kcal/liter).
e/ Lighting: (Number of rural electrified dwellings) x (120 W x 4 hrs. x 3,600) x (365 days) x (0.2389) x 10^3 Kcal/J).
f/ Cooking figure alone is 22,433,415 and heating, 1,478,408.
n.s. - Not specified.

Table 9.6
Rural Domestic Subsector Energy Consumption, 1970

Use	Firewood[a] Kcal x 10^12	%	Liquefied Gas[b] Kcal x 10^12	%	Light Oil[c][d] Kcal x 10^12	%	Electricity[e] Kcal x 10^12	%	Human Work Kcal x 10^12	%	Animal Work Kcal x 10^12	%	Total Kcal x 10^12	%	%
Cooking and Heating Water	99.0	97.7	0.03	n.s.	0.29	0.3	—	—	2.0	2.0	—	—	101.32	100	98.0
Heating	n.s.	n.s.	n.s.	n.s.	—	—	n.s.	n.s.	—	—	—	—	—	—	—
Lighting	n.s.	n.s.	n.s.	n.s.	2.0	93.5	0.14	6.5	—	—	—	—	2.14	100	2.0
Fetching Water and Products	—	—	—	—	—	—	—	—	n.s.	n.s.	n.s.	n.s.	—	—	—
Total	99.0	—	0.3	—	2.29	—	0.14	—	2.0	—	—	—	103.46	—	100

Source: Census data.

a/ Cooking: (Rural population consuming firewood) x (3.5 kg per capita/daily) x (365 days) x (4,000 Kcal/kg).
b/ Cooking: (Rural population cooking with gas) x (0.14 kg per capita/daily) x (365 days) x (12.248 Kcal/kg).
c/ Cooking: (Rural population consuming light oil) x (0.14 kg per capita/daily).
d/ Lighting: (Population lighting with light oil) x (16 liters per capita/year) x (9,221 Kcal/liter).
e/ Lighting: (Number of rural electrified dwellings) x (120 W x 4 hrs. x 3,600) x (365 days) x (0.2389) x (10^3 Kcal/J).
n.s. - Not specified.

TABLE 9.7
Energy Consumption in Rural Domestic Subsector in 1980

Use	Firewood a/ Kcal x 10^12	%	Liquefied Gas b/ Kcal x 10^12	%	Light Oil c/d/ Kcal x 10^12	%	Electricity e/ Kcal x 10^12	%	Human Work Kcal x 10^12	%	Animal Work Kcal x 10^12	%	Total Kcal x 10^12	%	%
Cooking and Heating Water	96.0	95.5	0.93	0.9	1.4	1.4	—	—	2.2	2.2	—	—	100.53	100	97.7
Heating	n.s.	n.s.	n.s.	n.s.	—	—	n.s.	n.s.	—	—	—	—	—	—	—
Lighting	n.s.	n.s.	n.s.	n.s.	2.2	91.3	0.21	8.7	—	—	—	—	2.41	100	2.3
Fetching Water and Products	—		—		—		—		n.s.	n.s.	n.s.	n.s.	—		
Total	96.0	—	0.93	—	3.6	—	0.21	—	2.2	—	—	—	102.94	—	100

Source: Census data.
a/ Cooking: (Rural population consuming firewood) x (3.5 kg per capita/daily) x (365 days) x (4,000 Kcal/kg).
b/ Cooking: (Rural population cooking with gas) x (0.14 kg per capita/daily) x (365 days) x (12.248 Kcal/kg).
c/ Cooking: (Rural population consuming light oil) x (0.14 kg per capita/daily).
d/ Cooking: (Population lighting with light oil) x (16 liters per capita/year) x (9,221 Kcal/liter).
e/ Lighting: (Number of rural electrified dwellings) x (120 W x 4 hrs. x 3,600) x (365 days) x (0.2389) x 10^3 Kcal/J).
n.s. - Not specified.

304

TABLE 9.8
Efficiency of Energy Devices Used in Rural Domestic Subsector, 1970-1980 (in percentages)

Use	Firewood	Liquefied Gas	Light Oil	Electricity	Human Work	Animal Work
Cooking						
Hearth	4-7	—	—	—	n.s.	—
Stove	—	30	30	—	n.s.	—
Other	—	—	—	—	n.s.	—
Heating Water						
Hearth	4-7	—	—	—	n.s.	—
Stove	—	30	30	—	n.s.	—
Other	—	—	—	—	n.s.	—
Heating						
Wood Burner	n.s.	—	—	n.s.	n.s.	—
Heater	—	n.s.	—	—	—	—
Other	—	—	—	—	—	—
Lighting						
Direct-Burning Ocote	n.s.	—	—	—	—	—
Lamp	—	n.s.	n.s.	5-10	—	—
Oil Lamp	—	—	—	—	—	—
Lightbulb	—	—	—	—	—	—
Fetching Water and Products	—	—	—	—	n.s.	n.s.

Source: Census data.

n.s. - Not specified.

TABLE 9.9
Commercial Production of Firewood and Coal (in thousands of m³ rolled)

Year	1	2	3	4	5	6	7	8	9
1965	—	—	763	763	573 a/	—	—	—	—
1970	—	—	769	769	—	—	—	428	939
1971	—	—	685	685	—	—	—	350	—
1972	—	—	—	625	—	—	—	333	—
1973	—	—	—	568	—	—	—	293	—
1974	—	—	—	534	—	—	—	283	—
1975	—	—	—	569	—	—	—	289	606
1976	—	—	—	593	—	—	—	608	—
1977	—	—	—	598	601	598	—	591	—
1978	—	—	—	598	—	598	642	—	—
1979	536	—	—	536	—	536	600	—	560
1980	485	485	—	—	—	485	—	—	—
1981	550	—	—	—	—	—	—	—	—
1982	—	—	—	—	—	—	400	—	—

Sources:

1. Secretaría de Programación y Presupuesto, *Agenda estadística 1981* (Mexico, 1982), p.171; *Agenda estadística 1982* (Mexico, 1983), p.171.

2. Subsecretaría Forestal y de la Fauna, *Vademecum forestal mexicano 1980* (Mexico, 1980), p.73.

3. Nacional Financiera, S.A., *La economía mexicana en cifras* (Mexico, 1974), p.119.

4. Nacional Financiera, S.A., *La economía mexicana en cifras* (Mexico, 1981), p.132.

5. Secretaría de Programación y Presupuesto, *Las actividades económicas en Mexico* (Mexico, 1980) pp. 106-108.

6. Secretaría de Programación y Presupuesto, *Anuario estadístico de los E.U.M., 1980* (México, 1982), p.114.

7. Salvador Vázquez Reta, "Recursos Forestales: Uso actual, crecimiento, rendimiento, residuos," in Secretaría de Agricultura y Recursos Hidráulicos and Subsecretaría Forestal y de la Fauna, *Simposio internacional: La biomasa forestal, recurso natural renovable y fuente de energía* (Mexico, 1981), p.109..

8. Secretaría de Programación y Presupuesto, *Manual de estadísticas básicas: Sector agropecuario y forestal* (Mexico, 1982), p.118.

9. Cited in Guzmán, Oscar, "Energía en el sector agrícola de subsistencia," in Wionczek, Miguel S., comp., *Energía en México: Ensayos sobre el pasado y el presente* (Mexico: El Colegio de México, 1982), p.110.

a/ Wood production destined for making charcoal.

TABLE 9.10
Estimates of Total Consumption of Firewood as Fuel

Year	Estimate		Source
	$10^3 m^3$	Kcal X 10^{12}	
1975	--	29.9	1
1976	--	20.4	2
1978	--	91.9	3
1979	9200	16.0	4
	8200	18.0	5
1980	--	65.9	6
	--	1.1	7

Sources:
1. IDEE

2. Cited in Guzmán, Oscar, "Energía en el sector agrícola de la subsistencia," in Wionczek, Miguel S., comp., Energía en México: Ensayos sobre el pasado y el presente (Mexico: El Colegio de México, 1982) p.119.
3. Sánchez, Vicente and Umana, P., "Análisis cuantitativo de la participación de la biomasa en el consumo energético de América Latina," Boletín Energético 21 (1981), p.108.
4. Larrañaga, Sergio, "Balance de energía," in Secretaría de Agricultura y Recursos Hidráulicos and Subsecretaría Forestal y de la Fauna, Simposio internacional: La biomasa forestal, recurso natural renovable y fuente de energía (Mexico, 1981), p.116.
5. Reta, Salvador Vázquez, "Recursos Forestales: Uso actual, crecimiento, rendimiento, residuos," in Secretaría de Agricultura y Recursos Hidráulicos and Subsecretaría Forestal y de la Fauna, Simposio internacional: La biomasa forestal, recurso natural renovable y fuente de energía (Mexico, 1981), p.119.
6. Asociación Nacional de Energía Solar, Curso de actualización sobre energía solar (Baja California Sur, 1979), p.120.
7. IV Informe de Gobierno, 1980, State of the Nation Address, José López Portillo.

Note: $1m^3 = 2.26$ X 10^6 Kcal.

TABLE 9.11
Wood Consumption per Capita (kg/day)

Location	Consumption	Source
Coscatlán de Los Reyes, Ver.	5-6	1
San Jerónimo Tulija, Chis.	3-4	1
La Guacamaya, Mich.	3-4	1
Amatlán, Morelos	1-3	1
N.E. Region of State of Puebla	4-2	2
Purificación Tepetitla, State of Mexico	2.1	3
Santa Catarina, State of Mexico	2.3	3
IIE	2.6	4

Sources:
1. Instituto de Investigaciones Eléctricas, Evaluation of Energy Supply and Demand at La Guacamaya, Mich., Mexico: Case Study (Mexico, 1983), p.109.
2. Secretaría de Agricultura y Recursos Hidráulicos and Subsecretaría Forestal y de la Fauna, Simposio internacional: La biomasa forestal, recurso natural renovable y fuente de energía (Mexico, 1981), p.115.
3. Evans, M., Aspectos socio-económicos de la carencia de combustibles domésticos: Un estudio empírico de México rural (Mexico, 1984), p.113.
4. Instituto de Investigaciones Eléctricas, "Evaluación de requerimientos y recursos energéticos en México a nivel rural: Estudio de casos," Mimeograph (Mexico, 1984), p.109. This figure was taken from 12 case studies in rural communities. However, it underestimates consumption when counting people in the population who do not use firewood.

Note: The Latin American average is 3 kg/day according to Organización Latinoamericana de Energía, Boletín Energético 21 (1981), p.69.

TABLE 9.12
Firewood Consumption

Use	1970 10^6 m^3	%	1980 10^6 m^3	%
As Fuel				
Rural Domestic Use	33.0 1/	85	23.0 2/	78
Commercial Use	0.7 1/	2	0.5 2/	1
Total	33.7 1/	87	32.5 2/	79
Non-Energy Uses	5.2 1/	13	8.5 2/	21
Grand Total	38.9	100	41.0	100

Sources:
1. Nacional Financiera, S.A., La economía mexicana en cifras (Mexico, 1981), p.117.
2. Subsecretaría Forestal y de la Fauna, Vademecum forestal mexicano 1980 (México: Dirección General de Información y Sistemas Forestales, 1980), p.193.

TABLE 9.13
Rural Sector: Energy Consumption Projections for 1990

Domestic Subsector

| Source | Energy Consumption | | | | Potential Savings (Kcal x 10^{12}) |
| | Without Measures | | With Measures | | |
	Kcal x 10^{12}	%	Kcal x 10^{12}	%	
Firewood	92.00	--	23.00	--	69.0
Light Oil (Cooking)	1.40	--	--	--	1.40
Liquefied Gas	2.00	--	3.00	--	-1.00
Electricity	0.22	--	0.04	--	0.18
Light Oil (Lighting)	2.23	--	2.23	--	--
Total	97.85	83.6	28.27	5.95	69.58
Productive Subsector					
Diesel	11.49	--	--	--	--
Kerosene	2.32	--	--	--	--
Electric Power	5.4	--	--	--	--
Total a/	19.21	16.4	19.21	40.5	--
Grand Total	117.06	100.0	47.48	100.0	69.58

Source: Estimates of authors.

a/ Does not include fertilizers, whose supply represents an energy
equivalent of 93.1 x 10^{12} Kcal.

TABLE 9.14
Energy Resources Available in Rural Zones

Resource	Amount	Unit	Energy Content	
Forest	54.0	m^3 rolls/year	121.5	10^{12} x Kcal
Wood Wastes	5.0	m^3 rolls/year	11.2	10^{12} x Kcal
Agricultural Wastes	38.3	tons/year	164.0	10^{12} x Kcal
Animal Wastes	356.9	tons/year	89.2	10^{12} x Kcal
Human Wastes	21.1	tons/year	49.3	10^{12} x Kcal
Land Under Cultivation				
Euphorbia Lathyris	25.0	bbl/hectare/year	38.0	10^6 x Kcal/hectare
Sorghum and Sugar	54-19	bbl/hectare/year	290-110	10^6 x Kcal/hectare
Forests	54-19	tons/hectare/year	225-81	10^6 x Kcal/hectare
Aquatic Vegetation	39.8	tons/hectare/year	160.0	10^6 x Kcal/hectare
Algae	18-88	tons/hectare/year	360-374	10^6 x Kcal/hectare
Solar Energy	400-500	cal/cm^2/day	1,150.0	10^6 x Kcal
Eolian Energy at				
La Ventosa, Mexico	6.8	m/sec/217d	8.3	10^{12} x Kcal

Source: Díaz, P., and Rodríguez, V., "Aspectos relevantes para reformular la estrategia energética en México," B.A. thesis (Mexico: Facultad de Ciencias, UNAM, 1984), p. 184.

TABLE 9.15
Policies and Energy Savings and Conservation Measures in the Rural Sector

Uses	Measures to Be in Practice by 1990	Measures to Be in Practice by 2000	Measures to Be in Practice by 2020
Cooking	• Substitute liquefied gas for light oil and firewood in specific localities. • Practice reforestation in areas where firewood is severely lacking. • Introduce mixed-type and Lorena-type stoves and pressure cookers.	• Substitute liquefied gas with firewood and biogas in specific localities. • Achieve total reforestation (40 x 10⁶ hectares). • Develop plans for stables.	• Use mixed stoves based on firewood and biogas. • Conserve forest resources. • Introduce solar cookers.
Lighting	• Promote the production and introduction of discharge lightbulbs (subsidized). • Construct or rehabilitate hydroelectric micropower stations.	• Reduce subsidies. • Introduce cells and air generators in specific localities.	• Practice efficient energy storage. • Achieve maximum electrification with air-generator cells. • Use thermal-solar cells.
Heating Water	• Selectively introduce flat heaters, i.e., install flat collectors in specific localities.	• Introduce passive systems. • Increase efficiency of flat collectors. Follow up.	• Use collectors. • Use passive systems. • Introduce pumps.
Farming	• Develop efficient animal-traction devices. • Select, maintain, and adequately operate tractors. • Introduce new methods and farm equipment.	• Substitute diesel engines with gas, or diesel with hydrogen. • Use energy crops. • Optimize animal traction with devices; coordinate stables in the domestic sector.	• Achieve total substitution by biogas or hydrogen engines.
Fertilizing	• Have programs to use fertilizers rationally. • Develop composte heaps. • Develop pilot program for stables.	• Use organic fertilizers based on biodigesters and composte heaps. • Use coordinated program of stables.	• Use biodigesters.
Irrigation	• Use water storage and containment in high-precipitation areas. • Save water with more efficient irrigation techniques (drop dispersion). • Replan irrigation systems.	• Introduce air pumps, air generators, and solar pumps in specific localities. • Develop improvements in drilling	• Irrigate with air pumps and solar pumps.

TABLE 9.16
Energy Consumption Outlook to 2020 (Kcal x 10^{12})

Use	Source						Total	Device Efficiency
	Fertilizers	Biogas	Firewood	Sun and Wind	Human Labor	Animal Labor		
Fertilization	(20)[a]						(20)	58.2 x 10^6 cows in stables for 5.82 x 10^6 biodigesters of 15 cm.
Irrigation		22.4[b]			1.1[c]		22.4	Electric pumps fed by biogas generators (.33 X 6)
Crops		26.6[d]					26.66	Biogas engines 0.3
Cooking		7.4[e]	15[f]		1.2[g]		23.6	Mixed-type stoves Firewood .2 Biogas .3
Heating Water				4.9[h]			4.9	Solar collectors 0.5
Lighting				0.1[i]			0.1	Self-generation : Solar cells : Microcenters : Fluorescent lightbulbs
Total	(20)[j]	56.4	15	5	2.3	k	78.7 +animal labor	

(continued)

TABLE 9.16 (continued)

a/ A 15-cm biodigestor fed with the excrement from 10 cows
   (25 kg each) produces .94 kg of nitrogen. At 200 kg of
   fertilizer per hectare, 5.82×10^6 biodigesters would
   be needed for the 10^7 hectares.

b/ Some 7.48×10^{12} Kcal of electricity were needed, according to the electric energy per hectare, in irri-
   gated areas by 1980: $\dfrac{3.2 \times 10^6 \text{ Kcal}}{4.3 \times 10^6 \text{ irrigated hectares}}$
   The efficiency of a gas generator is estimated at 33%.

c/ Human labor is calculated as 2×10^6 workers, working
   eight hours/day, five days a week all year, on 10^7 hectares, for all agricultural activities.

d/ Tractors would work 40 hectares each, implying one thousand hours a year of use.

e/ With a caloric content of 4.166 Kcal/cubic meter of
   biogas and five members per family, there would be 300
   Kcal of useful energy per capita. Biogas is burned in
   stoves with 30% efficiency.

f/ The remaining 400 Kcal/day per capita of useful energy
   needed for cooking will be obtained from 0.5 kg of fire-
   wood/day per capita and stoves with 20% efficiency.

g/ Human labor is calculated as one person per family, 4
   hours/day, 250 Kcal/hour.

h/ With a 50% collector efficiency, 600 Kcal/day per capita will be needed to heat 40 liters of water to 40°C
   every three days.

i/ Electricity is generated from the devices marked in the
   last column of the chart. The consumption indicated
   takes only the efficiency of the fluorescent lights into account and not those of sun, wood, or water conversion or electricity.

j/ A commercial fertilizer requires approximately 10^7 Kcal
   per ton of nitrogen. The equivalent is indicated between parentheses but is not included in the totals.

k/ Animal labor is included for all kinds of activities,
   but the data are not computed here because animal labor
   will be used in the other 30×10^6 hectares of the agricultural frontier. The 58 million animals will feed on
   6.4×10^6 hectares planted with corn or other crops,
   providing 10 tons of dry feed per hectare. Each cow
   eats 30 kg of dry feed a day.

APPENDIX TO CHAPTER 9

ESTIMATED ENERGY CONSUMPTION STATISTICS

The following details relate to the projected energy consumption by 1990 and 2020.

PROJECTIONS FOR 1990

Projections for the rural domestic subsector consider the probable growth of the total rural population and of the consumer population for each energy source by 1990 as well as maintaining current per capita energy consumption for that year. Therefore, energy consumption for 1990 would be 97.85 X 10^{12} Kcal, a decrease of less than 1.0% in 1980 consumption. This is the result of a decrease in the number of consumers using firewood.

For each source, the growth in the consumer population and the amount of demand by 1990 will be the following:

1. Firewood: The number of consumers will decrease at 3.5% annual rate for ten years. That is, 77% of the rural population will use firewood to cook and will need 92 X 10^{12} Kcal (30.7 X 10^6 cm of rolled paper).
2. Light Oil: Light oil for cooking will have the same number of consumers as in 1980, which is 9.5% of the 1990 rural population and a demand of 2.23 X 10^{12} Kcal. It will be used for cooking by 2.5% more people in rural areas than in 1980, or 65% of the population in 1990, using 2.23 X 10^{12} Kcal.

3. Liquefied Gas: The number of consumers will grow some 106% over 1980 figures. Thirteen percent of the rural population will use liquefied gas in 1990, requiring some 2 X 10^{12} Kcal of energy.
4. Electricity: It will be used mainly for illumination for 8.7% more users than in 1980, that is, 35% of the total 1990 rural population. The demand will be 0.22 X 10^{12} Kcal.

Energy projections for the productive subsector were calculated using the probable development of total energy consumption per hectare for each of the sources (hydrocarbons, fertilizers, and electricity) and of the amount of irrigated and rain-fed land:

Year	Irrigated Land (in millions of hectares)	Rain-Fed Land (in millions of hectares)
1960	3.5	8.7
1970	4.3	10.6
1980	5.5	11.8
1990	6.6	13.4

It is estimated that energy consumption in the productive subsector will grow at an average of 4% annually and reach 19.21 X 10^{12} Kcal in 1990, or 112.31 X 10^{12} Kcal, if fertilizers are included. With such parameters, the individual consumptions will be:

1. Diesel: 11.49 X 10^{12} Kcal. Land area: 19.4 X 10^6 hectares.
2. Kerosene: 2.32 X 10^{12} Kcal. Land area: 19.4 X 10^6 hectares.
3. Electricity: 5.4 X 10^{12} Kcal. Land area: 6 X 10^6 hectares.
4. Fertilizers: 93.1 X 10^{12} Kcal. Land area: 19.4 X 10^6 hectares.

PROJECTIONS FOR 2020

The following three starting points were used to construct the scenario for the rural sector:

1. Satisfied basic human needs so as to reduce the socioeconomic inequalities in the country

2. Endogenous self-sufficiency through participation and social control
3. Harmony with the environment

These objectives mark a series of social, economic and environmental preferences that in turn, determine the selection of sources and technologies that would integrate the pattern of energy consumption.

The preceding postulates can be translated into the following concrete premises for the scenario:

1. Only renewable resources will be used: sun, wind, water, firewood, and biomass
2. Self-sufficiency in food: The country will produce, within its boundaries, all the food needed to cover a basic diet satisfying the minimum nutritional needs of the entire population. Some 4.4 million to 17 million hectares will be destined for 120 million inhabitants, depending on the productivity obtained. The total agricultural frontier will be 40 million hectares.
3. Maximum mechanization and fertilization possible in 10 million hectares: This area will be open to intensive agriculture and cattle raising and will depend on the regeneration of the soil and an adequate planning of soil use.
4. In these 10 million hectares, the main source of renewable energy will be the biodigesters providing gas and fertilizers. Other sources could play an important role in the other 30×10^6 hectares.
5. The cooking, lighting, and hot-water needs of the 20,171,000 inhabitants making up the rural population will be satisfied. (It is not necessary to indicate if the uses mentioned will be satisfied because other needs, such as heating, food, refrigeration, and so on, are also important. Restricting it to three uses reflects only a simplification of the scenario.)
6. Effect the reforestation of no less than 40 million hectares with multiple-use species.

For the purpose of calculating the energy consumptions for each use, the following energy requirements were considered for the domestic sector:

. Cooking   700 Kcal/daily per capita
. Lighting   6.4 Kcal/daily per capita
. Heating Water 333 Kcal/daily per capita

We obtained the consumptions indicated in Table 9.13 as well as those for the productive sector by using these energy requirements and the efficiencies of each source.

The consumption pattern proposed also determines the requirements of appropriate technology. Therefore, the domestic sector will need the following:

. 4,034,000   Mixed biogas-firewood stoves
. 16 X 10^6 Fluorescent lightbulbs
. 6,700,000   Cubic meters of flat collector
. 5,829,000   Biodigesters

The productive sector will need the following:

. 250,000   Tractors run on biogas

10

Conclusions

It is apparent that over the past several years Mexico has required increasing amounts of energy. A detailed analysis of the economic trends and the energy requirements in the sectors producing and consuming energy indicates that this phenomenon cannot be explained exclusively by the growth process or by the development of larger segments of the population. Mexico has utilized its energy resources inefficiently and wastefully, especially since the middle of the 1970s when the mass extraction of hydrocarbons was well under way. As a consequence, the possibilities for conservation and efficient energy use are, without exaggeration, quite considerable.

To give the reader an idea of the potential energy savings involved, the estimates in the respective sectorial studies were totaled. The feasibility of these estimates depends on a series of variables and restrictions (economic, political, and technical) and on decisions made, at both national and specific levels, by the state and the corresponding agencies, by industries and companies, by regions, and so on. Consequently, there is no sound basis for predicting if the measures proposed will be put into practice and, if so, if they will have an immediate impact. The experience of other countries shows the impossibility of fully attaining these potential levels of savings and conservation and, moreover, that the impact of conservation programs of this type will be felt beyond the year 2000.

The estimates of potential energy savings for the years 1990 and 2000 are shown in Table 10.1. It is clear that the figures are highest for those areas where a precise study of energy consumption patterns was possible (CFE and the steel, cement, and sugar industries). From

TABLE 10.1
Potential Energy Savings in Mexico by 1990 and 2000

Sector	By 1990			By 2000			1984-1990		Cumulative 1991-2000		Total	
	10^{12} Kcal	mboe	US$ (millions)	10^{12} Kcal	mboe	US$ (millions)	10^{12} Kcal	US$ (millions)	10^{12} Kcal	US$ (millions)	US$ (millions)	%
PEMEX	46.8	37	1,004	91.2	71	1,954	178	3,823	658	14,108	17,931	17.7
CFE a/	35.0	27	743	150.0	117	3,217	133	2,859	1,082	23,203	26,062	25.7
Energy Subtotal	81.8	64	1,747	241.2	188	5,171	312	6,682	1,739	37,311	43,993	43.3
Transport	42.0	34	935	60.0	47	1,293	160	3,454	433	9,336	12,790	12.6
Industry	38.6	30	825	109.3	85	2,338	179	3,846	730	15,659	19,505	19.2
Steelmaking	10.2	8	220	33.1	26	715	39	837	216	4,633	5,470	
Cement	16.0	12	330	44.8	35	963	96	2,065	295	6,328	8,393	
Sugar	12.4	10	275	31.4	24	660	44	944	219	4,698	5,642	
RCPb/	7.8	6	165	23.4	18	495	30	644	169	4,641	5,285	5.2
Rural	69.6	54	1,485	92.6 c/	72	1,986	265	5,684	668	14,329	20,013	19.7
Grand Total	239.8	188	5,157	526.5	410	11,283	945	20,310	3,740	81,276	101,586	100

Sources: Estimates of authors.

a/ Data for HD. Cf. Table 5.18.
b/ Estimates considering technological innovations in refrigerators and television sets.
c/ Assumes that 23 x 10^{12} Kcal of firewood will no longer be consumed by the year 2000.
This figure was added to savings achieved in 1990, because of the policy of using forests in a renewable form.

these figures, we can see that for the year 1990 potential savings would be 240 Kcal X 10^{12}, that is, 188 mboe. If this amount of oil were exported, at current average prices (27.5 dollars/barrel), it would yield more than 5,000 million dollars. Cumulative savings from 1982-1984 to 1990 would be 945 X 10^{12} Kcal, or 20,310 million dollars. This is the equivalent of approximately one-fourth of Mexico's current foreign debt.

For the year 2000, potential savings are more than double what they are for 1990, that is, 527 X 10^{12} Kcal, or 410 mboe. This means more than 11,000 million dollars at current prices for Mexican crude. Cumulative savings from 1990 to 2000 would be 3,740 X 10^{12} Kcal, the equivalent of more than 81,000 million dollars. In dollars terms, the potential cumulative savings by the year 2000 would be approximately equivalent to Mexico's current foreign debt: 100,000 million dollars.

Even with these estimates, it would, of course, be an exaggeration to suppose that savings made by adopting policies of conservation and efficient energy use could pay a major part of Mexico's foreign debt. These figures are only an indicator of the magnitude of the potential savings and a reflection of how urgent and necessary it is to implement a policy of efficient energy use. This is all the more true if one considers the critical state of the domestic economy in Mexico and the country's extreme dependency on nonrenewable energy sources.

Official concern for energy waste was expressed first by the López Portillo administration in the Programa Nacional de Energéticos and again by the current administration in the Programa Nacional de Energéticos 1984-1988. However, corrective measures have only been applied in isolated situations.

Implementing programs of this nature requires precise studies on the patterns and development of energy consumption in production and end use and on overall, sectorial, and company levels. Once these patterns have been analyzed and compared with what is happening internationally, it will be possible to judge how inefficient and wasteful Mexico is with its energy resources. From this will come proposals for adopting global and concrete measures for the conservation and efficient use of these resources.

These were the precise objectives of the Project on the Conservation and Efficient Use of Energy, the results of which are presented in this book and are summarized again in the following sections.

GENERAL OBSERVATIONS

One possible explanation for the differences between the pattern and development of consumption in Mexico and those in other countries is derived from the differences in domestic energy prices during the 1970s and 1980s. Policies directed toward price increases seem, at first glance, easy for Mexico to adopt, given the state's monopolistic control of energy supplies. However, a diverse series of problems counteracts the benefits of such a plan. Private consumers, for example, are sensitive to price increases in the products of state-run companies, especially electricity and gasoline. General increases in energy prices are problematic because of inflation; such increases are passed on to the consumer by the private sector almost automatically.

Another problem for Mexico is determining a proper level for energy prices. Present emphasis is on a "policy of realistic prices." However, the costs incurred in producing energy are unknown. The alternative policy of stable prices, using existing international prices as a point of reference, would work against using the country's resources to promote development. There is undoubtedly a need to establish proper energy prices. To do this, however, production costs will have to be learned and a decision made about which sectors and social groups will shoulder the increases.

Other energy-related measures are also needed. A great number of state-owned companies have high energy consumptions, PEMEX and CFE among them. Prices of input and products do not play the same role in state-owned companies as they do in private companies: In many cases, prices are subordinate to other considerations. Thus, pricing policies have a limited effect on energy consumption in state-owned companies.

Other measures that could be adopted include fiscal and financial incentives, regulation, information and consultation, and increased research and development. The nationalization of the banks makes it possible to design a package of fiscal-financial incentives directed toward companies with investments in or investment programs for machinery, equipment, plants, and buildings designed to conserve energy. Some of these incentives are tax reductions, easily available credit or preferential interest rates for credit, and accelerated depreciation of machinery and equipment.

Measures designed to regulate energy consumption are varied. Some of those for private users and all of those for government concerns could be obligatory. Standards of efficiency that could be checked periodically through energy audits should be established. Large energy consumers should be made to adopt conservation measures and to report their progress periodically to the appropriate government authorities. Also, people should be appointed to handle energy conservation measures in government dependencies.

Energy consumption in the RCP sector could be regulated through restrictions in the use of heating and air conditioning, decorative lighting, and electric power during peak hours. Another measure to promote is the use of adequate insulation in building. Finally, city and highway traffic could be regulated, and the use of mass transportation could be promoted.

Such regulatory measures should be accompanied by information campaigns; consultation; publicity; and, most importantly, the promotion and support of technological research and development to discover means for energy efficiency and reductions in nonrenewable resource consumption.

PEMEX

In the energy sector, PEMEX is the energy producer with the highest energy consumption and the least efficient use of resources. Energy waste, typical of the company's entire range of extraction and transformation activities, has increased sharply since the mid-1970s because of the growth in production. The policies of giving priority to hydrocarbon extraction and export goals and of increasing the installed refining and petrochemical capacity in plants already among the world's largest disregarded efficient energy use or energy conservation.

The inadequacies in planning and executing construction work propitiated burning off enormous amounts of gas, one of the industry's main energy losses. The accelerated pace of oil extraction is evidence of the lack of interest in conserving resources. As a corollary, there was a tendency toward prematurely depleting resources, without making maximum use of the hydrocarbon reserves in the subsoil. Secondary recuperation measures did not produce the results expected, partly because of inadequate planning and execution. Therefore, the growing inefficiencies found in the industry's extraction phase before the 1980s originated principally in the economic and social policies that placed hydrocarbons at the center of development. The internal restrictions that were imposed as a result of the rate of production expansion and that delayed the meeting of technical and planning needs were all that was necessary to establish a pattern of energy waste.

With the industrial transformation of hydrocarbons into energy, petrochemicals and derived products had to adapt production to the strong domestic demand. The case studies presented on refining and basic petrochemicals indicate there is a margin for energy savings in both fields. The development in the specific consumptions of refineries shows a decrease in the energy efficiency of the processes during the 1970s. Comparisons with international norms show that improvements could be made, allowing savings of up to 60% in specific consumption.

The basic petrochemical industry, despite its modern industrial plants, could also consume energy more efficiently. It is clear from comparisons with international norms that some of the plants could achieve savings of up to 70%. In both refining and petrochemicals, the design and construction of plants has influenced their actual consumption. The design of these plants is based on technology from the United States, a country particularly wasteful of energy.

An overall diagnosis shows that important potential savings can be made in all the industry's activities. Taking advantage of these savings depends on conceiving and instrumenting an integral program for conserving and using energy efficiently. To do this, it is of prime importance to have energy audits of the companies that would reveal the way in which energy is consumed in each system of production and transportation. Once these studies are available, short-, medium-, and long-term measures can be formulated. A technical-economic evaluation should be made before putting the measures into practice.

The measures that should be considered cover extraction, transportation, distribution and storage, and industrial transformation. The programs for extraction and transportation that are already under way should be continued: minimize the burning of gas into the atmosphere; avoid dehydration losses of crude and water as well as storage losses; and optimize the transportation system, giving priority to moving products by pipeline, where technical and economic conditions permit. In industrial operations, the

generation and use of steam and the recuperation of residual heat from the stacks are improvements that can have a
significant impact on efficiency. Analyses of how the
steam system can be optimized and what the possibilities
are for cogeneration should be given priority. These
short- and medium-term measures have to be complemented by
long-term measures that include investments in technological innovations that can be integrated into the existing
production processes.

PEMEX has begun development of a three-stage program
of conservation and savings. If the proposed measures are
carried out, estimated potential savings would average a-
bout 20%, with an additional possible increase of 15% to
25% if, by the end of the 1980s, obsolete production systems are substituted with more modern ones.

Preserving hydrocarbon resources is an indispensable
step in a transition toward the use of other energy
sources, one that guarantees that the availability of these
sources will not slow down socioeconomic development.

CFE

The development of energy consumption in electric generation has been characterized by the growing importance
of thermoelectric plants in CFE's production. Consequently, there is greater dependency on hydrocarbons, especially bunker oil. This dependency affects the improvements
in efficiency made by the thermoelectric plants. The levels of efficiency attained are below international standards. These factors, in addition to the preponderance of
thermoelectric plants in Mexico, underscore the need not
only to use nonrenewable resources more efficiently but also to promote cogeneration and the diversification of primary sources for electric power in favor of renewable
sources.

With regard to these needs, experience has shown how
important it is that the design, construction, and quality
of equipment be congruous with one another. Maintenance
and care of the boilers and steam generators, as well as
the other equipment, would bring about considerable increases in plant efficiency, with no additional cost. Also,
efforts must be made to reduce the demand of nonproductive
users during peak hours.

Cogeneration is another important way to improve the
use and conservation of nonrenewable resources. It should

be promoted in industrial plants requiring steam and in
thermoelectric plants. This would notably reduce the pressure on CFE's energy supply. Combined cycle is a recent
technological innovation proven to make notable reductions
in overall specific energy consumption. Promoting its use
would be another effort toward increasing efficiency in
the subsector.

The growing dependency on nonrenewable resources for
generating electricity is a problem with no feasible solution in the near future. CFE itself has made substantial
reductions in its projections for the power generated by
hydroelectric plants. The current projection for the year
2000 is 60% lower than the projection made for 1980. The
dependency problem is magnified, however, by the fact that
CFE considers any increase in electric power demand beyond
planned production will be covered by plants using hydrocarbons. Therefore, even the most optimistic projections
foresee a greater dependency on nonrenewable sources. It
is important, therefore, to increase efforts to diversify
sources, expanding the use of renewable sources, as soon
as the country's economic situation permits.

TRANSPORTATION SECTOR

Meeting the transportation sector's needs resulted in
an important change in the sectorial composition of Mexico's end-use energy balances during the 1970s' Accelerated growth in demand, mainly of gasoline and diesel, not
only made this sector the largest end user of enerby but
also put strong pressure on the oil industry's productive
capacity. This complicated the transportation sector's expansion even more from 1975 on.

This situation is the result of a cumulative, three-
part process that began four decades ago. A transportation
system that was based on land transportation was established. The highway infrastructure, developed by the state,
has been complemented since the 1960s by the installation
and growth of Mexico's automobile industry. The harmonious
cooperation of the state and the transnational automobile
companies in integrating the country's development was supposed to be guaranteed by the supply of sufficient, oppor-
tune, and cheap fuel from the national oil industry. This
shaped Mexico's present transportation structure, which
was consolidated in the 1970s.

The current transportation system is determined by

two components: automobile transportation, both passenger
and freight, and hydrocarbon derivatives. The system is
distorted by the predominance of private automobiles and
by the displacement of the railroad. These factors have
all contributed to making this sector a highly inefficient
energy consumer. Other contributing factors are the relatively low consumption of diesel compared to gasoline, the
explosive urbanization of the country's main population
centers, and the lack of planning based on the country's
needs.

Excessively low diesel prices have not been enough of
an incentive to promote its use over gasoline. Low liquefied gas costs also have not produced the desired results.
The use of liquefied gas as a fuel in various cities has
created pressures that, together with residential area demands, have led to the need for gas imports at the expense
of hard currency. Thus, improving the efficiency of the
country's transportation system is justified not only on
economic grounds but also by the need to preserve the environment and raise the quality of people's lives.

Modifying current energy consumption patterns in
transportation means implementing measures related to the
sector's organization and structure. These measures would
help to quickly reduce excessive fuel use in urban centers
and to eliminate congestion on the highways. These measures include improving traffic flow in large urban centers
with an adequate and coordinated system of traffic lights,
strictly adhering to the laws regulating traffic, and modifying driving habits. These measures should be complemented by the encouraged use of mass transportation, the
increase in the number of passengers to each vehicle, and
the shift from highway to rail transportation for some
freight.

In the long run, reducing engine size, which has already been legislated in Mexico, and converting part of engine production from gasoline to diesel would result in
additional energy savings. However, one of the main ways
to improve energy efficiency and transportation services
is the long-term modification of the transportation structure itself. This would require improving and expanding
the railroad, subway, and other mass transportation systems and, at the same time, extending coastal freight
services.

Using fuels that are alternatives or are complementary to gasoline could reduce the pressure or demand. This
implies using biomass as a future energy source. However,

this does not seem particularly viable in Mexico considering current hydrocarbon availability.

INDUSTRIAL SECTOR

The industrial manufacturing sector did not appear to be one of the most inefficient energy users during the 1970s. However, little is known about where energy resources end up and how they are used at the production level to make a statement that is valid for all the branches and industries making up this sector. The case studies presented on the steel, cement, and sugar industries show the heterogeneous nature of each industry in regard to the energy efficiency of each industry's branches and even of each industry itself. Thus, the cement industry has developed in a way that distinguishes it sharply from the sugar industry. The sugar industry is characterized by production and energy disparities in the factories, high overall inefficiency, and a consequent waste of energy.

The detailed analysis of the production processes and their energy yields revealed that in these three industries considerable energy savings are possible. Decreasing specific consumptions will be conditioned by the degree to which measures are implemented. These measures include both short- and long-term considerations. A wide range of measures--from those with almost immediate effect and of relatively low cost, to those introducing changes in processes, incorporating new technology, and bringing large investments into play--can be applied.

During the 1970s, Mexico's steel industry tended to encourage production processes that had lower specific consumptions. However, an analysis of energy efficiency shows that this industry operated at efficiency levels below those obtained internationally during the mid-1970s. The production phases examined show that some specific consumptions are 15% to 40% higher than international consumptions.

There is wisdom in studying the feasibility of different energy efficiency measures. These measures include preparing materials; operating blast furnaces, soaking pits, and reheating and annealing furnaces; maintaining or replacing certain parts in areas of production where losses are concentrated; and improving instrumentation and process control. Cogeneration in the steel industry would not only improve plant efficiency but would also provide close to one-third of all electric power needs, thereby reducing demands on the network. These measures should reduce the specific consumptions of the different production phases. This could be done while the plants are in operation and in the transition toward a more modern and efficient productive structure based on smaller-sized units than currently used.

The cement industry has been quick to incorporate relatively new techniques into its processes and to increase production of puzzolanic cement, showing a marked tendency toward efficient energy use, in particular, of fuel. Notwithstanding the advances made by this industry in saving energy, there is still room for improvement because differences still exist between the industry's specific consumption and that achieved internationally. If we compare international levels with Mexico's there is a 26% margin for efficiency improvement.

The measures yielding the most important savings, modifying furnaces and increasing the number of preheating stages, are likewise those calling for the largest investments and the longest periods of repayment. However, losses can be reduced in the insulation and combustion systems without large expenditures. Increasing the use of hydraulic cements with extenders would also produce significant savings. The client's choice of cements plays a principal role in the development of energy efficiency. Mexico's cement industry is an example of a branch that is not outside the mainstream of modernized production but has not yet reached an efficiency comparable to international norms.

The sugar industry is the opposite of the cement industry. It combines stagnant production with greater specific consumption, thereby wasting energy, especially bunker oil. A study of the characteristics of sixty-six sugarcane factories does not show any relationship between their specific consumptions (and their variations) and installed production capacity, plant size, and the extent to which capacity is used. Differing trends have been apparent over the last few years: Some plants improve their efficiency, and the efficiency other plants gets considerably worse. The reasons for the increase in the specific consumptions of bunker oil in the sugar industry are beyond the technical considerations of this book. Also, bunker oil hides the inefficiency of the sugar-making process, especially the inadequate handling of the steam produced by an obsolete and low-efficiency system.

The heterogeneous nature of the plants making up the industry does facilitate making overall savings proposals for the sugarcane factories. It is clear that the generation and use of steam are areas for improvement. In this industry, waste is not exclusively technical in origin; it is also due to institutional, political, and economic reasons. Creating and applying an energy-saving program requires rigorous planning and the consensus of the interest groups connected with these productive activities. Based on comparisons with the Cuban sugarcane industry, potential savings of the order of 50% of the 1980 energy consumption level can be made.

The case studies presented on the steel, cement, and sugar industries represent an important advance in understanding energy consumption patterns and the degree of efficiency with which different phases of production are carried out. The studies show the need to analyze other industries that use energy intensively. The studies also point to the advantages of delving further into the technical, economic, and political-institutional viability of specific energy-saving programs contemplated by various industries.

This book presents the first approximation of an analysis of particular energy consumption features in the main industrial branches: mining-metallurgy, chemicals, cellulose and paper, glass, and brewing. The high level of energy used for heat, either directly as fuel or to generate steam, as opposed to that used for electricity, indicates that potential savings are possible even though we have not yet determined where. The large amount of steam produced in the chemical and paper industries, the dispersion of the specific intrabranch consumptions, and, of course, differences between Mexican and international norms, are factors contributing to this conclusion. In all of the industries examined, cogeneration offers an alternative for utilizing fuel better and shifting demand away from thermoelectric plants. The generation of steam-produced electricity, together with other uses of steam, could satisfy up to one-third of the industry's power demands as well as conserve energy resources.

From this industry analysis, we can also see that energy bills have had a limited effect so far on production costs in the different industries, illustrated by the fact that energy expenditures have little relation to industrial sales. In fact, even in extreme cases, energy costs were only 10% of branch sales in 1981. These figures not only reflect a policy of low prices but also encourage the wasting of energy during production. The phenomenon is even worse in state-owned industries, where energy is almost considered a free and unlimited resource.

RESIDENTIAL, COMMERCIAL, AND PUBLIC SECTOR (RCP)

The RCP sector's share of end-use energy is not very large. It is, however, important qualitatively because access to energy in all homes (residential subsector) is a way of improving social welfare. The principal forms of energy consumed in the sector are, in order of importance, liquefied gas and electricity. Of the three subsectors that make up the RCP, the residential subsector is the most important.

An analysis of this sector's consumption is difficult because of inadequate information. It was impossible to study liquefied gas consumption, and the information on electric power consumption is determined from tariffs set by CFE. There is also an overlap in CFE's definition of consumer groups; for example, commercial and industrial companies and public services have the same tariff.

The residential subsector showed considerable increases in the specific consumption of electricity, especially during the last ten years. The continual decrease in the real costs of electric power (especially in the tariffs for domestic use in hot climates) and the growing use of domestic and electronic appliances in the home are the reasons for this trend. Savings are possible by modifying both energy consumption in such appliances and electric power demands. Incorporating the best technology available in industrialized countries into the domestic appliance market is one way to reduce the domestic waste of electricity.

Power demands can be influenced both by price and by consumer information campaigns. The price influence, moreover, would have a positive effect on CFE finances. Several years ago the company initiated the Programa Nacional para el Uso Racional de la Electricidad (PRONURE, the National Program for the Rational Use of Electricity). The effects of this energy consumption program have yet to be evaluated.

Large portions of the population still do not have access to power in the home. At the other end of the scale, however, there are those households with sufficient purchasing power to acquire the most sophisticated domestic appliances. A plan to emphasize efficient energy use should be part of a strategy program with the objective of supplying electricity to all sectors currently without it. Expanding the electric power network and setting tariffs according to income level, area, or region, thus discriminating against the economically privileged consumer groups, would be one way to achieve both goals.

RURAL SECTOR

This is the first time in Mexico that a study of energy consumption patterns has attempted to treat the rural sector as a "consumer sector," transcending the divisions in energy balances. The concept of rural sector applied here includes both the productive and domestic activities of the country's rural areas. The limited information available had to be rearranged accordingly.

The rural energy problem was systematically left aside until the beginning of the 1980s. Such disregard was due to a general lack of knowledge and information and, above all, to the concept, deeply-rooted in some decision-making circles, that development is a linear process; in other words, the industrialization and urbanization associated with the growth of a mixed economy will make social margination and the problems linked with it disappear. In the area of energy use, this position meant disregarding nonconventional and noncommercial consumption patterns so that the basic needs of almost one-third of the country's population were not even considered.

The energy consumption of the rural sector was about 10% of total domestic consumption, including the energy sector. The brunt of the rural sector's demand falls on the domestic subsector and is characterized by a widespread and inefficient use of firewood as a fuel for cooking food and heating water. Other fuels are secondary compared to wood in terms of gross energy. The use of biomass as an energy source is derived, to a great extent, from the fact that vast sectors of the rural population do not have access to commercial fuels. This situation is made worse by the isolation and dispersion of rural communities and the limitations of commercial energy distribution. In those communities where there is distribution, people with economic resources combine wood with some other fuel, preferably liquefied gas.

In the production subsector, there is a strong polarization between entrepreneurial holdings and peasant holdings (that is, units of production and consumption). The mechanization of labor, fertilization, irrigation, and commercial energy are connected mainly with the entrepreneurial holdings, and human and animal work, irrigation by rain, and the absence of fuel characterize the productive conditions under which the peasants work.

Homes with electricity are fewer than statistics indicate because in communities with power lines, only the people with higher incomes use it. The rest of the population sues liquid fuels and, in extreme cases, ocote to supplement electricity, which is mainly used for lighting. Rural and Urban energy consumption patterns differ significantly because of the composition of and access to sources and because of the degree of efficiency in converting fuel into energy.

The use of firewood, together with the fact that the farming-cattle areas are growing and that forests are being cut down for non-energy purposes has meant increased deforestation. This has made access to energy more difficult for peasants and meant that a naturally renewable resource is being exploited less.

The relative underconsumption characterizing close to one-third of the country's population requires that an analysis of the rural sector's energy efficiency, savings, and conservation be done from a different point of view than analyses of the other sectors. This should not invalidate perspectives for using energy better. In the rural sector, better energy use has to be reconciled with the growth in consumption.

In Mexico, as in the rest of Latin America and in a large part of the countries where there is still a significant peasant population, improvements in living standards require energy and socioeconomic development policies to be conceived and implemented on the basis of a precise understanding of both the sector's overall and particular characteristics and problems. These characteristics and problems should be approached from a multidimensional viewpoint; should not be restricted by the economic laws of a nonexistent free-market economy; and should incorporate the social, cultural, and anthropological elements that define the essential features of a rural population whose ethnic diversity is a part of the substratum on which the state rests.

In rural areas, consumption patterns show a certain

uniformity in energy sources and habits that goes beyond the social heterogeneity mentioned. All energy policies should consider this as a central factor if a favorable reaction is to come from the rural population.

In the future, the incorporation of isolated communities and marginated peasant groups and the trend toward greater per capita energy consumption should not be at odds with a more efficient and nondepredatory use of finite or renewable energy resources. For this to occur, it is imperative energy and rural development policies be delineated in such a way as to harmonize differing objectives. Such objectives should include extending consumption to the entire rural population at a level adequate for its needs, encouraging the efficient use of energy, and conserving energy and natural resources. This should be carried out within a perspective of improving the population's living standards and recuperating and sustaining Mexico's self-sufficiency in food production.

Bibliography

Aguilar, Martiniano. Refinación petrolera en México: Desarrollo tecnológico actual. Mexico: Instituto de Investigaciones Eléctricas, 1978.

Asociación Nacional de Energía Solar. Curso de actualización sobre energía solar. Baja California Sur: Asociación Nacional de Energía Solar, 1979.

Azúcar, S.A. Estadísticas azucareras. Mexico: Azucar, S.A., 1983.

Bazán, Gerardo. "El perfil energético mexicano en 1982," mimeograph. Mexico, 1982.

Banco de México. Indicadores económicos. Mexico: Banco de México, May 1983.

Centro de Estudios de la Energía. Situación energética de la industria: Sector eléctrico. Madrid: Centro de la Energía, 1979.

Comisión de Energéticos. "Pronóstico de demanda de energía (modelos conjuntos)," mimeograph. Mexico, 1976.

_____. "Demanda interna, ahorro, sustitución y precios de los energéticos," mimeograph. Mexico, 1982.

_____. Energéticos: Boletín informativo del sector energético. Mexico: November 1981, April 1982, August 1982, and November 1982.

Comisión Federal de Electricidad. "Evolución de la eficiencia de conversión de energía térmica en energía eléctrica," mimeograph. Mexico: Gerencia de Estudios, July 1984.

_____. "Evolución de las tarifas de energía eléctrica en México 1962-1980." Mexico: Comisión Federal de Electricidad, June 1981.

_____. Plan nacional de electrificación rural 1979-1982. Mexico: Comisión Federal de Electricidad, July 1978.

_____. Sector eléctrico nacional: Estadísticas 1962-1982. Mexico: Comisión Federal de Electricidad, 1984.

_____. Informe de operación 1981. Mexico: Comisión Federal de Electricidad.

Coordinación General del Plan Nacional de Zonas Deprimidas y Grupos Marginados. Las necesidades esenciales de México. Mexico, 1982.

De Alba, Enrique. "Análisis de la demanda de energía en México: Un modelo de simulación," mimeograph. Mexico: Oficina de Asesores del C. Presidente, November 1982.

_____. "La demanda de energía en México: Versión preliminar," Document E 8301. Mexico: Instituto Tecnológico Autónomo de México, Departamento de Matemáticas, 1983.

Díaz, P., and V. Rodríguez. "Aspectos relevantes para reformular la estrategia energética en México," B.A. thesis. Facultad de Ciencias, Universidad Nacional Autónoma de México, 1984.

Diemex-Wharton. Proyecto automotriz. Mexico: Diemex-Wharton, November 1983.

Dobozi, István. "The Special Source of Alternative Energy: Comparing Energy Conservation Performance of the East and the West," mimeograph. Madrid, September 1983.

Evans, M. Aspectos socio-económicos de la carencia de combustibles domésticos: Un estudio empírico de México rural. Mexico, 1984.

Federal Energy Administration. "The Political for Energy Conservation in Nine Selected Industries." In Petroleum Refining, vol. 2. Washington, D.C.: Federal Energy Administration.

Food and Agriculture Organization. Informe sobre tracción animal. Rome: Food and Agriculture Organization, 1981.

Gastélum, Raúl, and Oscar M. Guzmán. "Posibilidades de ahorro de energía en el sector energético de México (Versión preliminar)," mimeograph. Mexico, November 1982.

Giesecke, R. et al. Leña y carbón vegetal: Su incorporación en la planificación y política energéticas. Managua: Nicaragua. and Instituto Nicaragüense de Energía, 1981.

Gordian Associates. An Energy Conservation Target for Industry. New York: Gordian Associates, 1976.

Grupo Intersectorial de Transporte. Consumo de energéticos por productos del sector transporte. Mexico: Grupo Intersectorial de Transporte, 1981.

Guzmán, Oscar M. "Energía y sector agrícola de subsistencia." In Energía en México: Ensayos sobre el pasado y el presente, compiled by Miguel S. Wionczek. Mexico: El Colegio de México, 1982.

Gyftopoulos, Lazanidis, and Witmar Gyftopoulos. Potential Fuel Effectiveness in Industry. 1978.

336

Haswell, M. Energy for Survival. Cambridge: 1981.

Hidalgo, C.H. "Aprovechamiento racional de la energía en centrales termoeléctricas," mimeograph. Mexico: Comisión Federal de Electricidad and Gerencia de Generación y Transmisión.

Ibarra, J. Los energéticos en el desarrollo revolucionario de México. Mexico: 1982.

Institute of Energy Economics. National Living Standards and Energy Demand. Tokyo: Institute of Energy Economics, 1980.

Instituto de Investigaciones Eléctricas. Evaluation of Energy Supply and Demand at La Guacamaya, Mich., Mexico: Case Study. Mexico: Instituto de Investigaciones Eléctricas, 1983

————. "Evaluación de requerimientos y recursos energéticos en México a nivel rural: Estudio de casos," mimeograph. Mexico: Instituto de Investigaciones Eléctricas, 1984.

————. "Evaluation of Energy Supply and Demand in Four Rural Communities," mimeograph. Mexico: Instituto de Investigaciones Eléctricas, 1984.

Instituto Mexicano del Petróleo. Serie Energéticos 1 (1973), 2 (1975).

————. Demanda de productos de la industria petrolera. Mexico: Subdirección de Estudios Económicos y Planeación Industrial, 1981.

International Energy Agency. Energy Policies and Programmes of IEA Countries. Paris: International Energy Agency, 1978.

————. Energy Policies and Programmes of IEA Countries. Paris: International Energy Agency, 1982.

Levy, Santiago. "Sobre el patrón de uso de energía en la economía mexicana," mimeograph. Mexico: Oficina de Asesores del C. Presidente, September 1982.

Nacional Financiera, S.A. La economía mexicana en cifras. Mexico: Nacional Financiera, S.A., 1974.

————. La economía mexicana en cifras. Mexico: Nacional Financiera, S.A., 1977.

————. La economía mexicana en cifras. Mexico: Nacional Financiera, S.A., 1981.

————. La economía mexicana en cifras. Mexico: Nacional Financiera, S.A., 1984.

Organización Latinoamericana de Energía. Balances energéticos de América Latina, Serie Documentos OLADE, No. 13. Quito: Organización Latinoamericana de Energía, 1981.

Petróleos Mexicanos. Anuario estadístico 1983. Mexico: Petróleos Mexicanos, 1984.

_____. Concentrado de las operaciones realizadas por las compañías distribuidoras. Mexico: Petróleos Mexicanos, 1983.

_____. Memorias de labores. Mexico: Petróleos Mexicanos, 1982.

_____. Memorias de labores. Mexico: Petróleos Mexicanos, 1983.

_____. México: Balance de energía, 1982. Mexico: Subdirección de Planeación y Coordinación, 1983.

_____. México: Balance de energía, 1983. Mexico: Subdirección de Planeación y Coordinación, 1984.

_____. Programa de conservación y ahorro de energía. Mexico: Petróleos Mexicanos, 1984.

Sánchez, X., and P. Umana. "Análisis cuantitativo de la participación de la biomasa en el consumo energético de América Latina." Boletín Energético (OLADE) 21 (1981).

Schutz E., Fernando. Uso eficiente de la energía en México. Mexico: Instituto de Investigaciones Eléctricas and Consejo Nacional de Ciencia y Tecnología, 1981.

Secretaría de Agricultura y Recursos Hidráulicos. Censo agropecuario y forestal. Mexico: Secretaría de Agricultura y Recursos Hidráulicos, 1970.

Secretaría de Comunicaciones y Transportes. Programa 1984-1989. Mexico: Secretaría de Comunicaciones y Transportes, 1984.

Secretaría de Energía, Minas e Industria Paraestatal. "Encuesta sobre el consumo de energía en la industria azucarera: Zafra 1982-1983," internal document. Mexico: Secretaría de Energía, Minas e Industria Paraestatal, 1983.

_____. Programa nacional de energéticos 1984-1988. Mexico: Secretaría de Energía, Minas e Industria Paraestatal, 1984.

Secretaría de Patrimonio y Fomento Industrial. Encuesta sobre el consumo de energía en la industria. Mexico: Secretaría de Patrimonio y Fomento Industrial, 1981.

_____. "First Seminar on Energy Economics." Mexico: Secretaría de Patrimonio y Fomento Industrial, August 1978.

_____. Programa de energía: Metas a 1990 y proyecciones al año 2000. Balances de energía y estudios complementarios. Mexico: Secretaría de Patrimonio y Fomento Industrial, 1980.

338

————. Programa de energía: Metas a 1990 y proyecciones al año 2000 (Resumen y conclusiones). Mexico: Secretaría de Patrimonio y Fomento Industrial, 1980.

————. Seminario de economías de energía (Eficiencia y ahorro de energéticos). Mexico: Secretaría de Patrimonio y Fomento Industrial, August 1978.

————. Balance de energía. Mexico: Secretaría de Patrimonio y Fomento Industrial, 1975-1981.

Secretaría de Programación y Presupuesto. Agenda estadística 1981. Mexico: Secretaría de Programación y Presupuesto, 1982.

————. Agenda estadística 1982. Mexico: Secretaría de Programación y Presupuesto, 1983.

————. Anuario estadístico 1981. Mexico: Secretaría de Programación y Presupuesto, 1981.

————. Anuario estadístico de los E.U.M. 1980. Mexico: Secretaría de Programación y Presupuesto, 1982.

————. Análisis y expectativas de la industria automotriz en México: 1982-1986. Mexico: Secretaría de Programación y Presupuesto, 1982.

————. Las actividades económicas en México. Mexico: Secretaría de Programación y Presupuesto, 1980.

————. Manual de estadísticas básicas: Sector agropecuario y forestal. Mexico: Secretaría de Programación y Presupuesto.

————. Sistema de cuentas nacionales. Mexico: Secretaría de Programación y Presupuesto.

Siddayao, Corazón Morales. "Energy Conservation Policies in the Asia-Pacific Region: Economic Evaluation," mimeograph. Manila, January 1982.

Sterner, Thomas. "Los precios de la gasolina: Un reflejo de la política energética," mimeograph. Gothenburg: University of Gothenburg, August 1983.

————. "Tecnología y estructura en el sector manufacturero: Factores para explicar el uso de energéticos," mimeograph. Gothenburg, February 1983.

Subsecretaría Forestal y de la Fauna. Vademecum forestal mexicano, 1980. Mexico: Subsecretaría Forestal y de la Fauna, 1980.

United Nations. Anuario estadístico de América Latina. Santiago: CEPAL 1981.

————. Small Scale Power Generation. New York: Department of Economic and Social Affairs, 1967.

Vclar, S. "China's Energetics: A System Analysis." In Energy in the Developing World. Oxford, 1980.

Vázquez Reta, Salvador. "Recursos forestales: Uso actual, crecimiento, rendimiento, residuos." In Simposio internacional: La biomasa forestal, recurso natural renovable y fuente de energía. Mexico: Secretaría de Agricultura y Recursos Hidráulicos and Subsecretaría Forestal y de la Fauna, 1981.

Villagómez, Alejandro. "Crecimiento económico y consumo de energía en el sector manufacturero, 1965-1979." Economía Mexicana 5 (1983).

Willars, Jaime Mario. "El papel del petróleo durante los ochentas: Elementos de política y perspectivas," mimeograph. Mexico, August 1983.

_____. "Perspectivas de la demanda interna y posibilidades de ahorro y sustitución de energéticos en Mexico." In Cuadernos sobre Prospectiva Energética, No. 36. Mexico: El Colegio de México, 1983.

_____. "Evolución del sector de hidrocarburos en México: Efectos macroeconómicos, elementos de política y perspectivas," mimeograph. Mexico, November 1983.

Acronyms and Abbreviations

AAGR	Average annual growth rate
AHMSA	Altos Hornos de México, S.A.
BDE	Balances de energía (Energy balances)
CANACEM	Cámara Nacional del Cemento (National Chamber of Cement)
CANACERO	Cámara Nacional de la Industria del Hierro y Acero (National Chamber of the Iron and Steel Industry)
CEPAL	Comisión Nacional para América Latina
CFE	Comisión Federal de Electricidad (Federal Commission of Electricity)
COPLAMAR	Coordinación General del Plan Nacional de Zonas Deprimidas
EAP	Economically active population
FMSA	Fundidora Monterrey, S.A.
GDIP	Gross domestic industrial product
GDP	Gross domestic product
GNP	Gross national product
HD	High diversification
HYLSA	Hojalata y Lámina, S.A. (Sheet Metal and Laminates, S.A.)
IIASA	International Institute for Applied Systems Analysis
IIE	Instituto de Investigaciones Eléctricas (Institute of Electrical Research)
IMP	Instituto Mexicano de Petróleo (Mexican Institute of Petroleum)
LDC	Less-developed countries
mbce	Millions of barrels of crude equivalent
MD	Moderate diversification
mdcf	Millions of daily cubic feet
MTBE	Methyletherbutilic ether
MTSC	Metric ton of sugarcane
NAFINSA	Nacional Financiera, S.A. (National Finance Corporation, S.A.)
NIC	Newly industrialized country

OCDE	Organization for Economic Cooperation and Development
OLADE	Organización Latinoamericana de Energía (Latin American Energy Organization)
PEMEX	Petróleos Mexicanos (Mexican Petroleum Company)
PNE	Programa Nacional de Energía de 1984 (National Energy Program for 1984)
PRONURE	Programa Nacional para el uso racional de la electricidad (National Program for the Rational Use of Electricity)
RCP	Residential, commercial, and public
SARH	Secretaría de Agricultura y Recursos Hidráulicos (Secretariat of Agriculture and Hydraulic Resources)
SCT	Secretaría de Comunicaciones y Transportes (Secretariat of Communications and Transport)
SEMIP	Secretaría de Energía, Minas e Industria Paraestatal (Secretariat of Energy, Mines, and State-Owned Industry)
SEPAFIN	Secretaría de Patrimonio y Fomento Industrial (Secretariat of Patrimony and Industrial Promotion)
SFF	Subsecretaría Forestal y de la Fauna (Subsecretariat of Forestry and Fauna)
SICARTSA	Siderúrgica Lázaro Cárdenas-Las Truchas, S.A. (Lázaro Cárdenas-Las Truchas Steel Works, S.A.
SPP	Secretaría de Programación y Presupuesto (Secretariat of Programming and Budget)
TAMSA	Tubos de Acero de México, S.A. (Iron Tubes of Mexico, S.A.)
tb	Thousands of barrels
tbd	Thousands of barrels daily
tbdce	Thousands of barrels of daily crude equivalent
tpe	Total primary energy

Index

344